Deliberation, Dismissal, and Democracy

Deliberation, Dismissal, and Democracy

DAVID SCHRAUB

OXFORD
UNIVERSITY PRESS

OXFORD
UNIVERSITY PRESS

Oxford University Press is a department of the University of Oxford. It furthers the University's objective of excellence in research, scholarship, and education by publishing worldwide. Oxford is a registered trade mark of Oxford University Press in the UK and in certain other countries.

Published in the United States of America by Oxford University Press
198 Madison Avenue, New York, NY 10016, United States of America.

CIP data is on file at the Library of Congress.

ISBN 9780197816394

ISBN 9780197816387 (hbk.)

DOI: 10.1093/9780197816424.001.0001

Paperback printed by Marquis Book Printing, Canada

Hardback printed by Lightning Source, Inc., United States of America

The manufacturer's authorized representative in the EU for product safety is Oxford University Press España S.A., Parque Empresarial San Fernando de Henares, Avenida de Castilla, 2 – 28830 Madrid (www.oup.es/en or product.safety@oup.com). OUP España S.A. also acts as importer into Spain of products made by the manufacturer.

FSC
www.fsc.org
MIX
Paper | Supporting responsible forestry
FSC® C103567

Contents

Foreword

Perhaps even more than most books, this manuscript is the product not just of "its time" but of many times. The bulk of the book was written in 2019–2020 as my dissertation project, though portions of it come from projects written considerably earlier than that, and I continued to make updates and revisions through 2024 and into early 2025. The topics I explore are, both fortunately and unfortunately for me, timely and constantly evolving, and so it often felt as if as soon as I completed (or revised) one section, events would transpire to make my work, if not obsolete, then at least obviously incomplete.

To take one example: the majority of Chapter 9, on protests, was initially drafted in the spring of 2023. I was concentrating on campus politics at the time, and my main motivating example was a highly disruptive protest at Stanford Law School of Fifth Circuit Court of Appeals judge Kyle Duncan that had occurred earlier that year. This protest was to me the culmination of a particular kind of disruption attempting to block controversial speakers from presenting that had long occupied the attention of academics and commentators on academic affairs trying to parse questions of free speech on campus—prominent other examples include scheduled speeches delivered by Ben Shapiro and Milo Yiannopoulos at UC-Berkeley, Christina Hoff Sommers at Lewis & Clark Law School (before my arrival there), and Moshe Halbertal at the University of Minnesota Law School.

Just a few months later, however, Hamas's October 7 attack on Israel, and Israel's ensuing war in the Gaza Strip, thrust a new protest "case" into the public eye—the pro-Palestine encampments that began at Columbia University and soon spread to campuses across the country. These encampments did not exactly falsify any of the arguments I had made previously about campus protests, but they were clearly distinct from the "shout-down" style of protests targeting particular speakers I had focused on before. More to the point, there was an obvious absurdity in having a chapter on campus protests that did not cover the encampment protests which had gripped the attention of the nation—it would read as embarrassingly incomplete. So I dutifully attempted to incorporate these protests into my discussion (in Chapter 9 and throughout the book) of deliberation and dismissal. And by the time I had made these additions, Donald Trump had been inaugurated for his second term in office, and yet another wave of protests—this time featuring elected officials challenging Trump administration initiatives seeking to obliterate USAID or handing over sensitive financial data to Elon Musk and his "Department of Governmental Efficiency" again presented a new paradigm of public disruption that was neither inconsistent with nor fully incorporated by what I had written before. The world keeps turning.

More broadly, the public and academic valence of issues like free speech and dismissal has shifted considerably over the decade this book has been under way, and my own opinions have been evolving as well. The earliest incarnations of this project were deeply attached to and had an abiding faith in the importance of open-minded and fearless consideration as an indispensable feature of healthy democratic living and deliberative practice. With the benefit of reflection, that faith in some ways feels very much of a time—a period when many observers' worries about free speech took the form of worries about "free speech culture" and attendant problems of cancelation, silencing, and epistemic bubbles. Even in this period I'd like to think I was offering a distinctive contribution—while persons speaking in the register of "free speech culture" often presented claims of discrimination (racism, antisemitism, and the like) as the paradigmatic problem (allegedly used to shut down conversations), I instead presented the reflexive *dismissal* of these allegations as a quintessential example of malformed free speech culture. Chapter 4, which was based on an article published in 2016 and thus written before any other portion of this book, is dedicated to this argument. I believed then, and still believe now, that as a deliberative community we should be far more attentive to and considering of allegations of racism, misogyny, antisemitism, and other forms of discrimination, and that one of the most common occasions when people shut down a conversation is not when they "play the race card" but when they defiantly refuse to consider any possibility of racism (often by flippantly complaining "Oh, they're just playing the race card").

Still, it quickly became apparent that my enthusiasm for open-minded consideration needed to be cut with a healthy acknowledgment of the limits of that project and recognition of the occasional—but very real—value of *not* listening and *not* considering. If anything, in today's political climate the old worries about preserving climates of open-minded debate and fair-minded consideration seem almost quaint. The United States is going through a period of democratic backsliding that is arguably unprecedented since the post-Reconstruction era. It took the Trump administration mere days into its second term to launch a full-scale assault on established legal rules and processes—to say nothing of bedrock American values of equal citizenship and dignity—that dwarfed even the extremities of his previous tenure in office. It is not exaggeration or alarmism to say this represents a global crisis. And it feels naïve at best, appeasing at worst, to think that Trump or his loyalists will be talked out of their radical illiberal agenda or that there is some underlying humanitarian impulse behind efforts to strip birthright citizenship or to torment transgender Americans. Opposition to Trumpism almost certainly will need to take forms of protest, resistance, and confrontation, not exclusively or even primarily contemplative debate. Those who respond even to a Nazi salute with calls for equanimity and grace are profoundly missing the demands of the moment.

Despite these changes in circumstance, I am glad I did not swing too far in the opposite direction. The push and pull between the competing values of consideration and dismissal is a theme present throughout this book, and properly so. Indeed, I believe that it is especially essential now to recall the virtues of open-mindedness and interpretative charity and the importance of not unduly evading grappling with hard or challenging thoughts. That's not because these instincts must always or in all circumstances prevail. Rather, it is because these instincts must not be *forgotten*, and it is very easy in times of crisis to discount their value entirely. The situation America faces now is not a normal one, and even the features of a righteous resistance are not ones conducive to a sustainably healthy democracy over the long term. Street protests may be good when responding to efforts to loot the American treasury on behalf of unaccountable plutocrats (notwithstanding that a street protest is hardly a medium conducive to open-minded exchanges of reasoned argument), but it would very much not be good if every political dispute over traffic laws or tax policy was resolved primarily by marches and sit-ins. That we are in the realm where the former is necessary not just occasionally but systematically is the crisis, and part of our goal should be to return ourselves to the latter domain—ordinary politics normally hashed out by the ordinary virtues of political dialogue. When the reign of the witches passes—and it will, not automatically or inexorably, but by the sustained and heroic efforts of fearless advocates, activists, and ordinary patriots—we need to remember those virtues in order to ensure that the democracy we wish to see can truly flourish.

There are a great many people who deserve thanks for making this book possible, and all of them deserve more thanks than can be adequately communicated in an acknowledgment section. First and foremost is my wife, Jill, who is the best person in my life. There have been many ups and downs over the past several years, and she has been a rock (albeit a comfortable, soft rock who gives great hugs) throughout all of them. I can scarcely think of any accomplishment in my adult life I can imagine having done without her, and this book assuredly is no exception.

My parents and family have always been there for me. My dad is an intellectual role model whose wit, humor, and storytelling are not just entertaining but also taught me much about how to speak and write in a manner that is both engaging and rigorous. My mom is an endless fount of support and encouragement, and has been for as long as I can remember. My brother is grounded in the real world in a way that I can't be myself but I certainly admire greatly. I'm blessed with many wonderful cousins, aunts, uncles, and other relatives across the country who I don't see nearly enough but who have made a tremendous impact on me nonetheless. Finally, in the midst of revising this manuscript for publication, I had a much more important "publication" enter my life in the form of my first son. The year 2025 was simultaneously a great and a terrible time to welcome a new soul into the world, but I hope that this book may contribute in some small way to cultivating the sort of healthy democratic and deliberative climate I want him to grow up in.

I was incredibly fortunate to have a tremendous dissertation committee—Sarah Song, Mark Bevir, Josh Cohen, and Chris Kutz—all of whom have played integral roles in supporting me throughout the doctoral process and later in converting this project into a book manuscript. I hope no offense is taken if I give special thanks to Sarah, who has truly gone far above and beyond as the chair of my committee to become a true mentor, colleague, and friend. To say I am honored to call myself her student surges past understatement. I also want to thank several professors at Berkeley who were not on my committee but were helpful in various ways. I asked Avani Sood to be on my committee, which she agreed to do and then did not hold it against me when the project turned in a different direction and I ended up replacing her. While she is not formally involved in this project, her influence still can be felt in several of the chapters that are more psychological in focus. Kinch Hockstra, Dan Lee, and Wendy Brown were likewise generous with their time and feedback on various side projects despite the fact that I was never officially one of "their" students, and I'm grateful for it. (Kinch gets an additional shoutout for chairing my prospectus committee.) I count myself lucky that my colleagues among the Berkeley political science graduate students were fun people to hang out with and become friends with. I've heard tales of graduate programs where students are rivals with one another and in competition with one another, which sounds like an awful experience I'm glad I did not have to go through.

Outside of Berkeley, there were many influences in my academic life who helped set me on the path I am on today. I was blessed with many fantastic teachers in elementary, middle, and high school who helped nurture me in my academic growth. (And with the benefit of hindsight I have to imagine I wasn't the easiest student to teach.) At Carleton College I had a surplus of wonderful mentors, among them Kim Smith, Louis Newman, Melvin Rogers, and Anna Moltchanova. I remain in contact with each of them to this day, and Carleton remains my model for what academia should be. The University of Chicago Law School was its own intellectual feast (I am among the few, I think, who without any irony will say "I loved my time in law school"), and once again I was privileged to be supported by some superb faculty members, including David Strauss, Emily Buss, Lisa Bernstein, Martha Nussbaum, and Aziz Huq. All of them are of course renowned and accomplished scholars who nonetheless have been unfailingly generous with their time and support for me not only when I was their student but for years after graduation as well. I also am tremendously grateful to my colleagues at Lewis & Clark Law School, who were nothing but supportive as I pursued a somewhat untraditional—from the vantage of legal academia, anyway—academic project. One often has little control over where one lands in academia, and I count myself exceptionally fortunate to teach at a college filled with gracious, warm, and insightful colleagues who have enabled me to flourish.

Finally, I'm grateful to the editors at the Oxford University Press, particularly David McBride, who helped shepherd this book through a long and winding review process. As a first-time author, I found the endeavor of going from submission to publication especially opaque and prone to triggering neurosis, and he was always patient with my questions and concerns in the course of guiding this book forward.

As mentioned, the book itself is a compilation of several different projects—some brand new, some previously published, and some which I had written before but never had put into publishable form until now. They were honed and fine-tuned across many conferences, workshops, and casual conversations—too many for me to recount now. Academia is a village, and I've benefited greatly from the contributions of the entire intellectual community in creating this corner of my own.

Introduction

On November 2, 2001, Javad Iqbal was arrested. He was one of the more than 1,000 people questioned in the immediate aftermath of the September 11th attacks as the FBI sought to identify persons connected to the attacks or to terrorist activity more generally. Iqbal was a cable television installer from Hicksville, New York; he was also a Pakistani American Muslim. The FBI designated him a person of "high interest," which caused him to be held in restrictive custody for months while awaiting trial. During his incarceration, Iqbal claimed that he was routinely abused by prison staff. Prison officers allegedly turned the air conditioning on in the winter and the heat on in the summer to make cell conditions unbearable. They were said to have interfered with his attempts to pray and engage in other religious rituals. And they conducted multiple unwarranted and gratuitous strip and body cavity searches in an attempt to humiliate him. Ultimately, Iqbal was convicted of identity fraud for using another man's Social Security card, and he was released from prison in 2003.

In May 2004, Iqbal filed suit. Not only did his conditions of confinement violate constitutional due process guarantees, but Iqbal asserted that the decision to label him a "high interest" detainee was on account of his racial and religious background. More important, Iqbal's complaint did not attribute this treatment to a few overzealous low-level field agents. He made a far more explosive allegation: that the decision to designate him and other Muslim detainees "high interest" was part of an official government policy approved at the highest levels of the American government. Among the persons Iqbal claimed were involved in the decision were Attorney General John Ashcroft and FBI Director Robert Mueller.

A typical piece of federal civil litigation can be roughly divided into three stages: pleading, discovery, and trial. The pleading stage begins when the plaintiff officially files a complaint. The purpose of the complaint is to place the defendant on notice regarding what the case is about and what laws have allegedly been violated, and accordingly the federal rules prescribe that a complaint should consist only of "a short and plain statement of the claim showing that the pleader is entitled to relief."[1] "Short and plain" is a relative term—Iqbal's

[1] Federal Rules of Civil Procedure, Rule 8(a)(2), https://www.law.cornell.edu/rules/frcp/rule_8.

Deliberation, Dismissal, and Democracy. David Schraub, Oxford University Press. © Oxford University Press (2025). DOI: 10.1093/9780197816424.003.0001

complaint was 45 pages long and contained 20 separate causes of action—but the point of the pleading stage is not to prove or even investigate the truth or falsity of the allegations but rather to ascertain that they are the sort of allegation that a court has jurisdiction to hear and which (assuming the plaintiff proves his or her case) would entitle the claimant to judicial remediation. If the claim does not even on its face allege the sort of wrongdoing courts are empowered to redress, there is no point in wasting time proceeding to the subsequent (and more costly) stages of discovery and trial.

Hence, standing between pleading and discovery is the defendant's first opportunity to dispose of a case: the motion to dismiss. In urging that a case should be dismissed, the defendant generally argues that the plaintiff's claim "fail[s] to state a claim upon which relief can be granted."[2] To take a simple example, imagine a plaintiff who filed suit alleging that a particular defendant was "a jerk." The problem, of course, is that there is no law prohibiting persons from being jerks, and thus the claim is not of the sort upon which the court could grant relief. Consequently, there would be no point in proceeding to the subsequent litigation stages: even if depositions and discovery provided smoking-gun evidence that the defendant was indeed a jerk, and even if at trial a jury was completely persuaded that the defendant was a jerk, it would not do the plaintiff any good because he still would not have established any *legal* wrong courts are empowered to redress. Of course, in most filed cases the question of whether the claim is properly legal in character is less straightforward. But hopefully this illustrates why the preemptory character of dismissal is so valuable to defendants: discovery is expensive, time-consuming, and runs the risk of disclosing embarrassing information. Where a case is dismissed, most of the hard work of investigating and verifying the claim can be skipped over entirely.

The government defendants had moved to dismiss Iqbal's case, and in September 2005 the district court was prepared to rule on the motion.[3] This was, to the say the least, an awkward time for a claim like Iqbal's to emerge. The detention of "enemy combatants" at Guantanamo Bay without trial was already proving controversial, and debates over "waterboarding" and "extraordinary rendition" (the transfer of captured terrorism suspects to foreign countries that would, presumably, torture them under interrogation) were on the horizon as well. Perhaps the most politically salient iteration of the issue came with the revelation of abusive

[2] Federal Rules of Civil Procedure, Rule 12(b)(6), https://www.law.cornell.edu/rules/frcp/rule_12.

[3] The district court opinion in Iqbal's case can be found at Elmaghraby v. Ashcroft, 2005 U.S. Dist. LEXIS 21434 (E.D.N.Y. Sept. 27, 2005). The United States Court of Appeals for the Second Circuit largely affirmed the district court, Iqbal v. Hasty, 490 F.3d 143 (2007), but the Supreme Court reversed with respect to the high-level governmental officials and dismissed the claims against them, Ashcroft v. Iqbal, 556 U.S. 662 (2009).

practices by U.S. soldiers at the Abu Ghraib prison in Baghdad. Eleven primarily low-level operators were convicted, but questions were percolating about the degree to which inhumane and abusive treatment, justified by the war on terror, was not the province of a few "bad apples" but rather derived from official policies approved by high-level American representatives. For a country that had long prided itself as being a "beacon of democracy" and a model of human rights, and which was currently engaged in an attempt to win the hearts and minds of a global populace caught amid the larger war on terror, this presented a disturbing counternarrative to the story favored by the American political and legal establishment.

We never did find out whether Iqbal's allegations were true. In 2009, the Supreme Court decided that Iqbal's claim could not proceed against the upper-level administrative officials.[4] Specifically, it concluded that Iqbal's complaint did not satisfy the (newly announced) "plausibility" standard, requiring that "the pleaded factual content allows the court to draw the reasonable inference that the defendant is liable for the misconduct alleged."[5] Conceding that Iqbal had made allegations "consistent with petitioners' purposefully designating detainees 'of high interest' because of their race, religion, or national origin," the Court nonetheless declined to allow the case to proceed because "given more likely explanations," the contents of the complaint "do not plausibly establish this purpose."[6]

Because the case was dismissed, it never proceeded to discovery, and so neither judges nor the public ever got the opportunity to examine or evaluate the record regarding treatment of Muslim prisoners in the aftermath of 9/11. It is possible that none of the misconduct Iqbal alleged occurred, and it's possible that if it did happen it was entirely unattributable to upper-level governmental policy. But the only fact we know is that we don't actually know one way or the other.

Claims like Iqbal's can be very disconcerting. It is one thing, after all, to accept that the occasional rogue operator or misplaced brute will engage in unsanctioned acts of abuse. It is quite another to reckon with the possibility that such actions are *not* illicit exceptions but rather are honest representations of one's own country and its political leadership. Given a choice, people would rather not think such hard thoughts. We are much happier believing that our political system is normally just, that people usually get what they deserve, that we can be

[4] 556 U.S. 662 (2009).

[5] *Id.* at 678. A prior decision, *Twombly v. Bell Atlantic*, had introduced the plausibility standard, but *Iqbal* was the first to clearly state that these rules applied to all civil actions. Together, these two cases are said to have "revolutionized" federal pleading rules. Kevin M. Clermont, "Three Myths about *Twombly-Iqbal*," *Wake Forest Law Review* 45 (Winter 2010): 1337.

[6] *Iqbal*, 556 U.S. at 681.

proud of the community we inhabit and of the nation we swear allegiance to, and that what injustices do occur are rare and exceptional. Honest political deliberation requires recognizing the possibility that such beliefs are not, or are not always, warranted. Yet often when faced with such a challenge, we shy away. We search for reasons to evade having to honestly reckon with this uncomfortable possibility—to avoid hearing it, to deny its merits, or to dismiss its legitimacy. We are, in short, dismissive. And it is this act of dismissal of the hard thoughts—inside but, perhaps more importantly, outside the courtroom as well—that is the primary subject of this book.

If "dismissal" is the theme of the book, its partner and counterweight is consideration. Chapter 1 explores the idea of "taking up" the challenging, disconcerting, but nonetheless important contentions that often are both central to core cases of political morality but which also are most prone to being dismissed (what I term the "hard thoughts"). It also provides an introduction to several of the core cases which will be returned to throughout the book, such as the propensity to dismiss discrimination claims, and outlines how such claims might be effectively taken up notwithstanding continued disagreement regarding the very contour of the term "discrimination." Likewise, the chapter confirms that while the problems associated with dismissal can often be linked to certain deliberative vices—such as close-mindedness or prejudice against particular claimants—such agential misconduct is not necessary for the phenomenon to emerge. There can be structural conditions which facilitate (wrongful) dismissal, ones which transcend any obvious "bad behavior" by a particular actor but which nonetheless facilitate an overall failure for certain sorts of claims that seem to have a valid claim on our collective attention to be effectively taken up and considered.

Chapter 2 provides a direct articulation of dismissal itself. Inspired by the concept in civil procedure, I define "dismissal" as the practice of dispensing with a proffered claim *without* analyzing it on its merits. I situate dismissal as part of a broader "continuum" of motivated cognition bracketed by ignorance, on one side, and evaluative motivated cognition, on the other. These together represent a trio of cognitive checkpoints which assist in evading consideration of challenging or disconcerting claims—the "hard thoughts" of Chapter 1. If one is ignorant of a claim, one need not (and indeed cannot) consider it; if one becomes aware of a claim, one can still dismiss it (again, forgoing consideration); and finally, if one is forced to actually engage in the process of articulating and defending reasons for one's conclusion, one can do so in a motivated fashion that is slanted toward one's preferred outcome. Most of the psychological literature in this area has focused on the final step (evaluative motivated cognition); a burgeoning segment of philosophical literature—typically drawing on James Baldwin—has explored the normative implications of the first step (ignorance). The middle segment of dismissal, by contrast, is relatively underdeveloped.

Chapter 3 focuses on the specific problems associated with dismissal. I begin by describing several mechanisms by which dismissal may operate. We may *desire disagreement*—intentionally refusing points of commonality or overlapping consensus in order to preserve an antagonistic and dismissive posture toward a political or social movement we oppose. We also can engage in *replacement epistemology*, where we successfully replace an outgroup's intended communicative offering with one of our own—and, importantly, successfully and authoritatively impute that meaning as being the one intended by the outgroup. I then proceed to articulate the distinctive harms that may be associated with dismissal. Drawing on Miranda Fricker's work on epistemic injustice, I contend that dismissal comes with specific dignitary and deliberative harms that are not fully encompassed by other deliberative malfunctions. These harms deserve their own distinct analysis.

Chapter 4 offers a deep dive into perhaps the paradigm case of dismissal: that which afflicts claims of discrimination. Responding to a claim of racism by alleging that the aggrieved party is "just playing the race card" and a claim of antisemitism by accusing the claimant of actually wishing only to "silence criticism of Israel" are depressingly common features of rhetoric in this area. Indeed, to a large extent they overshadow the entire field. Importantly, such replies do *not* typically even purport to respond to the discrimination claim on its substance—they do not say "No, this is not racist or antisemitic for X, Y, and Z reasons." Rather, they present such claims as somehow outside the boundaries of legitimate public conversation altogether. This is what makes them cases of *dismissal*. Continuing to pull from Fricker, I argue that this form of dismissal represents a testimonial injustice and cannot be justified by the fact that some discrimination claims are, in fact, ill-taken.

As noted, the implied counterpart to dismissal is consideration. But what does the obligation of consideration actually demand of us? Chapter 5 explores this question via a familiar source: John Stuart Mill's classic text *On Liberty*. There is a tendency at least in some popular writing to link Mill too closely with purely jurisprudential limits on speech—tackling "censorship" as a question of *de jure* limits on what is permitted to be spoken, written, or published. Yet law is not Mill's focus, and in many ways it is his easiest case. Rules against formal legal censorship are of at most indirect utility when seeking to resolve many of the high-profile "free speech" controversies that have exploded into public view over the past few years. Questions of trigger warnings, campus climate, no-platforming proposals, and the like cannot be easily resolved by analogy to the (im)permissibility of legal proscriptions on certain forms of speech. I argue, however, that a reading of Mill that concentrates on the value of *listening* rather than *speaking* can provide a more illuminating gloss on how to approach these issues. This orientation de-emphasizes questions of rules and rights (which naturally lend themselves to a jurisprudential focus) in favor of promoting certain deliberative *virtues*—values like open-mindedness, curiosity, and a willingness to lean into the difficulty of challenging claims.

If Chapter 5 is the most aggressive defense of consideration as an essential deliberative value, Chapter 6 is meant to pump the brakes by considering circumstances when it might not be obligatory or even advisable to listen. Shifting from Mill to Nietzsche, I suggest that in many circumstances the capacity (whether exercised or not) to *not* listen—to ignore, overlook, or discount—is an important component of human freedom and autonomy. This value is especially important in national independence and decolonization movements, many of which are expressly motivated by a desire to *no longer* listen to their prior colonial overlords or masters. The traditional liberal account centers deliberation because it imagines a collaborative process where all parties consider the needs and interests of one another and ultimately agree to give what is due. But in many cases involving decolonization, the desire is *not* to enter this deliberative space, even in a context where one's needs are being successfully recognized by the erstwhile oppressing party. Rather, the goal is to be in a position where one's needs and interests can be protected *regardless* of whether the oppressor consents or not. To be sure, this is a matter of capacity, not actualization—I do not suggest that it would be either possible or desirable for even the hitherto oppressed to fully withdraw from the processes of mutual consideration and deliberation. But the insight still matters because it once again centers the deliberative ethos of consideration as a *choice*, not a mandate. What is required is the cultivation of particular virtues rather than the fiated insistence that one is always at all times obligated to come to the discursive table.

Chapter 7 fleshes out how these deliberative virtues might be developed. Drawing on Alexis de Tocqueville, I argue that an unintended consequence of increased deliberative equality—perhaps most noticeable in the rise of social media circumventing legacy media gatekeepers—is the development of a deliberative terrain where, paradoxically, nobody trusts anyone. The cynical belief that it is futile to expect truth from any source enables people to justify indulging in epistemic siloing—if every source is a liar, one might as well seek out the lies one already wants to hear. What's needed are sources of epistemic friction—something that can break up the flattened deliberative landscape and retrigger critical thinking capacities that would otherwise atrophy—and one potential source of such friction is cultivating social diversity in our deliberative spaces. This account of the virtues of diverse deliberative spaces is less about the importance of representation or substantive equality (though those may be important) and more instrumental—it posits that we deliberate better when exposed to social diversity. I then apply that insight to assess a common criticism about contemporary progressive social discourses—that practices like "safe spaces" and other efforts to be inclusive toward historical outgroups undermine deliberative diversity and unintentionally hurt those they mean to help. I argue instead that, while there is not nothing to this criticism, a fuller account of the actual social situation these groups occupy strongly suggests that these concerns are overblown. Simply put, "safe spaces" or no, it is not plausible to suggest that members of social minorities are unaware of arguments or contentions commonly asserted by dominant social castes, and so efforts to provide them with some provisional and contingent respite from engaging with these arguments is not the same thing as a complete and utter insulation from them.

The root of dismissal, as a concept, is legal. Chapter 8 returns to law and explores how the judiciary might occupy a unique niche in the deliberative ecosystem enabling it to better overcome some of the problems of dismissal, some of the time. Nobody can force Congress to hold a hearing on your bill, or the president to grant you an audience, or the newspaper to publish your column, or even your neighbor to have a conversation with you. But courts are different. If a claim checks off the requisite doctrinal boxes—and admittedly, that's a big "if"—courts are *compelled* to listen when other deliberative institutions are not. In other words, we've noted that one of the recurrent dilemmas around dismissal is that it is resistant to the establishment of hard and fast rules requiring consideration. But precisely because it is restricted to a limited (legal) space—an attribute that has frequently made courts objects of suspicion by deliberative democrats—the judiciary can craft rule-based regimes which limit its discretion to simply ignore a "hard thought" and therefore can compel consideration. This certainly is not the whole game—marginalized groups which successfully have their claims considered by the judiciary still can and often do lose. But it is not nothing either. For groups accustomed to being ignored, overlooked, unheard, or dismissed, simply getting to the space where arguments are heard and reasons must be given may well be a significant victory in and of itself.

Chapter 9 concludes with an attempt to synthesize the insights of the prior chapters in order to tackle one of the most nettlesome arenas of free speech controversies: the college campus. The past decade has seen repeated free speech contretemps explode into broader social view, from disputes over "safe spaces" and "trigger warnings," to "shout-downs" or other obstructions of controversial speakers, to crackdowns on protest activities surrounding Israel's war in the Gaza Strip following the October 7 attacks. Political commentators seem to oscillate between favoring and indicting speech protections at a dizzying pace—in one breath decrying censorial attitudes and an inability to tolerate challenging views, in the next demanding conscious interventions to diminish speech perceived as threatening or offensive. Is this simply a matter of bog-standard political hypocrisy? Perhaps in many cases. But at least some of the problem can be chalked up to confusion regarding what we mean by free speech in the first place. In particular, I will argue that colleges seek to regulate speech across different domains—what it can and can't prohibit, but also what ethical values and orientations it wishes to cultivate vis-à-vis the speech practices of its members. Steps which seek to validly advance a regulatory interest in one domain can often place severe and improper pressure on others. These tensions are difficult enough to untangle under the best of circumstances; they can be nigh impossible to harmonize when we conflate all of the relevant considerations under a single, unqualified banner of "free speech."

1
Taking Up Hard Thoughts

If dismissal is the subject—and, at least initially, the villain—of this book, what is its alternative? What do we do if we do *not* dismiss? The answer, as I'll argue in this chapter, is something along the lines of *consideration*. Dismissal is not, at root, concerned with what ideas are ultimately accepted or acted upon. Rather, it looks at which deliberative offerings are and are not *taken up*—given suitable deliberative attention—which makes it possible (but by no means guarantees) that they will ultimately gain approval.

It is a given that many if not most claims which are seriously debated in a democratic society will not ultimately prevail in a legislature, court of law, or court of public opinion. This is not itself a problem; it is almost certainly unavoidable. What could be a problem is if important claims, ones that should occupy our attention as democratic deliberators, are successfully blocked from even reaching this threshold of consideration—that is, are not taken up at all. In this chapter, I am particularly concerned about our collective ability to take up the "hard thoughts": potentialities that are deeply threatening to our personal or collective sensibilities and so tend to be avoided, even though (if valid) they would represent crucial areas upon which a virtuous citizen would feel compelled to deliberate.

With respect to dismissal, our core worry is that some sorts of claims, ones which would contribute to the quality of political debate, are systematically obstructed from being taken up by relevant deliberative actors. To be sure, there are some sorts of claims which regularly fail to be taken up for discussion for which this "failure" is hardly a failure at all. Some claims are, from a deliberative perspective, useless, trivial, or frivolous. It might be hard to accept the claim that one's spouse is secretly a space monster from the Andromeda Galaxy, but fortunately that is also a profoundly stupid proposition. Likewise, our concern is for "systematic" failures, which excludes momentary or ephemeral reasons for why one would not want to consider a given claim (e.g., declining to consider a powerful and epistemically useful argument because it is 1:00 a.m. and one wants to go to sleep).

On the other hand, if our central worry is dismissal—systematically avoiding consideration of certain claims even though (I'll argue) they frequently deserve our attention—those thoughts which we must regularly attend to are by definition outside the parameters of the problem. That said, the mere fact that

Deliberation, Dismissal, and Democracy. David Schraub, Oxford University Press. © Oxford University Press (2025). DOI: 10.1093/9780197816424.003.0002

a given challenging idea is *sometimes* considered does not mean the problem of dismissal disappears. For one, occasionally circumstances conspire to force to the table issues or claims typically ignored. And for two, that a given claim was in fact taken up does not necessarily prove that the deliberator could not have successfully avoided taking it up if he or she had so wished. Some people are particularly virtuous (or masochistic) in their deliberations, and that is to their credit. But their unusual willingness to proactively tackle difficult questions—where it is indeed an *unusual* characteristic—does not tell us much about the general degree of access such ideas can claim upon the deliberative agenda.

What we're left with are cases where one seeks to, and frequently is empowered to, "insulate [oneself] from demands made by others."[1] Certain thoughts, if entertained, could compel us to respond in ways we'd rather not do—so we do our best to avoid entertaining them. Martha Nussbaum gives the example of casting blame on the poor for their poverty, thus refusing them compassion for their plight: this "is very convenient . . . [for i]f we think this way, we don't have to do anything about the situation of the poor."[2] Regina Rini makes a similar observation regarding the propensity to dismiss racial minority claimants as "bitter": "When a woman or person of color tries to express anger at social oppression, people who benefit from privilege have a (possibly unconscious) incentive to interpret the expression as irrational bitterness rather than as reasonable anger because attributing reasonableness would mean acknowledging the existence of pervasive oppression. If a person attempts anger but is constructed as bitter instead, her complaint can be ignored, and everyone else can go on without the trouble of confronting injustice."[3] There are a multitude of reasons for which persons might seek out this sort of insulation: the claim may threaten the interests of the deliberator; it may threaten to produce cultural, cognitive, or political dissonance in the deliberator; or it may threaten to cause other members of the deliberative community to view the deliberator adversely.

Return then to the *Iqbal* case, discussed in the introduction. How does it fit into this discussion? To begin, surely whether or not high-level government officials endorsed abusive treatment of detainees on the basis of their religion or ethnicity is an extraordinarily important question that a healthy democracy must investigate. Equally surely, if it were proven to be true it would significantly destabilize important narratives about America as a nation and the basic legitimacy of

[1] Martha C. Nussbaum, *Political Emotions: Why Love Matters for Justice* (Belknap, 2013), 158.

[2] *Id.* Consider also the words of James Baldwin: "White America remains unable to believe that Black America's grievances are real; they are unable to believe this because they cannot face what this fact says about themselves and their country." James Baldwin, *The Price of the Ticket* (St. Martin's Press, 1985), 536.

[3] Regina Rini, "How to Take Offense: Responding to Microaggressions," *Journal of the American Philosophical Association* 4, no. 3 (2018): 340.

core governmental institutions. Judges, as themselves high-ranking government officials, carry their own investment in the core justness of the American system and thus may be ideologically resistant to concluding that such abuse could have occurred. And even beyond the need to avoid dissonance, judges have a more prosaic interest in avoiding "bombshell" confrontations with the executive branch. The accusation that the president and top cabinet members engaged in not just unlawful conduct but ethnic or religious abuse would necessarily pit the courts against the executive in a manner that is deeply politically fraught.

So *Iqbal* presents both an important contribution to public debate that deserves to be "taken up" and one that deliberators (including the judicial deliberators in the American court system) have good reason to want to systematically avoid. The last element I suggested was germane to the question of hard thoughts is whether the deliberator can systematically (albeit not always) avoid taking up questions such as these. In Iqbal's case, of course, the court successfully managed such avoidance—and set precedent making it even easier for it do so again in future cases. Many have expounded on what Alexander Bickel calls the "passive virtues" that allow courts to engage in such evasion as a matter of course, particularly on controversial or politically sensitive subjects.[4] Nonetheless, I want to bracket this element for now. In Chapter 8, I will return to courts as a special epistemic arena which may—*Iqbal* notwithstanding—be especially productive at *forcing* consideration of otherwise "hard" thoughts.

Hard Thoughts and Political Openness

Political argument, when functioning properly, anyway, comprises the giving and taking of reasons. Once we agree to engage in the project of interpretation, Jürgen Habermas tells us, we commit ourselves to a particular posture vis-à-vis our interlocutors. Most notably, we agree to at least potentially alter or revise our own views in response to their contributions. Interpreters, Habermas writes, "are drawn, at least potentially, into negotiations about the meaning and validity of utterances. . . . Within a process of reaching understanding, actual or potential, it is impossible to decide a priori who is to learn from whom."[5]

When engaged in political discussion—by which I mean discussion that, whether formal or informal, is geared toward orienting or legitimating collective social action[6]—we present claims for our interlocutors to consider and

[4] Alexander M. Bickel, "The Passive Virtues," *Harvard Law Review* 75, no. 1 (1961): 40–79.

[5] Jürgen Habermas, *Moral Consciousness and Communicative Action*, trans. Christian Lenhardt and Shierry Weber Nicholsen (MIT Press, 1990), 26.

[6] Some discussions about politics—such as those geared toward solidifying or reinforcing membership in a particular group or tribe—rest uneasily with this definition. But I would argue that to the

symmetrically agree to consider the assertions of others. Implicit in this project is an openness on behalf of all parties to at least potentially change their minds. In Iris Marion Young's formulation, entrants in public conversation must come to the table with the aim—though by no means the guarantee—of agreement, a requirement which cannot be met if participants have pre-committed to *never* altering their positions, come hell or high water.[7] Part of successful democratic practice, after all, is a willingness to (re)consider—to accept that the way we have done things or the thoughts we have thought have not been as successful as we might have hoped. Where this openness is not present, much of the value of democratic *deliberation* is lost. As Elizabeth Anderson observes, "If the people themselves are hidebound and dogmatic, thinking, for example, that social arrangements *must* follow tradition, or revert to principles laid down in an ancient religious text, they will not be prepared to take the untoward consequences of current habits, or policies following ancient principles, as evidence disconfirming their claim to practical success."[8]

One does not need to engage in political argument if all parties agree on all the relevant particulars. (Indeed, Anderson argues that democracy is *least* relevant in circumstances where voters are homogeneous.)[9] The (or at least a) purpose of argument is to persuade, or if not that, then at least to modulate. Democratic citizenship does not require universal agreement on contested issues. But it does require that we commit to giving each other's claims a fair hearing and due consideration.[10] Our concerns about free speech, Alexander Meiklejohn writes, are not primarily "for the protection of those intellectual aristocrats who pursue knowledge solely for the fun of the game."[11] We care about speech because we

extent such discussion is purely inward-facing as a preparatory maneuver in *advance* of a collective discussion, it is better characterized as prepolitical precisely because it could not legitimate action by the broader group. And insofar as these intragroup discussions can be characterized as legitimating collective action among the group members (e.g., legitimating what tactic or approach they will take once they do converse with other members of their polity beyond their own tribe), then I would agree that they are political but would also insist that they allow for the possibility that new dialogic offerings in the discussion might change minds or alter trajectory.

[7] Iris Marion Young, *Inclusion and Democracy* (Oxford University Press, 2000), 24. At the founding, Roger Sherman raised a similar argument in explaining why the people should not have a right of "instruction" whereby they could dictate how their representatives would vote in Congress. The purpose of convening in a Congress, Sherman argued, is to "meet others from the different parts of the Union, and consult. . . . If they were to be guided by instructions, there would be no use in deliberation." Quoted in Joseph Gales, ed., *The Annals of Congress* (Gales and Seaton, 1834), 763–64.

[8] Elizabeth Anderson, "The Epistemology of Democracy," *Episteme* 3, nos. 1–2 (June 2006): 14.

[9] *Id.* at 11.

[10] Brandon Morgan-Olsen, "A Duty to Listen: Epistemic Obligations and Public Deliberation," *Social Theory & Practice* 39, no. 2 (2013): 188 ("There is no conduit from a citizen's lips to the exercise of political power save the ears of others, and to fail to listen fair-mindedly in the public square can thereby represent a failure to acknowledge another's status as citizen.").

[11] Alexander Meiklejohn, *Free Speech and Its Relation to Self-Government* (Harper & Bros., 1948), 45.

use speech to come to practical conclusions about practical problems that face us as members of political and social collectivities.

This is all easy to commit to in the abstract. But some arguments—allegations, claims, potentialities—are harder to face than others. As José Medina observes, "[W]e all have things we would rather avoid: things that are hard to hear, things that are difficult to accept or even to acknowledge."[12] Questions such as "Am I a racist?," "Is this social movement I am a member of antisemitic?," or "Are my consumption patterns compatible with continued environmental sustainability?" are tremendously important for members of a healthy polity to take seriously and think about carefully.[13] They also are among the questions which many people are most resistant to considering in all but the most superficial fashion.

These are what I call the "hard thoughts." Hard thoughts matter because they are simultaneously among the most important issues for which well-functioning political consideration is necessary, and the ones where our practices of political consideration are most likely to malfunction. Claims which should be heard are ignored; arguments which should be considered fail to be taken up.

Democratic society expects, if not demands, that people will consider claims that threaten their narrow self-interest or which conflict with their prior cultural or political attachments.[14] No matter how controversial or disconcerting, "[w]hen a question of policy is 'before the house,'" Meiklejohn writes, "free men choose to meet it not with their eyes shut, but with their eyes open."[15] Yet for most of us this prospect is not fun, and there are a wealth of mechanisms available by which we can skirt our obligations. Thomas Hobbes anticipated the literature on motivated cognition by centuries when he observed, "As oft as reason is against a man, so oft will a man be against reason."[16] But this tendency is not simply a matter of individual vice and virtue. There is a distributional quality to the problem—whose claims are most likely to fit the criteria of a "hard thought," and so be occluded from the general practices of public reasoning, are likely to track preexisting lines of social, political, and economic power. This maldistribution, in turn, seriously undermines the democratic value of "deliberation" tout court. Lynn Sanders makes this point in powerful fashion:

[12] José Medina, *The Epistemology of Resistance: Gender and Racial Oppression, Epistemic Injustice, and Resistant Imaginations* (Oxford University Press, 2013), 34.

[13] Of course, for different people different thoughts might be hard. Some, for example, might find "Are fetuses moral 'persons'?" or "How can we justly incapacitate unrepentant criminals?" to be hard.

[14] See Alasdair MacIntyre, "Relativism, Power, and Philosophy," in *After Philosophy: End or Transformation?*, ed. Kenneth Baynes, James Bohman, and Thomas McCarthy (MIT Press, 1987), 408.

[15] Meiklejohn, *Free Speech*, 27.

[16] Thomas Hobbes, *The Elements of Law Natural and Politic* (1650), ed. J. C. A. Gaskin (Oxford University Press, 1994), 19.

> [S]ome Americans are apparently less likely than others to be listened to, even when their arguments are stated according to conventions of reason, they are more likely to be disregarded. Although deliberators will always choose to disregard some arguments, when this disregard is systematically associated with the arguments made by those we know already to be systematically disadvantaged, we should at least reevaluate our assumptions about deliberation's democratic potential. Deliberation requires not only equality in resources and the guarantee of equal opportunity to articulate persuasive arguments but also equality in "epistemological authority," in the capacity to evoke acknowledgment of one's arguments.[17]

The distributional element of deliberative ethics deserves closer scrutiny. It is of pressing importance given the relatively aggressive requirements for appropriate dialogic conditions imposed by many writers concentrating on ethics as a feature of discourse. Seyla Benhabib argues that dialogue, "to be distinguished from cajoling, propaganda, brainwashing, and strategic bargaining," requires recognition of the "right to equal participation between conversation partners," defined as "all whose interests are actually or potentially affected by the courses of action and decisions which may ensue from such conversations." And all participants, in turn, "have an equal right to suggest topics of conversation, to introduce new points of view, questions, and criticism into the conversation, and to challenge the rules of the conversation insofar as they seem to exclude the voice of some and privilege that of others."[18]

These requirements are effectively impossible to meet in practice, at least across the board. If we cannot in fact ensure that *all* whose interests are potentially affected are included and neither can we guarantee that *everyone* has equal right to place arguments, claims, or criticisms on the public agenda—and we can't—then how those scarce deliberative resources are distributed becomes a question of paramount importance, even if the standard Benhabib (and others) present nonetheless seems to stand at the center of a compelling ideal conception of deliberative ethics. In addressing that scarcity problem, it seems reasonable to hold that questions which press upon the fundamental justice or legitimacy of our social practices deserve heightened deliberative attention. Even if we cannot simply will ourselves to believe or disbelieve given propositions, "we can (and often do) voluntarily select what evidence we look for and how we choose to interpret it and weigh it," and therefore can "exercise indirect long-term control over many of our beliefs by choosing how we engage in inquiry,

[17] Lynn Sanders, "Against Deliberation," *Political Theory* 25, no. 3 (1997): 349.
[18] Seyla Benhabib, *The Claims of Culture: Equality and Diversity in the Global Era* (Princeton University Press, 2002), 36–37.

what sources we look to, etc."[19] These voluntary choices are properly given an ethical valence. Insofar as our political structures channel these choices in particular directions—either encouraging us to confront challenging but important pieces of epistemic data or allowing us to indulge our preference to remain safely cocooned—they cannot be confined to the realm of epistemology but are of political interest as well. As a result, democratic theorists "need to take one problem as primary. This problem is how more of the people who routinely speak less—who, through various mechanisms or accidents of birth and fortune, are least expressive in and most alienated from conventional American politics—might take part and be heard and how those who typically dominate might be made to attend to the views of others."[20]

Unfortunately, it seems likely that our current practices of deliberation do not prioritize full and fair consideration of such hard thoughts; if anything, they're geared toward deprioritizing them. Increasingly, our epistemic lives are structured so that we hear what we *want* to hear, and just as frequently what we *want* to hear is quite distant from what a healthy democratic space *requires* us to hear and consider. In such a case, the very success in meeting our epistemic desires is itself a sign of a deliberative space that is not functioning.[21]

What Does It Mean to "Take Up" a Claim?

The ambition of a deliberative ideal that takes these distributional concerns seriously is that hard thoughts are not systematically dismissed and shunted aside but rather are "taken up." "Taken up" implies a certain level of consideration beyond simply hearing or even responding to the proffered thought. It entails treating the claim in question as a live possibility, the sort of contribution which genuinely *could* be true or just or useful, and thus at the very least cannot be dismissed *prior* to actually working through the relevant analysis. In that respect, "taking up" is a public-facing concept—though I do not want to insist that in all

[19] Rima Basu, "What We Epistemically Owe to Each Other," *Philosophical Studies* 176, no. 4 (2019): 917n3; see also Pamela Hieronymi, "Controlling Attitudes," *Pacific Philosophical Quarterly* 87, no. 1 (2006): 45–74; Pamela Hieronymi, "Responsibility for Believing," *Synthese* 16, no. 3 (3008): 357–73.

[20] Sanders, "Against Deliberation," 352.

[21] Cass R. Sunstein, *#Republic: Divided Democracy in the Age of Social Media* (Princeton University Press, 2017), ix ("In a well-functioning democracy, people do not live in echo chambers or information cocoons. They see and hear a wide range of topics and ideas. They do so even if they did not, and would not, choose to see and hear those topics and those ideas in advance."). But see Andrew M. Guess, "(Almost) Everything in Moderation: New Evidence on Americans' Social Media Diets," *American Journal of Political Science* 65, no. 4 (October 2021): 1007–22 (finding significant overlaps in news sources consumed by Democrats and Republicans on social media, but that those who do silo into uniformly liberal or conservative media diets are those most likely to vote in primary and general elections).

cases it must take the form of a literal interpersonal back and forth. The reason "taken up" is public facing is because it relates to ideas that exist in a social context and our obligations to claims made by others which we are bound to consider. This obligation can, in some circumstances, be fulfilled via relatively solitary reflection—one encounters a claim and retreats to one's room to ponder and deliberate over it. But it must at some point reemerge into the public sphere as part of a conversation with the original claimant that takes them seriously as a deliberative participant.

To flesh this out: Imagine a group of friends discussing where to go for dinner. Mary suggests the local pizza place; Nate immediately replies, "No, we're not doing that." Mary would seem quite justified in objecting, "You didn't even consider it!" In that sense, even though there has been an interpersonal exchange of ideas, Mary's reply is a claim that her suggestion was not in fact taken up for discussion.

Of course, there might be scenarios where this objection is not well-taken: perhaps Mary has suggested pizza every week, and the group has already gone through and considered why it does not want to accede to the proposal. In this case, Nate could be thought to be simply incorporating that discussion by reference. But absent such special circumstances, it seems Mary is right to view her proposal as not being taken up by the group. And if we consider some of the other possibilities for why it was met with such a flip rejection—anything from "Nate doesn't like pizza and wants to short-circuit an idea which might have traction with the broader group but which is personally distasteful to him (in circumstances where the group isn't necessarily pursuing unanimity)" to "Nate dislikes Mary and wants to denigrate her standing in the group"—it is also fair for Mary to find this treatment objectionable.

Keeping with this example (and ascribing exaggerated ethical weight to proper dinner deliberations), what would it mean for Mary's suggestion to be taken up? I propose that to take up a proffered claim means to treat it as at least a plausible candidate for truth (or advisability, validity, or whatever the proper success-condition is, given the sort of claim at issue) that accordingly requires listeners give appropriate attention and consideration to reasons and arguments which support or undermine the claim. One does not "take up" the possibility that one's spouse is an Andromedan space monster because one does not treat it as even plausibly true, and thus does not begin the process of attending to reasons which might support or reject its veracity. One takes up a dinner suggestion by slotting it into the broader decisional criteria the group uses for deciding where to go for dinner (is it affordable, is it well-reviewed, does it have menu items everyone enjoys, and so on). This need not be a particularly involved process; often it might be quite cursory (either because the proposal obviously fails a dispositive criterion or because the stakes are sufficiently low that "appropriate attention and consideration" is rather minimal). And it by no means requires that Mary's suggestion ultimately carry the day. "Taken up" refers to the *process* of reasoning, not its conclusion.[22] Nonetheless, it is distinct from Nate's immediate, prima facie dismissal.

What is the proper angle of approach toward taking up a proffered *political* claim? Start with Ian Shapiro's articulation of "political deliberation" as "involving the solicitous search for right solutions in circumstances of conflict."[23] "Solicitous" is meant to evoke a collective practice of seeking the views and perspective of others, contrasting "deliberation" with "reflection," which can be done as a matter of isolated contemplation.[24] The "deliberative turn" in political theory was characterized, in part, by a shift away from such solitary reflection into actual interpersonal engagement—often face to face, at the very least involving an active give and take of views by interested parties.[25]

For my part, while the "solicitude" is important, I again do not wish to overemphasize the interpersonal character of the discussion.[26] It is likely that all or nearly all subjects of political consideration—whether done in a "deliberative" or "reflective" fashion—at least begin from hearing a claim or argument put forward by another. Even in its reflective guise, the goal of engaging in political reasoning "is not to arrive at some generalities, certainly not generalizations about social interaction or principles of justice. Instead, we are looking for just solutions to particular problems in a particular social context."[27] We engage in political reason not for its own sake but in response to particular problems, claims, and issues that emerge from our connections to other people. Yet it is certainly possible to be solicitous of the views of others through "reflective"

[22] Indeed, it seems possible for a claim to be *accepted* without being "taken up." Imagine that Mary was instead the "Queen Bee" of her social group, such that her dinner suggestions were sycophantically agreed to without any consideration whatsoever. Of course, it is likely that this sort of uncritical acceptance would be paired with uncritical rejection of the offerings of other group members (at least, when they conflict with Mary's proposals). But we can also imagine that this sort of behavior could have certain debilitating effects on Mary herself, for example, degrading her ability to actually anticipate and tailor her suggestions to the needs of others. Medina goes into these possibilities in detail in *The Epistemology of Resistance*.

[23] Ian Shapiro, "Optimal Deliberation?," *Journal of Political Philosophy* 10, no. 2 (2002): 196.

[24] *Id.* at 197. I do not agree with all of Shapiro's taxonimization; in particular, his indication that appellate courts are not "deliberative" because they "do not engage in deliberative exchange with their readers." *Id.* While it is true that judges are not necessarily in an ongoing dialogic relationship with the broader political community after the decision is announced, Shapiro overlooks the more basic feature of the judicial hearing—that cases are decided only after involved parties have full opportunity to air their arguments. In a real sense, judges are compelled to solicit the opinions of others before finalizing their own views.

[25] Robert E. Goodin and Simon J. Niemeyer, "When Does Deliberation Begin? Internal Reflection versus Public Discussion in Deliberative Democracy," *Political Studies* 51, no. 4 (2003): 627–49.

[26] See also Young, *Inclusion and Democracy*, 44–47.

[27] *Id.* at 113.

practices. For example, your friend tells you that you should become a vegetarian. You listen to his case and promise that you'll consider it. That evening, you go home and really do contemplate his arguments. Ultimately, you decide you will remain omnivorous. Here, consideration is "reflective" but nonetheless solicitous—it is prompted by, and attentive to, the arguments and claims made by others.

Now, one could rejoin that a single night's pondering is insufficient when it comes to an important ethical issue like vegetarianism. You should have returned to your friend and given him the opportunity to respond to your omnivorous conclusions, or perhaps you should have affirmatively gone out and consulted a wider array of perspectives than just your buddy's. This criticism suggests that one hasn't been sufficiently solicitous given the matter under consideration, and it suggests an instrumental rationale for favoring interpersonal deliberation over reflection: it is more solicitude *eliciting*. It is harder to avoid considering the perspectives of others when they are being put directly to one's face than when one is alone in one's bedroom. But while I concede this may be practically true in many cases, it is not a conceptual requirement: there are all manner of ways to resist taking up the views of others expressed directly in one's presence, and virtuous, curious individuals can very much pursue alternative perspectives in nonpublic settings. This is why the proper emphasis, when thinking of how persons ought to take up hard thoughts, should be on the solicitude and not on the interpersonal character per se.

Taking Up Discrimination Claims

If we move away from dinner planning and into more contentious political debates, the importance of what arguments are successfully taken up—and how we justify *avoiding* taking them up—becomes much more evident. Consider claims of discrimination.[28] Certainly, claims of discrimination are exceedingly important ones for any political or social actor, ones which on the face of it deserve considerable critical engagement and deliberative attention. Yet it is also the case that discrimination claims are often among the quickest to be *dismissed* out of hand; it seems probable that discrimination claims are—once weighted for their relative social importance—among the *least* likely claims to be successfully

[28] In addition to discrimination, there is a cluster of related wrongs—including individual discriminatory or oppressive acts, public manifestations of hatred or bias, as well as contentions of structural oppression. Although the term "discrimination" in isolation does not fully capture each of these different wrongs (e.g., it is not clear that public expression of hateful views is necessarily discrimination if unattached to any deprivation of economic, political, or social opportunity), for brevity's sake I include all under this single umbrella insofar as they are similar issues vis-à-vis a propensity toward dismissal.

taken up in public or private deliberative exchanges. This case will be discussed in detail in Chapter 4. Here, however, I want to leverage the case of discrimination claims to more fully articulate what I mean when I speak of an argument or assertion being taken up.

Those who do engage in such early dismissal of discrimination claims typically justify (if they do so at all) their failure to take up the claim on the grounds that the claims are distractions, made in bad faith—and that we can know they are made in bad faith because they are immediately and transparently false. Yet at the moment a claim of the form "This law (act, practice, belief) is discriminatory" is made, we generally cannot immediately say with certainty whether that claim is valid or not. The veracity of the claim will no doubt depend on several considerations which have yet to be determined. For starters, it almost certainly relies on certain factual assertions (about the world, about the claimant, about the target, etc.)—assertions which may or may not be accurate. Moreover, whether or not we ascribe validity to the charge often will depend on our understanding of the term "discrimination" itself. In cases such as these, Amy Gutmann and Dennis Thompson observe, "[t]o presume that we know what the right resolution is before we hear from others who will also be affected by our decisions is not only arrogant but also unjustified in light of the complexity of the issues and interests that are so often at stake."[29]

Despite its status as one of the most important concepts relating to political ethics and behavior, there is no commonly agreed-upon definition of "discrimination" even in the scholarly literature, let alone popular discourse. A charge of discrimination might be perfectly accurate along one understanding of the term, while transparently ludicrous along another.[30] This has important consequences when considering when and how such claims should be taken up. Consider the following examples:

(1) Jan joined the Ku Klux Klan, and that is racist.
(2) Jan gave a Black student a below-average grade, and that is racist.
(3) Jan supports the war on drugs, and that is racist.

Assume that in each of these examples the first clause is verifiably true: Jan really did join the KKK, gave the subpar grade, or supports the war on drugs. In the first example, there is probably widespread agreement that this behavior is indeed properly referred to as racist; assuming that Jan did in fact join the KKK, we

[29] Amy Gutmann and Dennis Thompson, *Why Deliberative Democracy?* (Princeton University Press, 2004), 12.

[30] See Dov Waxman, David Schraub, and Adam Hosein, "Arguing about Antisemitism: Why We Disagree about Antisemitism, and What We Can Do About It," *Ethnic & Racial Studies* 45, no. 9 (2022): 1803–24.

can be pretty immediately confident that the inference of racism is accurate. The second example, by contrast, seems to demand deeper factual investigation. If Jan gave the student an inferior grade simply because the work was of lower quality, then that would provide strong evidence that the claim is false. But if it could be shown that Jan held discriminatory attitudes toward Black students or that she harbored certain implicit and prejudicial biases against them, then that would provide evidence which favors the validity of the claim. In this circumstance, our pre-investigative intuitions about whether the challenged behavior is racist or not cannot provide much guidance into the actual merits of the dispute. Finally, the validity of the third claim could also depend on similar factual assessments about (for example) Jan's state of mind—if she favors aggressive drug enforcement "because of, not in spite of" its disparate impact on minority communities.[31] But it might also turn on disputes regarding what "racism" means in principle—whether it requires conscious malignant intent or whether it might encompass disparate impact scenarios or cases of structural bias. (These considerations could also come into play in the second example.) Once again, while we might have intuitions about whether Jan's support for the war on drugs is racist, it would be difficult to hold them with any degree of confidence until after we figure out the governing principle of racism and then any factual disputes which are relevant to applying that principle to Jan's case.

At this stage in the game—when we know there is a claim of discrimination on the table but little else—we have what might be called a "discrimination candidate."[32] Thinking of the claim as a candidate for discrimination—not yet known to be valid or not—accounts for several uncertainties that exist at this preliminary stage of inquiry. Most obviously, we do not know whether the facts underlying the claim are true or not. Julie Suk observes that a particular claim of racism may stand self-consciously outside prevailing understandings of the term, with the goal of "enlarging and evolving the definition of racism, which in turn enlarges the concept of responsibility for racism."[33] It is, to be sure, likely that at the end of the discussion we eventually will have to settle on a particular understanding of "racism" or "discrimination," and that might not incorporate

[31] See Personal Administrator of Massachusetts v. Feeney, 442 U.S. 256, 279 (1979) (A discriminatory purpose exists where an action is taken "because of, not merely in spite of, its adverse effects upon an identifiable group") (internal quotations omitted).

[32] Cf. Nicholas Rescher, "Foundationalism, Coherentism, and the Idea of Cognitive Systematization," *Journal of Philosophy* 71, no. 19 (1974): 703 (discussing "truth-candidates" in the context of coherentism as those claims which "are not certified truths (or even probable truths) but theses that are in a position to make some claims upon us for acceptance").

[33] Julie Suk, "Race without Cards," *Stanford Journal of Civil Rights and Civil Liberties* 5, no. 1 (April 2009): 114. See also Martha Minow, "Interpreting Rights: An Essay for Robert Cover," *Yale Law Journal* 96, no. 8 (1987): 1867 ("[R]ights represent articulations—public or private, formal or informal—of claims that people use to persuade others (and themselves) about how they should be treated and about what they should be granted.").

the speaker's claim of wrong. But that's a conclusion, not a starting point—at the outset it is no response to simply declare "That's not discrimination," because part of the controversy might precisely be over how to properly conceptualize what discrimination means. Consequently, properly appraising such a claim requires the listener to evaluate not just factual assertions but also the collective understanding of what discrimination means.[34]

A discrimination candidate hence includes any type of assertion which could be seen as a claim of discrimination under any plausible understanding of what discrimination is. A plausible understanding is meant to be broad, but not infinitely so: it is similar to William James's concept of a "live hypothesis" that is actually perceived as "a real possibility" (rather than, for example, a pure thought experiment).[35] A "discrimination candidate" thus would probably not include the statement "Jan ate an orange for lunch, and that is racist," because the idea that eating an orange on its own would be a form of racism is not a "live hypothesis" held by anyone. Nonetheless, discrimination candidates make up a very expansive category.

The set of discrimination candidates consists of every type of behavior which might fall under every plausible understanding of discrimination, and there is considerable heterodoxy in how we understand concepts like discrimination. For example, one definition of "discrimination" is "engaging in differential behavior *because of* the [identity] of the target."[36] Another view objects to a focus on the conscious thought process of the alleged perpetrator and instead looks to how a particular group is (differentially) treated.[37] Still others concentrate on the "systematic aspects of oppression . . . that are often drowned out by the more common focus upon explicitly held beliefs and attitudes."[38] The important thing is not to resolve this debate but to recognize that it is extant and ongoing. That there are sharp normative disputes about the meaning of discrimination blurs controversies over what "counts" as discrimination—a critique that may

[34] See Elizabeth S. Anderson, "Integration, Affirmative Action, and Strict Scrutiny," *New York University Law Review* 77, no. 5 (2002): 1266–67 (distinguishing between persons who oppose affirmative action because of specific factual appraisals about the state of racial affairs versus those who oppose it due to a principled commitment to the ideology of "color-blindness"); Russell K. Robinson, "Perceptual Segregation," *Columbia Law Review* 108, no. 5 (2008): 1117 ("A critical racial difference is that blacks and whites are likely to differ on the very definition of racial discrimination. Because they are using different definitions, blacks may reasonably conclude that discrimination has occurred even as whites may reasonably disagree.").

[35] William James, "The Will to Believe," in *The Will to Believe and Other Essays in Popular Philosophy* (Longmans Green, 1905), 2.

[36] Lisa Feldman Barrett and Janet K. Swim, "Appraisals of Prejudice and Discrimination," in *Prejudice: The Target's Perspective*, ed. Janet K. Swim and Charles Stangor (Elsevier, 1998), 14.

[37] Ann C. McGinley, "*¡Viva la Evolucion!* Recognizing Unconscious Motive in Title VII," *Cornell Journal of Law & Public Policy* 9, no. 2 (2000): 420.

[38] Michael J. Monahan, "The Concept of Privilege: A Critical Appraisal," *South African Journal of Philosophy* 33, no. 1 (2014): 73.

be about fundamental principles can masquerade as a simple misappraisal of facts.[39] From the vantage of dismissal, this is important because frequently discrimination claims are dismissed on the basis of a particular understanding of discrimination whose contested status is not acknowledged—meaning that a live point of controversy (what the correct conception of discrimination should be) ultimately avoids scrutiny.

Hopefully it is evident that a discrimination candidate is emphatically *not* a particular theory of what discrimination is. Discrimination candidates are just that—candidates—and so not every discrimination candidate will turn out to be actually discriminatory. But they could be, at least as far as we know *prior* to actually engaging in any substantive investigation. The idea of discrimination candidates is meant to focus our attention on the *claim*, not the *conclusion*. In particular, the breadth of what I am including under "discrimination" does not necessarily imply that discrimination should be a broad concept—certainly not so expansive as to include all discrimination candidates. No cohesive theory of discrimination could ever encompass all discrimination candidates. Some discrimination candidates are mutually contradictory—a pure anti-classificationist who thinks racial discrimination means the public use of racial categories would likely consider affirmative action discriminatory, while someone who views discrimination as failing to meet certain specific substantive obligations vis-à-vis marginalized groups might conclude that failing to provide for affirmative action is discriminatory. And even were that not the case, it seems implausible that any serious theory of discrimination would include each and every instance or event that has ever been so labeled.

It likewise should be apparent that the uncertainties latent in discrimination candidates need not be *factual* uncertainties. To be sure, sometimes facts are the problem—determining whether Jan did or did not harbor animus toward Black persons may be the decisive question in deciding whether her challenged conduct is discriminatory. But sometimes the uncertainty exists because there is a dispute over principles—what does it *mean* to say that an action was discriminatory?[40] Again, the conflict between an anti-classification approach and a substantive obligations approach provides an illustration: we might have complete agreement on the facts of a particular controversy and yet still be unsure whether a given behavior is properly labeled discriminatory if there remains a

[39] Samuel R. Bagenstos, "Implicit Bias, 'Science,' and Antidiscrimination Law," *Harvard Law & Policy Review* 1, no. 2 (2007): 480 (critiquing prominent arguments that purport to attack the "science" behind implicit bias as actually "rest[ing] on a particular set of normative views about the kinds of bias to which antidiscrimination law ought properly to respond").

[40] See Waxman Schraub, and Hosein, "Arguing about Antisemitism."

dispute over which of these two competing understandings should be accorded primacy.

The idea of discrimination candidates, in short, is not meant to present a theory of discrimination—even (especially) an "ideal" theory of discrimination. It looks to the beginning of social discussion, not the conclusion. At the moment a discrimination candidate is put on the table, there is often too much uncertainty surrounding it to determine with any confidence its truth or falsity. Do all participants in the conversation share a common understanding of the meaning of discrimination? If so, how does the claim map onto that understanding? If not, whose understanding is correct, and how does the claim fit into *that* understanding? Discrimination candidates are the building blocks upon which discussion of what discrimination "means"—which claims are valid and which are not—can proceed. And until that discussion commences, we cannot know (in advance) the validity of a particular discrimination claim. Discrimination, as a social concept, does not exist in an idealized form prior to our discussions over its meaning.

Debates about discrimination claims should recognize and duly account for the claim's initial position as a discrimination candidate that very rarely can be dismissed offhand. In particular, participants should recognize that the theory of discrimination being appealed to might not be one that (for example) entails labeling the alleged discriminator as a moral monster or that attributes the wrong to intentional malign intent. Ideally, due epistemic diligence would have us methodically explore the proposed underlying theory of discrimination to see what it has to offer as well as examine the relevant factual accounts to see if the claim can be sustained under the forwarded theory. The obligation is not to ultimately agree with the discrimination claim but rather to fairly consider it. And further, even if the claim ultimately is rejected, this would not in itself support an inference that the claim was brought in bad faith. A plausible claim of discrimination made under a plausible theory of discrimination is a valid entrant into social conversation even if, after sustained examination, it turns out to be wrong.

To sum up: What would it mean to take up a discrimination claim, such as "This law is racist"? It cannot, under normal circumstances, permit a cavalier dismissal or a rejection out of hand. It would instead entail treating the claim as a live possibility, including by being open to the possibility that the concept of racism being appealed to is different from our own pre-interactive view. While continued interpersonal engagement with a claimant is not strictly necessary, such engagement will often be the most direct avenue toward *soliciting* the actual conceptual architecture undergirding the claim and thereby allow our own response to it to develop accordingly.

Motive and Structure in Taking Up the Hard Thoughts

Hard thoughts are in large part defined by the existence of a significant motivated desire to avoid taking them up. That said, it is important to clarify that the definition of a hard thought does *not* require that, if the claim is not taken up, the *reason* it is not considered be directly attributable to the motivational rationale. Rather, the reality wherein a given claim is routinely avoided or dismissed can result from features embedded in social structures, requiring little to no conscious effort at directing. Here we see the problem of the hard thoughts taking on a structural form, divorced from avaricious individual behavior.

This accounts for the many cases where persons are sufficiently insulated from hard thoughts such that they do not, in fact, have to expend any effort to avoid taking them up. Although they do have reasons to systematically avoid considering them, they're in luck: they do not need to deploy those reasons in order to successfully evade the thought. Consider the following examples:

- Adam suspects that Betty may think he's misogynist. This prospect hurts Adam—he doesn't like to think of himself that way, and he worries about his public reputation if he is successfully deemed a misogynist—so he strives to limit the circumstances where he or his colleagues might be forced to consider Betty's view of him.
- Cheryl is a staunch liberal and believes that conservatives are nitwits. Evidence that would suggest some conservative ideas are worthwhile would deeply unsettle her whole worldview. Fortunately, Cheryl lives in an overwhelmingly liberal area and thus, through no particular effort on her part, she does not normally encounter conservative views—including those right-wing views which might be reasonable and therefore conflict with her underlying view of inveterate conservative foolishness.

In the first example, Adam's motivating reason for desiring not to take up the proffered claim is why the claim is obstructed. In the second, Cheryl possesses a similar motivated reason, but it does not play a causal role in why she can avoid taking up the claim (at least not directly). Nonetheless, under my definition both of these cases qualify as hard thoughts. And it should be apparent that, even though Cheryl's attitudes don't play a direct role in insulating her from having to encounter well-reasoned conservative views, the deliberative position she occupies nonetheless could be thought of as problematic for a host of reasons.

It is fair to wonder why I omit a strong requirement that the motivated reason be causally connected to the failure to take up the claim. There might be all sorts of potentially difficult claims which we, by pure good fortune, happen never to be forced to think about. If, as I expressed at the outset, my concern is about certain deliberative *malfunctions*, it is easy to spot how a personal motivated desire to avoid certain conversational topics could qualify as a problem. But what is the misfire that occurs in circumstances where that motivated incentive is causally detached from the failure to take up the argument? Arguments fail to be taken up all the time, and while deliberate efforts to squelch uncomfortable points of view may be obvious misconduct, the unfortunate passing of two ships in the night is perhaps of lesser concern.

The answer here is that we are not dealing simply with matters of fortune. It is not—or at least not always, and perhaps not even often—the case that the arguments that we are or are not forced to consider are distributed arbitrarily or haphazardly.[41] They are not a random sample; they track the usual grooves of power. "If you have power," Carol Gilligan once said, "you can opt not to listen. And you do so with impunity."[42] The clichéd cinematic moment when a gun is pulled and "Now are you listening?" is shouted out is an overwrought illustration, but an illustration nonetheless. Relationships of power condition what we listen to and when we can opt not to listen. And since "power," in the relevant sense, is not even primarily (let alone exclusively) the act of waving a gun, its influence permeates the entire deliberative ecosystem. As Miranda Fricker aptly observes, "social power is a capacity we have as social agents to influence how things go in the social world"—a capacity which can be exercised actively or passively.[43] Well beyond obvious cases of threat or coercion, where one stands in society in large part channels which claims one is forced to consider and which one can avoid. And Fricker further suggests that power can operate in a sufficiently dispersed and distributed fashion such that it is wholly structural—lacking any particular subject even passively exercising agency.[44]

Cheryl's case can illustrate how hard thoughts often are embedded into our social structure. In her articulation of "structure" as a site of potential injustice, Young notes that structure accounts for cases where disadvantages or wrongs

[41] Discussing her concept of hermeneutical injustice, Miranda Fricker observes that anybody might, by sheer bad luck, have an experience that is unintelligible in the prevailing argot of the time. What makes this state of affairs an *injustice* is when it is not simply a state of bad luck, when it "is no accident that their experience had been falling down the hermeneutical cracks." Miranda Fricker, *Epistemic Injustice: Power and the Ethics of Knowing* (Oxford University Press, 2007), 153.

[42] "Feminist Discourse, Moral Values, and the Law—A Conversation: The 1984 James McCormick Mitchell Lecture," *Buffalo Law Review* 34, no. 1 (1985): 62 (Isabel Marcus and Paul J. Spiegelman, moderators; Ellen C. DuBois, Mary C. Dunlap, Carol J. Gilligan, Catherine A. MacKinnon, and Carrie Menkel-Meadow, participants).

[43] Fricker, *Epistemic Injustice*, 9. Fricker uses the example of a traffic cop, who can exercise power actively (by writing a ticket) and passively (in that her mere presence—or the thought of her presence—causes drivers to alter her behavior).

[44] *Id.* at 10–11. While Fricker does make this point, others have observed that much of the work that followed has been exceedingly "culprit-based" in its approach to epistemic injustice, neglecting its structural dimension. Michael Doan, "Resisting Structural Epistemic Injustice," *Feminist Philosophical Quarterly* 4, no. 4 (2018).

are not caused by any one individual's agential choice nor direct policies of oppression or repression by governmental or institutional actors, but which are the products neither of random chance nor of misfortune.[45] What structure does is "create 'channels' for the actions of individuals, guiding and constraining them in certain directions but not disabling their flow."[46]

Even in Cheryl's case this is evident. Cheryl, we stipulated, can avoid hearing or considering more sophisticated conservative views because of the community where she lives and works. But her residence in *that* community (as against others) is hardly likely to be random, in the sense of being completely disconnected from her deliberative preferences. Persons of her political, cultural, and social milieu are likely to be channeled, via a variety of mechanisms, into communities of just this sort. Likewise, the conservative testifier who might wish to contest Cheryl's default assumptions about his or her ideology will find himself or herself uniquely obstructed from gaining Cheryl's attention. The easy routes in—being her neighbor, working at her firm, or being published in her newspaper—are likely unavailable. Even if these could be circumvented, the testifier may also lack the markers of credibility that put Cheryl on notice that this is an opinion worthy of credence. If, as Fricker tells us, a good informant must be one who is not just competent and trustworthy but also bears the *markers* of these qualities (the latter attribute Fricker terms "credibility"), then we are faced with potentially regular scenarios where there is a mismatch between those thought to possess rational authority to testify on a subject (are "credible") and those who actually do possess that authority (are in fact competent and trustworthy).[47]

One might think that these mismatches, if they occur, will be self-correcting over time: people have an incentive to collect true beliefs, so if their indicia of credibility do not actually map onto trustworthiness and competence, then the credibility indicators will have to shift. But Cheryl's case offers a scenario where this correction seems unlikely to occur. Cheryl, after all, is probably quite content with the state of affairs outlined above. An inchoate but nonetheless quite real sense of "comfort" or "being at home" might attach. Even those who relish a good political debate typically do not wish to be on call 24/7. Compared to the nagging anxiety or stress (or even, for some, exhilaration) that attaches to Thanksgiving dinner with her conservative in-laws, where people are no longer "on the same page" and foundational premises cannot be assumed to be shared,

[45] Iris Marion Young, *Responsibility for Justice* (Oxford University Press, 2011), ch. 2.

[46] *Id.* at 53, citing Jeffrey Reiman, *Justice and Modern Moral Philosophy* (Yale University Press, 1989), 213.

[47] Miranda Fricker, "Rational Authority and Social Power: Towards a Truly Social Epistemology," in *Social Epistemology: Essential Readings*, ed. Alvin I. Goldman and Dennis Whitcomb (Oxford University Press, 2011), 57, 60.

it can be downright relaxing to simply be in a place where the core political and social values are basically taken for granted.

The broader point is that social discourse and social debate occur within a social structure that is built up and conditioned by a huge network of decisions—many in the distant past—that we cannot control.[48] We don't reason in an austere way, unmediated by the social environment. Much the opposite. "In securing our knowledge," Steven Shapin writes, "we rely upon others, and we cannot dispense with that reliance."[49] Commenting on this passage, Fricker observes that this reliance has an unavoidably political valence: "[E]pistemic subjects are socially constituted individuals who stand in relations of power."[50] We rely on others to produce, warrant, ratify, and confirm the knowledge we possess—but who is in a position to (and/or who is recognized as possessing the authority to) provide this evidentiary support is neither a matter of chance nor the product of an equal or a democratic distribution.

Finally, an optimistic commentator on this structural problem of dismissal might assume that it will self-correct if and to the extent that the structural channeling of persons like Cheryl toward "wrong" beliefs (i.e., about the deficiencies of conservativism) will, via "natural" processes, prompt reassessment and reconsideration. Certain theories of free speech influenced via a classical liberal approach, for example, suggest that under conditions where there is no direct coercion and ideas are allowed to compete in the open marketplace of ideas, "bad" beliefs will progressively be supplanted by better ones. One need not be attentive to structure, under this view, because individual choices and interactions will suffice to purge mistaken views from the populace.[51]

The problem with this view is that markets supply what customers demand, and it is far from clear that deliberative actors demand "good" ideas (at least as defined by a philosopher or a reflective democrat). In part, this is because deliberative participants may simply engage in satisficing—gaining enough knowledge to adequately meet their everyday interest, but having little desire to go any

[48] Young, *Responsibility for Justice*, 54–55.

[49] Steven Shapin, *A Social History of Truth—Civility and Science in Seventeenth-Century England* (University of Chicago Press, 1994), xxv. Tocqueville makes a similar point: "There is no philosopher in the world so great that he does not believe a million things on faith in others or does not suppose many more truths than he establishes." Alexis de Tocqueville, *Democracy in America* (1840), ed. and trans. Harvey C. Mansfield and Delba Winthrop (University of Chicago Press, 2000), 408.

[50] Fricker, "Rational Authority and Social Power," 54.

[51] Cf. Brian K. Miller, "There's No Need to Compel Speech. The Marketplace of Ideas Is Working," *Forbes*, December 4, 20,217), https://www.forbes.com/sites/briankmiller/2017/12/04/theres-no-need-to-compel-speech-the-marketplace-of-ideas-is-working/?sh=538873ab4e68. Miller is an attorney at the Center of Individual Rights and wrote this column in defense of the Supreme Court's *Janus* and *Masterpiece Cakeshop* decisions, arguing that to the extent some persons are coming to the "wrong" conclusions regarding the merits of gay marriage or public-sector unionism, the marketplace of ideas would naturally allow the superior argument to eventually prevail.

further than that even when more information might be optimal.[52] But worse still, it is quite feasible that participants in the deliberative market will not just drop out of the bazaar upon attaining a satisfactory base of knowledge, but in fact actively desire and demand *irrational* or distorted views across a wide range of cases. Bryan Caplan's model of "rational irrationality" offers further detail.[53] Rational irrationality refers to the decision to hold onto an "irrational" (in the sense of generating distorted predictions) belief because the person gains private benefits from holding the belief that outweigh the material or social consequences of disturbing it.[54] A deeply religious person, for example, might experience more distress from abandoning a belief in creationism than he would see material benefits from adopting a belief in evolution.[55] Outside a few scientific disciplines, after all, few of us actually need to believe in evolution in order to generate useful predictions on a day-to-day basis. For most people the primary benefits of believing in evolution are intangible—it is in harmony with the views of our peers or is consonant with deeply set personal, cultural, or ideological beliefs. Persons with a different group of peers or priors will have a different calculus of incentives. Rational irrationality provides an explanatory framework for why people do not just lack information but actively shun it—certainly, it can encompass why they may be content living in epistemic universes where some truthful information is systematically occluded from them. It also explains why persons who lack information about their beliefs may nonetheless assert them with considerable ferocity: "[I]t is not too pleasant to affirm unreasonable views with a healthy dose of skepticism."[56] Indeed, some research distressingly suggests that where people have a significant ideological attachment to a position, correcting misinformation can actually *strengthen* the conviction with which people hold the mistaken belief.[57]

That our (social) epistemic lives will frequently be sorted in such a way as to reflect ideological preferences and minimize (for those with power, anyway) forced confrontations with dissonant or dispiriting ideas might not be straightforwardly caused by motivated avoidance—at least not in the very overt form seen in Adam's case—but it is by no means a "fortuitous" accident either. If we

[52] On satisficing, see Herbert A. Simon, "Rational Choice and the Structure of the Environment," *Psychological Review* 63, no. 2 (1956): 136.

[53] See, e.g., Bryan Caplan, "Rational Irrationality: A Framework for the Neoclassical-Behavioral Debate," *Eastern Economics Journal* 26, no. 2 (2000): 191–211; Bryan Caplan, "Rational Ignorance versus Rational Irrationality," *Kyklos* 54, no. 1 (2003): 3–26.

[54] Caplan, "Framework," 194–95.

[55] Caplan, "Rational Ignorance," 8–9 ("[A] fundamentalist's bliss belief might be that the earth is 6000 years old; it pains him to believe that the earth's age is either more or less.").

[56] *Id.* at 10.

[57] Brendan Nyhan and Jason Reifler, "When Corrections Fail: The Persistence of Political Misconceptions," *Political Behavior* 32, no. 2 (2010): 323.

think that sort of self-segregation is politically problematic for people who still are asked to engage in political reasoning with a broader, heterogeneous set of interlocutors, then I suggest this sort of circumstance is a central form of the broader problem of dismissal. And so it is that this idea of dismissal—the core focus of the book—takes center stage in the next chapter.

2
Ignorance, Dismissal, and Motivated Cognition

People have preferences about the beliefs that they hold.[1] That is to say, they do not simply want to know the unvarnished truth; they want to believe what they *want* to believe. And by the same token, there are also invariably thoughts they would rather sweep under the rug: "[W]e all have things we would rather avoid: things that are hard to hear, things that are difficult to accept or even to acknowledge."[2] Such beliefs are often uncomfortably dissonant with our core ideologies or self-conceptions, and so people try their best to remove them from our epistemic lives.[3] This realization is what makes the problem of "hard thoughts" so central to proper democratic deliberation.

This chapter offers a critical account and expansion of the literature on motivated cognition to help flesh out the concept of the hard thoughts. I suggest that motivated cognition be thought of as a continuum consisting of several "cognitive checkpoints"—ignorance, dismissal, and (evaluative) motivated reasoning—each of which offers a unique obstruction to considering hard thoughts. In the following chapter, I will link this process, and in particular the act of dismissal, to Miranda Fricker's concept of "epistemic injustice"—wronging someone in their capacity as a knower.[4] The act of avoiding consideration of

[1] This chapter, as well as parts of Chapters 3 and 8, are adapted from portions of David Schraub, "Deliberation and Dismissal," *University of Pennsylvania Journal of Constitutional Law* 22, no. 5 (August 2020): 1319–87.

[2] Jose Medina, *The Epistemology of Resistance: Gender and Racial Oppression, Epistemic Injustice, and Resistant Imaginations* (Oxford University Press, 2013), 34.

[3] James H. Kuklinski, Paul J. Quirk, Jennifer Jerit, David Schwieder, and Robert F. Rich, "Misinformation and the Currency of Democratic Citizenship," *Journal of Politics* 62, no. 3 (2000): 794 ("[I]nconsistency causes dissonances. Because dissonance is uncomfortable, the individual seeks to avoid it. Better, then, to make inferences that fit one's existing beliefs and attitudes than not."); Daniel T. Gilbert, Elizabeth C. Pinel, Timothy D. Wilson, Stephen J. Blumberg, and Thalia P. Wheatley, "Immune Neglect: A Source of Durability Bias in Affective Forecasting," *Journal of Personality & Social Psychology* 75, no. 3 (1998): 619 (discussing our "psychological immune system" that fights against hostile information threatening to our sense of self); E. Tory Higgins, "Self-Discrepancy: A Theory Relating Self and Affect," *Psychology Review* 94, no. 3 (1987): 319 ("The notion that people who hold conflicting or incompatible beliefs are likely to experience discomfort has had a long history in psychology.").

[4] Miranda Fricker, *Epistemic Injustice: Power and the Ethics of Knowing* (Oxford University Press, 2007), 20.

Deliberation, Dismissal, and Democracy. David Schraub, Oxford University Press. © Oxford University Press (2025). DOI: 10.1093/9780197816424.003.0003

the hard thoughts, while obviously troublesome insofar as it obstructs public consideration of important social problems, also functions as an ethical wrong.

* * *

Motivated cognition, or motivated reasoning,[5] describes the "less-than-conscious tendency to reason toward one's preferred result."[6] "Everyday experience confirms that people's judgments are often biased by their beliefs, desires, and vested interests,"[7] and legal scholarship has not ignored the problem. Typically, however, it has analyzed motivated cognition through one particular mechanism: biased evaluation of ambiguous situations. For example, a judge considering whether to exclude evidence from an arguably unlawful search may be influenced by the egregiousness of the underlying crime; her desire to punish a particularly vicious act may slant her appraisal of the underlying legal issues.[8] I term this "evaluative motivated reasoning."

But evaluative motivated reasoning is only part of a larger continuum of motivated cognition. Biased reasoning is necessary only if one needs to consider an argument in the first place. If it can be dismissed out of hand—or is never heard in the first place—then much taxing cognitive effort can be avoided altogether. Hence, there are two prior "cognitive checkpoints" that also serve to ward off discomforting thoughts—what I call "ignorance" and "dismissal." Precisely because these latter maneuvers elide the need to substantively reason at all, they can be far more effective—and far more dangerous—than their more commonly acknowledged cousin.

Ignorance is, as one might expect, the state of simply not knowing the challenging information. This can be purely coincidental, but it also encompasses acts or structures whereby persons are able to effectively shun sources of information which they predict will yield dissonance—for example, liberals refusing to watch Fox News while conservatives skip past MSNBC. Yet even if one does end up hearing a claim, one often can still elect not to examine, investigate, or otherwise consider its details or particulars. This is an act of *dismissal*—it parallels the civil procedure concept, which also acts to terminate (judicial) consideration of a given (legal) claim prior to the discovery process. I position these

[5] See generally Ziva Kunda, "The Case for Motivated Reasoning," *Psychological Bulletin* 108, no. 3 (1990): 480–98. Technically speaking, one can refer to both directionally based and accuracy-based reasoning as "motivated cognition." (One is motivated either by direction or by accuracy.) See *id.* at 480–81. For purposes of this chapter, I consider "motivated cognition" to refer exclusively to the former.

[6] Avani Mehta Sood, "Cognitive Cleansing: Experimental Psychology and the Exclusionary Rule," *Georgetown Law Journal* 103, no. 6 (2015): 1547.

[7] David K. Sherman and Geoffrey L. Cohen, "Accepting Threatening Information: Self-Affirmation and the Reduction of Defensive Biases," *Current Directions in Psychological Science* 11, no. 4 (2002): 119.

[8] See generally Sood, "Cognitive Cleansing."

three mechanisms—ignorance, dismissal, and evaluative moral reasoning—as part of a continuum[9] of motivated cognition whereby we protect ourselves from adopting beliefs inconsistent with our priors.[10]

To illustrate the difference between the three concepts, consider the following example. Dana believes that racial discrimination in America, particularly by authority figures, is rare and getting rarer. She is attached to this viewpoint due to various ideological and social bonds, and therefore does not like hearing about cases and circumstances which challenge her optimistic view regarding America's racial state. Josh is a person of color who claims to have been racially profiled by the police. How might Dana successfully dissipate the threat Josh's allegation poses to her worldview?

The first answer is that Dana might remain *ignorant* about the allegation altogether. Of course, there are all sorts of innocent reasons why Dana might never hear about Josh's incident—but there are also ways in which she can stack the deliberative deck.[11] For example, Dana might (consciously or not) think that persons of color are more likely to make discomforting allegations of racial prejudice and therefore she may be less likely to socialize with members of other racial groups so as to reduce the probability that she will encounter such a claim. Beyond her set of personal acquaintances, Dana might tailor her media consumption to favor outlets which are less likely to devote attention to discrimination claims and thus are less likely to pass along Josh's story. If she successfully avoids hearing about the claim, she need not expend any additional effort rationalizing it.

Suppose, though, that Dana does become aware of Josh's claim. Maybe a friend raises Josh's complaint, or maybe his story happened to be picked up

[9] The description of motivated cognition as a continuum suggests that there are not sharp boundaries between ignorance, dismissal, and evaluative motivated reasoning. Just how much awareness moves a listener from ignorance to dismissal, or how much consideration is necessary to convert dismissal into evaluative motivated reasoning, are matters of judgment. That each may sometimes shade into the others does not significantly affect the concepts' clarity.

[10] In other words, all three processes—ignorance, dismissal, and evaluative motivated reasoning—can fit under the broader umbrella of motivated cognition. There is potential for confusion, since in the literature "motivated reasoning" and "motivated cognition" are typically used interchangeably. Sood suggests that motivated cognition is the superior term because it encompasses "not only active reasoning" (what I am terming evaluative motivated reasoning) "but also more immediate forms of acquiring knowledge and understanding, such as visual perception." Avani Mehta Sood, "Motivated Cognition in Legal Judgments—An Analytic Review," *Annual Review of Law & Social Science* 9 (2013): 309. So one could simply call this final step in the continuum "motivated reasoning" and the broader phenomenon "motivated cognition." But this would be idiosyncratic, and so to avoid confusion I use the label "evaluative motivated reasoning" to distinguish it from other forms of motivated cognition which do not engage in explicit analysis of the proffered claim.

[11] Consider James Baldwin's searing indictment of the "innocence" of White people in the face of ongoing racial injustice: "[T]hey have destroyed and are destroying hundreds of thousands of lives and do not know it and do not want to know it. . . . [I]t is not permissible that the authors of devastation should also be innocent. *It is the innocence which constitutes the crime.*" James Baldwin, *The Fire Next Time* (Vintage, 1993), 5–6 (emphasis added).

by the nightly news. Even so, it is rarely if ever the case that all the details of a given situation emerge before the recipient of the information has time to react. Though Dana now is aware of the basics of the issue—that Josh alleges he was the victim of profiling—she need not entertain it as a live possibility worthy of her time. She can also *dismiss* it as unworthy of attention—"He's just playing the race card"—and thus justify refraining from delving into the details that would ultimately ratify whether the claim was a legitimate one or not.

Despite her best efforts, however, there are circumstances where Dana might be effectively forced to take Josh's claims seriously. She might be Josh's friend (in which case accusing him of "playing the race card" would be at the very least rude, and at worst would fracture their relationship outright); she might encounter Josh's case as part of the assigned reading in an academic seminar; or she might be a jury member in Josh's civil suit. In these cases, powerful norms exist which compel Dana to listen to the whole story and actually weigh the evidence presented. And this is the stage where evaluative motivated reasoning comes into play. If the case is ambiguous or the evidence unclear, Dana is likely to subtly interpret these ambiguities in ways which are consistent with her worldview. Josh *was* exceeding the speed limit (even if by only 10 miles per hour), and the police officer *did* say that his demeanor was suspicious given the time and neighborhood.

This last step—*evaluative motivated reasoning*—is often given outsized attention. But it is actually best thought of as the final checkpoint on a cognitive continuum that also includes ignorance and dismissal. Far from being the sine qua non of motivated cognition, it is often the move of last resort. Exploring how ignorance and dismissal interact with their more familiar cousin provides a richer understanding of the psychological processes which enable us to protect deeply felt beliefs from external challenges. They also front-load a problem I identified in Chapter 1: the maldistribution of deliberative expenditures to favor the sorts of claims which are amenable to dominant social groups. As a psychological tic, anyone can (and likely does) engage in evaluative motivated reasoning. But as we will see, ignorance and (especially) dismissal are particularly likely to facilitate inequalities in which sorts of claims and arguments successfully penetrate into widespread public discourse.

Before we dive into these checkpoints, however, it is worth briefly exploring why people are "motivated" to believe anything other than true or at least well-warranted assertions. Put differently: why isn't the truth motivation enough? It's important to stress that the problem here stretches significantly beyond mere lack of information. Well before the development of the motivated cognition literature, scholars had been exploring why people lacked critical information about basic political questions and other seemingly important issues. On this point, Anthony Downs pioneered the idea of "rational ignorance," arguing that where increased knowledge is unlikely to result in tangible benefits to a person, it is rational for that person to remain ignorant on the matter.[12] Voting was the paradigmatic example—the likelihood that a single voter will meaningfully affect policy decisions is incalculably slim; hence there is no reason for voters to become informed about public policy. Herbert Simon provides a more general account with his idea of "satisficing"—that agents, far from seeking perfect results (insisting on using the very best tool, picking the most qualified candidate, and so on), will typically be content with a "good enough" choice.[13] A tool which gets the job done is perfectly acceptable to use, even if there is a better tool out there if one continued to look. An applicant who can fill the role is perfectly acceptable to hire, even if holding the search open might yield an even better choice. When it comes to acquiring knowledge (truthful or otherwise), the same considerations apply, and there is little reason to think people will consciously seek out more than they need to satisfactorily achieve their desired ends.

Rational ignorance explains why persons often possess very little information about seemingly important concepts, such as public policy issues. But "there is an important distinction between being *un*informed and being *mis*informed."[14] The focus on rational failed to explain several seemingly essential facts about citizen (mis)information. First, while it could explain widespread ignorance, it could not explain any particular patterns of ignorance. If pure lack of information was the problem, beliefs would be distributed somewhat randomly. Yet it seemed clear that low-information voters exhibited patterns of misunderstandings. Patterns of misinformation—not just the lack of knowledge but a slant for or against a particular worldview—are hard to attribute to rational ignorance. A rationally ignorant person is not actively averse to knowledge—knowledge might not be actively sought out, but neither is it discounted or ignored if it should happen to fall into one's lap. So if rational ignorance was the sole or primary driver of political (un)information we should still see a weak and fitful tendency toward accurate beliefs. Second, the theory of rational ignorance would predict a correlation between the amount of knowledge a person possessed about a subject and the amount of confidence or certitude with which they held their views. A person lacking information might have a tentative belief on a given matter, but knowing how little they knew they should readily acknowledge the possibility

[12] See generally Anthony Downs, *An Economic Theory of Democracy* (Harper & Row, 1957); Anthony Downs, "An Economic Theory of Political Action in a Democracy," *Journal of Political Economy* 65, no. 2 (April 1957): 146–47.

[13] Herbert A. Simon, "Rational Choice and the Structure of the Environment," *Psychological Review* 63, no. 2 (1956): 136 ("A 'satisficing' path [is] a path that will permit satisfaction at some specified level of all [an actor's] needs.").

[14] Brendan Nyhan and Jason Reifler, "When Corrections Fail: The Persistence of Political Misconceptions," *Political Behavior* 32, no. 2 (2010): 304.

that an alternative conclusion was actually correct.[15] Yet this is not borne out by the empirical research either—people regularly express exceptional confidence in their conclusions on topics they know very little about.[16]

In short, people have preferences about the beliefs they hold. Part of the utility of holding a certain belief is that it generates accurate predictions which make it easier to achieve one's (external) preferences. But there are often intrinsic values to holding certain beliefs which do not depend on their being accurate or not—such as consonance with deeply felt ideological commitments or solidarity with one's peer group.[17] For many categories of belief, the latter type of utility will be implicated far more regularly than the former. This is most obvious in the case of beliefs that don't correspond to any truth-statement (e.g., whether it is better to root for the Dodgers or the Giants). Even though the decision regarding one's favorite baseball team could not assist in rendering any predictions about the world, it is not the case that such beliefs are randomly distributed, and it is not the case that these beliefs don't color how we appraise ambiguous information (e.g., about a controversial call).[18] And even in circumstances where there is truth to be had, when it comes to general normative questions of the sort that are the subject of widespread political debate it is probably quite rare that the average person will derive more expected benefit from being accurate than from maintaining a psyche-pleasing perspective.

In addition to the desire to express cultural solidarity, another line of research suggests that persons are motivated to protect their self-integrity, that is, "the sense that, on the whole, one is a good and appropriate person," as would be understood by the relevant cultural institutions.[19] As David Sherman and Geoffrey Cohen observe, this sense of self spends much of the day under threat from events and mishaps which challenge how we would prefer to think about ourselves.[20] Sometimes we accommodate the challenging information and alter our attitudes or behavior, but often we will look for ways to sublimate the threat by

[15] But see Justin Kruger and David Dunning, "Unskilled and Unaware of It: How Difficulties in Recognizing One's Own Incompetence Lead to Inflated Self-Assessments," *Journal of Personality and Social Psychology* 77, no. 6 (1999): 1121–34.

[16] See James H. Kuklinski, Paul J. Quirk, Jennifer Jerit, David Schwieder, and Robert F. Rich, "Misinformation and the Currency of Democratic Citizenship," *Journal of Politics* 62, no. 3 (August 2000): 809 (concluding that people are often not just wrong but confidently wrong in their political beliefs).

[17] See Dan M. Kahan, "Neutral Principles, Motivated Cognition, and Some Problems for Constitutional Law," *Harvard Law Review* 125, no. 1 (November 2011): 20 (noting that "[a]ffirming one's membership in an important reference group" can be a powerful sort of goal that motivates one's cognitive processes).

[18] See generally Albert H. Hastorf and Hadley Cantril, "They Saw a Game: A Case Study," *Journal of Abnormal and Social Psychology* 49, no. 1 (1954): 129–34.

[19] David K. Sherman and Geoffrey L. Cohen, "The Psychology of Self-Defense: Self-Affirmation Theory," *Advances in Experimental Social Psychology* 38 (2006): 185–86. See generally Claude M. Steele, "The Psychology of Self-Affirmation: Sustaining the Integrity of the Self," *Advances in Experimental Social Psychology* 21 (1988): 261–302.

[20] Sherman and Cohen, "Psychology of Self-Defense," 183–84.

"dismissing, denying, or avoiding the threat in some way."[21] All of this contributes to what Daniel Gilbert and his cohorts call a psychological "immune system" that fights against hostile information threatening to our sense of self.[22]

Ignorance

Evaluative motivated reasoning—the subject of most of the literature on motivated cognition—allows for people to rationalize around received information so that they do not threaten one's cultural or ideological priors. It relies on biased appraisal of evidence—faced with a discussion about, say, gun control or global warming, persons will selectively read the arguments so as to fit within their preexisting beliefs.[23] In other words, this form of reasoning kicks in at the point where one is already relatively deeply enmeshed in the merits of the dispute.

Hopefully, it is obvious why motivated reasoning of this sort does not account for anything close to the majority of scenarios where a given claim is not ratified by surrounding social actors. The overwhelming majority of claims are not accepted as true not because they are evaluated and discounted in a biased (or nonbiased) manner but because they are never heard at all. Most people, obviously, remain unaware of most claims. They do not read, hear, or otherwise encounter them, and so they never have any occasion to appraise them (whether dispassionately or not). And so a discussion of the continuum of motivated cognition cannot begin with cases of biased evaluation (even though that concept, as the dominant player in the literature, necessarily lurks in the background),[24] but rather must commence by exploring the phenomenon of *ignorance*.

On its own, ignorance might not seem especially worthy of much concern. There are limits to the amount of information anyone can reasonably be expected to process, and so the fact that most claims won't be appraised is true only in the trivial and banal sense that a great many claims will never be given attention. This might be all that needs to be said on the subject were it the case that the distribution of heard and unheard claims was random. But this is exceptionally unlikely to be true. It is quite clear that people frequently structure

[21] *Id.* at 186.

[22] Gilbert et al., "Immune Neglect," 619.

[23] *See* Dan M. Kahan, Ellen Peters, Erica Dawson, and Paul Slovic, "Motivated Numeracy and Enlightened Self-Government," *Behavioural Public Policy* 1, no. 1 (2017): 69.

[24] I place this chapter's three subsections in the order that they are because this reflects the temporal priority with which one encounters them—one starts off ignorant, if ignorance is overcome then one can dismiss, and if one cannot dismiss then one can engage in evaluative motivated cognition. But because the existing literature I draw on is so heavily centered on the final step, it is impossible to discuss ignorance and dismissal without at least some allusion to evaluative motivated cognition—if only to articulate what the latter concept does not encompass and cannot explain.

their social worlds so that they are relatively unlikely to hear claims that they'd rather not consider. The most obvious and well-known form this practice, as discussed above, comes in the form of media selection—liberals don't watch Fox, conservatives avoid MSNBC.[25]

Hence the first cognitive checkpoint that helps ward off thoughts we'd rather not think is simply remaining ignorant about them in the first place. "Ignorance," Shannon Sullivan and Nancy Tuana observe, "often is thought of as a gap in knowledge, as an epistemic oversight that easily could be remedied once it has been noticed. It can seem to be an accidental by-product of the limited time and resources that human beings have to investigate and understand their world."[26] But ignorance can be quite conscious and volitional: we specifically construct our social spheres so as to minimize the situations where we come face to face with discomfiting claims.[27] The Fox/MSNBC divide provides a stark demonstration that ignorance is more than just an acknowledgment of the inevitable limits of our attention and cognitive resources and can instead represent an active attempt to distribute said resources to problems amenable to our ideological or cultural desires.

Ignorance can also be an implicit or unconscious phenomenon. Consider the concept of "aversive racism," which plays a significant role in the related literature on implicit bias.[28] Aversive racism generally refers to the interplay between conscious egalitarian commitments and subconscious racial prejudice,

[25] Pew Research Center for the People and the Press, "Americans Spending More Time Following the News," September 12, 2010, http://www.people-press.org/2010/09/12/americans-spending-more-time-following-the-news/ (finding that three-quarters of Fox viewers are conservative and three-quarters of MSNBC viewers are liberal or moderates).

[26] Shannon Sullivan and Nancy Tuana, "Introduction," in *Race and Epistemologies of Ignorance*, ed. Shannon Sullivan and Nancy Tuana (SUNY Press, 2007), 1.

[27] Bernhard Salow argues that we cannot intentionally select evidence that is biased in favor of our own preferred outcomes because we should assess such evidence only in relation to whether it is more or less persuasive than one would expect from a source we know to be biased. So, for example, while a prosecutor's case may in the abstract provide evidence only for the defendant's guilt, since we know that this is the prosecutor's explicit objective we should find his case to *actually* be evidence for the defendant's guilt only if it is stronger than expected given our knowledge of its objective. If it's *weaker* than expected, by contrast, we should actually take that as evidence of the defendant's innocence (on a sort of "Is that all you've got?" logic). Bernhard Salow, "The Externalist's Guide to Fishing for Compliments," *Mind* 127, no. 507 (July 2018): 697–99. However, Salow concedes that *in practice* this sort of biased evidentiary accumulation may well generate biased formation of beliefs, albeit "only by exploiting our failure to conform our beliefs to our total evidence." *Id.* at 699n10. And his account also seems to allow for the *unintentional* selection of biased evidence, which likely accounts for the structural ignorance cases discussed below.

[28] See, e.g., John F. Dovidio and Samuel L. Gaertner, "Aversive Racism," *Advances in Experimental Social Psychology* 36 (2004): 1–52 [hereinafter Dovidio and Gaertner, "Aversive Racism"]; John F. Dovidio and Samuel L. Gaertner, "Aversive Racism and Selection Decisions: 1989 and 1999," *Psychological Science* 11, no. 4 (2000): 315–19 [hereinafter Dovidio and Gaertner, *Selection Decisions*]; Samuel L. Gaertner and John F. Dovidio, "The Aversive Form of Racism," in *Prejudice, Discrimination, and Racism*, ed. John F. Dovidio and Samuel L. Gaertner (Academic Press, 1986), 61–89 [hereinafter Gaertner and Dovidio, "Aversive Form"].

resulting in the imposition of racial inequalities only when they can be justified by neutral rationales.[29] But the "aversive" in "aversive racism" refers to a practice of avoidance—because people feel the dissonance between their conscious desire for egalitarianism and their subconscious prejudice, they learn to associate interracial interaction with anxiety and discomfort and so become "averse" to and avoid such engagements.[30] In this way, the anxiety often felt toward interracial interaction, and the ensuing self-segregation, can be seen as a form of (motivated) ignorance.[31]

But ignorance need not be sought out—even subconsciously—to have normative significance. It can also have a structural component that transcends anyone's conscious or unconscious choice to avoid hearing certain types of assertions. Even absent such a decision, the sorts of claims that are likely to emerge out of the infinite din of human experience and make it onto the broader social radar screen are not randomly distributed. This is true for at least two reasons. First, the default package of socially salient issues that is immediately accessible without effort typically reflects that which is important to particular empowered classes. "Ignorance" can in some cases simply reflect a lack of epistemic curiosity: people accept the default offerings and feel no desire to interrogate further.[32] Moreover, "social stratification" often helps insulate the beneficiaries of unjust systems "from their effects; they experience all of the pleasure and see none of the pain."[33] Residential segregation, narrowly focused media, and government responsiveness to the interests of certain social classes over others, all contribute to an unequal distribution of claims which receive meaningful attention.

Second, even where social actors are affirmatively engaged listeners it still might be the case that claims favored by particular groups will be less able to be rendered intelligible and therefore will not be expressed. This is what Fricker refers to as a "hermeneutical injustice."[34] A hermeneutical injustice refers to the problem whereby "relations of unequal power can skew shared hermeneutical resources" such that the perspectives of the powerful are easily expressed through normal, well-understood social narratives, while the powerless find that

[29] See Dovidio and Gaertner, "Aversive Racism," 7.

[30] Gaertner and Dovidio, "Aversive Form," 64.

[31] See Clarissa Hayward, "Responsibility and Ignorance: On Dismantling Structural Injustice," *Journal of Politics* 79, no. 2 (2017): 396–408; Charles W. Mills, "White Ignorance," in Sullivan and Tuana, *Race and Epistemologies of Ignorance*, 13.

[32] See Medina, *Epistemology of Resistance*, 33 (describing the epistemic vice resulting "from the privilege of not needing to know[:] a lack of curiosity about those areas of life or those social domains that one has learned to avoid or not to concern oneself with").

[33] David Schraub, "Sticky Slopes," *California Law Review* 101, no. 5 (2013): 1304. *See also* Robin DiAngelo, "White Fragility," *International Journal of Critical Pedagogy* 3, no. 3 (2011): 58 ("Growing up in segregated environments . . . white interests and perspectives are almost always central. An inability to see or consider significance in the perspectives of people of color results.").

[34] Fricker, *Epistemic Injustice*, 147.

their understanding of their own experiences is not quite as intelligible under these standard modes of communication.[35] Sexual harassment, prior to the popularization of the term, is a paradigmatic example of a harm that was difficult to elucidate, even for women, not just because of overt biases but also because the relevant public knowledge for understanding it as a conceptually cohesive wrong had yet to be developed.[36] Prior to the 1970s or 1980s, men could remain ignorant of the problem of sexual harassment simply because there was not yet any widely accepted language available that would render a claim of "sexual harassment" intelligible.

The practical effects of ignorance, in its systematic dimension, are to render certain types of opinions normal and others rare or aberrant. A person who very infrequently hears claims of racial profiling will find the exceptions to be, well, exceptional (even if the reason they're an exception is not because of their infrequency but rather because most of the others were unaired or otherwise failed to register). And in turn, the content of the "normal" or "typical" opinions registered in a particular social context has an impact on what opinions are likely to be presented in the future. People do not simply blurt out any thought or claim on their mind; they are far more likely to do so when they feel their arguments are in tune with the opinions of those around them, and are far more likely to keep silent when they do not.[37] This reticence has a cascading effect: persons do not voice opinions they think are unpopular, further marginalizing their public salience and making it even less likely that such thoughts will gain airing in the future.[38] The result is what Elisabeth Noelle-Neumann calls a "spiral of silence."[39] And the hermeneutical maldistribution identified by Fricker amplifies the effect:

[35] *Id.* at 148.

[36] *See id.* at 149–51. *See generally* Catherine A. MacKinnon, *Sexual Harassment of Working Women* (Yale University Press, 1979).

[37] Frances Bowen and Kate Blackmon, "Spirals of Silence: The Dynamic Effects of Diversity on Organizational Voice," *Journal of Management Studies* 40, no. 6 (2003): 1396 ("People's willingness to express their opinions is influenced not only by their own personal opinions, but also by their external environment, particularly what they perceive as the prevailing 'climate of opinion.' When they are not sure that they agree with the majority, people are reluctant to express their opinions.").

[38] See *id.* ("When people perceive that they share the dominant opinion they will speak out, strengthening this position, whilst those who perceive that they hold the minority opinion will become more silent, diminishing their position."). Compare Timur Kuran and Cass R. Sunstein, "Availability Cascades and Risk Regulation," *Stanford Law Review* 51, no. 4 (1999): 685 (arguing that prevalent or expressed opinions have a tendency to "cascade"—they "trigger chains of individual responses that make these perceptions appear increasingly plausible through their rising availability in public discourse").

[39] Elisabeth Noelle-Neumann, "The Spiral of Silence: A Theory of Public Opinion," *Journal of Communication* 24, no. 2 (1974): 44 ("The more individuals perceive these tendencies and adapt their views accordingly, the more the one faction appears to dominate and the other to be on the downgrade. Thus the tendency of the one to speak up and the other to be silent starts off a spiraling process which increasingly establishes one opinion as the prevailing one."). See generally Elisabeth Noelle-Neumann, *The Spiral of Silence. A Theory of Public Opinion—Our Social Skin* (University of Chicago Press, 1984).

it limits the rhetorical resources available even for dissidents who are willing to buck the dominant trend. In this way, patterns of ignorance are able to replicate and sustain themselves with considerable vigor and longevity.

Dismissal

Another form of suppressing—or more accurately, evading—dissonance is through dismissal. Dismissal is a species of motivated cognition in that it is a form of direction-oriented (rather than accuracy-oriented) reasoning.[40] But unlike evaluative motivated reasoning, which is a (biased) means for assessing the evidence of a proposition, dismissal occurs when one refuses to consider the claim at all.

In Chapter 4, I will offer a keynote example of the dismissal: the case of the "bad faith" response to charges of discrimination (e.g., alleging that a discrimination claimant is just "playing the race card"). For now, it suffices to note that the key attribute of the bad faith response—what makes it a form of *dismissal*—is that it dispenses with the claim without having to engage with it on its merits. To say that someone is "playing the race card" is to say that their claim is fundamentally illicit—a ploy done for tactical advantage rather than an organic attempt to advance discussion—and therefore need not be taken seriously. This maneuver justifies refraining from engaging in reasoned deliberation over the discrimination claim, which in turn dissipates the risk that one might have to accept its validity.

In many circumstances, dismissal can be thought of as a special case of what Fricker calls a "testimonial injustice." A testimonial injustice occurs where "prejudice on the hearer's part causes him to give the speaker less credibility than he would otherwise have given."[41] Often the decision to dismiss is indeed tied to assessments about the claimant's reliability that are explicitly prejudicial. The rhetoric surrounding the "race card" claim, for example, frequently relies upon notions that marginalized persons are epistemically incredible—that they lack objectivity or dispassionate neutrality compared to putatively unmarked majoritarian observers.[42] Calling into question the capacity of marginalized persons to

[40] See Kunda, "Motivated Reasoning," 480–81.

[41] Fricker, *Epistemic Injustice*, 4.

[42] Derrick Bell, "The Rules of Racial Standing," in *Faces at the Bottom of the Well: The Permanence of Racism* (Basic, 1992), 113 (noting that Black people speaking about racism will be viewed as "less effective witnesses than are whites . . . reflect[ing] a widespread assumption that blacks, unlike whites, cannot be objective on racial issues"). Bell also provides for an important exception: when members of marginalized groups criticize members of their *own* community, then their testimony will be accorded enhanced weight. *Id.* at 114–15.

make credible claims in the public sphere is an easy means of dispensing with their arguments without having to engage with their substance.

But like ignorance, dismissal can also result from structural factors that do not necessarily implicate even implicit personal biases. For example, our priors about what is likely to be relevant or useful information in carrying inquiry forward may cause us to discount particular testimonial offerings—refusing to engage with them as part of an ongoing political or social debate.[43] Return to Fricker's concept of a "hermeneutical injustice," whereby we lack the relevant language to understand a given claim as part of a generalizable or systematic experience recognized as wrong. Fricker focuses on the knower who can't effectively articulate her own experience. But there is a related problem for the listener who fails to adequately perceive potentially valid claims due to an overly cramped and partial account of the relevant principles. These are two sides of the same coin: the shared problem is that differing hermeneutical resources make certain types of claims (favored by certain types of persons) easy to process while rendering others opaque.[44]

In the discrimination context, for example, the prevailing narrative of the concept might cast discrimination as something extreme (Nazi- or Klan-like) and/or rare.[45] If this is how discrimination is understood, then a discrimination claim which lacks these characteristics (e.g., complaining about microaggressions or paternalism) might feel discordant or ridiculous even to one who does not believe that the claimant's class should generally have their credibility discounted. Such listeners would justify brushing this sort of discrimination claim aside because it refers to something too minor, or to something that would implicate too many people, to be properly labeled "discrimination."[46]

It is possible, of course, that the person who rejects a claim of discrimination on the grounds that the challenged conduct was insufficiently serious does so because they believe a measure of seriousness is properly incorporated into the

[43] Christopher Hookway, "Some Varieties of Epistemic Injustice: Reflections on Fricker," *Episteme* 7, no. 2 (2010): 157–58 ("There could be a form of injustice related to assertion and testimony that consisted, not in a silencing refusal to take the testimony to be true or expressing knowledge, but in a refusal to take seriously the ability of the agent to provide information that is relevant in the current context.").

[44] See John S. Dryzek, *Deliberative Democracy and Beyond: Liberals, Critics, Contestations* (Oxford University Press, 2000), 70–71 (contending that political argument "involves communication in the terms set by the powerful, who almost by definition are those best able to articulate their arguments in terms of the dominative speech culture of a society").

[45] See Taunya Lovell Banks, "Exploring White Resistance to Racial Reconciliation in the United States," *Rutgers Law Review* 55, no. 4 (2003): 948 ("The dominant perception of a 'racist' is only the most extreme example—a person who rabidly hates, often to the point of violence, persons from other racialized groups.").

[46] *See* Corne v. Bausch and Lomb, Inc., 390 F. Supp. 161, 163 (D. Ariz. 1975) (rejecting an early attempt to bring suit on a sexual harassment theory because "holding such activity to be actionable under Title VII would be a potential federal lawsuit every time any employee made amorous or sexually oriented advances toward another").

definition of the term. They might define "discrimination" to mean something like "unjustified differential treatment on account of a protected identity that passes some threshold of severity," and then claim the case at issue fails the last proviso. Assuming such a person is willing to engage in the meta-debate over whether that definition is correct, this would not be dismissal.

But one wonders if those who appear to dismiss claims of discrimination on account of their "minor" character truly conceive of themselves as adding a "severity" rider to their definition of the term. Certainly, it is not implausible that some might desire to bracket off certain terms as referring only to the most serious cases—this is part of what motivates Lawrence Blum to call for "a more varied and nuanced moral vocabulary for talking about the domain of race" beyond just "racism."[47] Yet if that is what is happening, the dispute is primarily a semantic one, and moreover it invites the creation of additional, alternative terms to encompass "unjustified differential treatment" that falls short of the severity threshold—"microaggression," for instance. Notably, it does not seem the case that those who complain about "discrimination" wrongfully being applied to less sweeping cases have typically overlapped with those who have praised the introduction of "microaggression" into our lexicon as a welcome expansion and pluralization of our taxonomy.[48] In practice, the attempt to negate a discrimination claim on account of its allegedly trivial character is, more often than not, an act of dismissal.

In any event, hopefully it is clear how these two bases for dismissal—the testimonial and the hermeneutical—can end up reinforcing one another and further foster harmful attitudes and practices toward marginalized persons. If marginalized persons regularly level claims which feel groundless because they fall into a hermeneutical gap, it is easy to arrive at the mistaken belief that these persons simply lack a reasoned or "objective" view of the relevant facts or principles and can therefore be discounted. Likewise, to the extent that marginalized persons are most likely to perceive a lacuna in the dominant understanding of important social norms, a testimonial injustice which preemptively discredits minority perspectives makes it more difficult for their observations to receive

[47] Lawrence Blum, "*I'm Not a Racist, But . . .*": *The Moral Quandary of Race* (Cornell University Press, 2002), 2.

[48] It seems that in most cases what we're seeing is a variant on Charles Stevenson's concept of the "persuasive definition." The idea is that, in addition to its propositional content, the term "discrimination" carries a certain emotive power that renders it inappropriately applied to cases which should not generate such powerful sentiments of disgust or outrage. Charles Leslie Stevenson, "Persuasive Definitions," *Mind* 47, no. 187 (July 1938): 331–50; see also Keith Burgess-Jackson, "Rape and Persuasive Definition," *Canadian Journal of Philosophy* 25, no. 3 (1995): 415–54. Yet it is far from clear that this alleged mismatch in affective power should count as a valid refutation in circumstances where the conduct at issue does appear to propositionally meet the requirements of the term's definition.

fair consideration or for their understandings to be incorporated in publicly intelligible conceptions of the relevant principles.

Other scholars have recognized that people often act to prescreen extant claims on criteria which have little to do with the claim's substantive merits. In discussing their idea of a psychological "immune system," Gilbert and his colleagues present a very simple example: the decision to "dismiss[,] as a rule[,] all remarks that begin with 'You drooling imbecile.'"[49] This dismissal is done as a substitution for actually engaging with the substantive merits of the remark (which, given the introduction, are likely to be hurtful or at least unsettling). Eileen Braman has made the important contribution of connecting this phenomenon to legal behavior; her research found that decisions regarding "threshold" legal questions like standing were significantly influenced by study participants' views of the underlying claim (at least in ambiguous cases with no controlling legal precedent).[50] Even though standing decisions nominally are wholly apart from the substantive merits of a legal case, there is a greater propensity to dismiss cases on standing grounds when doing so will forestall having to consider a potentially hostile claim on its merits.

Like all forms of motivated cognition, it is easy to think of dismissal in purely negative, even opportunistic terms. So it is important to stress that, just as with ignorance, dismissal begins from a simple and important truth: there are many demands upon our cognitive facilities throughout the day, and we must prioritize what areas receive our attention. "The quantity and variety of social stimulation available at any time is vastly greater than a person can process or even attend to. Therefore, individuals are necessarily selective in what they notice, learn, remember, or infer in any situation."[51] Gilbert's "drooling imbecile" example perhaps provides a fine case of a circumstance where dismissal may be perfectly appropriate—a reasonable screen for what is worth paying attention to, on the grounds that few if any comments of serious value or incisiveness begin in that fashion. Dismissal, to reiterate, can be done with good reason; not every motivation we have for dismissal boils down to a desire to evade consideration of hard thoughts.

Yet it is evident why discursive dismissal carries significant potential for abuse. To the extent that "drooling imbecile" suggests that incivility is a valid screen—and again, in many cases it may be—it is worth reflecting upon Mill's own caution against being too quick at dismissing speech on the grounds that it lacks "temperate" character. As will be discussed in Chapter 5, Mill was well aware not

[49] Gilbert et al., "Immune Neglect," 619.

[50] Eileen Braman, "Reasoning on the Threshold: Testing the Separability of Preferences in Legal Decision Making," *Journal of Politics* 68, no. 2 (2006): 315.

[51] Hazel Markus, "Self-Schemata and Processing Information about the Self," *Journal of Personality and Social Psychology* 35, no. 2 (1977): 63.

just of the difficulty of drawing consistent lines but also of the ease of recoding nearly any troublesome challenge as uncivil, no matter how politely put. "Drooling imbecile" is too clear a case to be of much use; relying too heavily on it risks creating an exception that swallows the rule. Mari Matsuda, for example, points out the nigh impossibility of crafting a complaint about racism that does *not* come off as "uncivil": "No matter how politely you put it, the message 'You are racist and doubly so if you allow racism to persist in a place where you have the power to change business as usual' [will be] seen as a direct challenge to status and safety and familiar pajamas."[52]

Meanwhile, what sorts of claims strike us as facially implausible will depend greatly on our past experiences, and hence social stratification can yield wide gaps in what sorts of statements seem reasonable versus farcical even among well-meaning deliberators.[53] After all, "[p]lausibility, like beauty, is usually in the eye of the beholder."[54] Persons who occupy epistemically privileged positions—who are unused to having their cognitive authority questioned or whose social appraisals are generally accorded respect—may be ill-equipped to critically reconsider their instincts in response to unfamiliar challenges.[55] And when we reckon with the fact that people also have motivated reasons for preferring to grapple with certain sorts of claims while ignoring others, the problem intensifies further still.[56] Dismissal is motivationally useful because it obviates the need to consider arguments or evidence that might be brought to bear in favor of threatening claims. Structuring our thought processes such that claim classes likely to be discomforting are coded as facially implausible or ludicrous allows for potentially dissonant claims to be headed off without having to do the hard cognitive work of actually reasoning around the merits of the case.

Moreover, if we are refraining from considering a given claim solely because we need to triage scarce deliberative resources, then we have no grounds to speak to the potential validity of the claim. We should, as Fricker observes, reserve judgment on its merit until such time as it can be given proper attention.[57] The fact that dismissal so frequently comes attached to evaluative statements about

[52] Mari J. Matsuda, "Are We Dead Yet? The Lies We Tell to Keep Moving Forward without Feeling," *Connecticut Law Review* 40, no. 4 (2008): 1041.

[53] *See* Russell K. Robinson, "Perceptual Segregation," *Columbia Law Review* 108, no. 5 (2008): 1106–17 (providing empirical evidence supporting significant gaps in how men and women, and White and Black individuals perceive the potential cases of discrimination); David R. Maines, "Information Pools and Racialized Narrative Structures," *Sociological Quarterly* 40, no. 2 (1999): 317–26 (explaining that social stratification causes Black and White people to draw from different "pools" in terms of where they get background information).

[54] Brian Leiter, "The Death of God and the Death of Morality," *Monist* 102, no. 3 (2019): 396.

[55] *See* Medina, *Epistemology of Resistance*, 30 (discussing the problem of being epistemically "spoiled").

[56] *See* Robinson, "Perceptual Segregation," 1124 (noting that "an individual's social position shapes his willingness to pursue information about a particular topic").

[57] Fricker, *Epistemic Injustice*, 172.

the claimant (through terms like "bad faith," "implausible," "playing the race card," and so on), however, suggests that more is going on than dispassionate attempts at prioritization.

And while anyone is capable of dismissal, it carries particular potency when conjoined with social power. One of the more important attributes of power, after all, is that "you can opt not to listen. And you do so with impunity."[58] Persons with power can often unilaterally set the conceptual boundaries of a given conversation and thereby "preemptively silence" perspectives which might—if given due consideration—present an effective challenge.[59] By contrast, a position of vulnerability makes it more likely "that one will need to attend to what others are likely to notice."[60] While marginalized persons certainly can (under the right circumstances) argue against the principles or assertions of the dominant classes, they are rarely in a position to simply wave them aside outright.[61] At the same time, persons holding epistemic power—who are in a privileged position to articulate what counts as valid knowledge and who are considered to be valid exponents of potential claims—have every incentive to preserve their advantaged status. Dismissing the perspectives of those who are members of marginalized groups helps preserve this epistemic primacy.

(The Limits of) Evaluative Motivated Reasoning

The structure and importance of evaluative motivated reasoning have been analyzed in great detail elsewhere, so I will not give more than a basic sketch here. Instead my focus is on how, despite the outsized attention paid to it in the literature, this particular form of motivated cognition is only a partial and in some ways unideal solution to the threat posed by a discomfiting allegation. The purpose is not to discount evaluative motivated reasoning as an important

[58] Carol Gilligan said this in a roundtable discussion hosted at Buffalo Law School. "Feminist Discourse, Moral Values, and the Law—A Conversation: The 1984 James McCormick Mitchell Lecture," *Buffalo Law Review* 34, no. 1 (1985): 62 (Isabel Marcus and Paul J. Spiegelman, moderators; Ellen C. DuBois, Mary C. Dunlap, Carol J. Gilligan, Catherine A. MacKinnon, and Carrie Menkel-Meadow, participants).

[59] Eric Reitan, "Rape as an Essentially Contested Concept," *Hypatia* 16, no. 2 (2001): 49 ("[I]f any one party has the power to unilaterally determine the conceptual framework that will be used in assessing a normative problem, that party will be able to preemptively silence certain dissenting voices.").

[60] Gaile Pohlhaus Jr., "Relational Knowing and Epistemic Injustice: Toward a Theory of *Willful Hermeneutical Ignorance*," *Hypatia* 27, no. 4 (2012): 721.

[61] Medina, *Epistemology of Resistance*, 44 (noting that marginalized persons are often forced to understand and consider seriously the perspectives of dominant groups as a condition of social survival). The inequality in the ability to dismiss, in turn, presages how a capacity to "not listen" can also be an important part of political freedom, as I argue in Chapter 6.

phenomenon, but rather to situate it as one part of a broader continuum of cognitive practices.

Evaluative motivated reasoning describes "the unconscious tendency of individuals to process information in a manner that suits some end or goal extrinsic to the formation of accurate beliefs."[62] It refers to how we process received information. We *see* the protest, we *listen* to the witness. In this, it differs significantly from both ignorance and dismissal. In an ignorance scenario, of course, there is no received information to be processed—the listener is unaware that the relevant charge has been made. And in a dismissal case, the listener has elected to refrain from taking up most of the relevant information—they are eliminating the allegation as a valid or worthy hypothesis prior to engaging with it on its merits.

Focusing on the biased appraisal of received evidence, evaluative motivated reasoning understates how biases affect not just how we process information but how we make initial decisions regarding what sort of information is worthy of our attention. One recent study used visual-attention trackers to see how people observed videos documenting physical altercations between members of an outgroup and the police.[63] It found that persons devoted more of their visual attention to the party they were predisposed to see as the wrongdoer. (So persons hostile to the police looked more at the police; those with negative attitudes toward the outgroup looked more at the civilian.)[64] Reacting to the study, which he labeled "the run-away winner in the contest for 'coolest study of the year,'" Dan Kahan wrote:

> Before reading this study, I would have assumed the effect of cultural cognition was generated in the process of recollection: that people were fitting bits and pieces of recalled images onto narrative templates featuring police force and the like.
>
> But [these] findings suggest the dynamic that generates opposing perceptions in these cases commences much earlier, *before* the subjects even take in the visual images.
>
> The identity-protective impressions people form originate in a kind of biased sampling: by training their attention on the actor who they have the greatest stake in identifying as the wrongdoer, people are . . . prospecting in that

[62] Dan M. Kahan, "Neutral Principles, Motivated Cognition, and Some Problems for Constitutional Law," *Harvard Law Review* 125, no. 1 (2011): 19.

[63] Yael Granot, Emily Balcetis, Kristin E. Schneider, and Tom R. Tyler, "Justice Is Not Blind: Visual Attention Exaggerates Effects of Group Identification on Legal Punishment," *Journal of Experimental Psychology* 143, no. 6 (2014): 2196–208.

[64] *Id.* at 2205.

portion of the visual landscape most likely to contain veins of data that fit their preconceptions.[65]

In other words, what made the study so fascinating was that it revealed just how early in the deliberative life-cycle motivational concerns came into play. They did not only affect how people reasoned through received information; they also played a dramatic role in determining what sort of information people elected to focus on in the first place.

To be sure, the assumption that persons have received and are analyzing (albeit in a biased manner) substantial information is a valid one in certain contexts. A juror in a civil or criminal case feels obligated (one hopes) to pay close attention to the statements of a witness. A student in a classroom feels obligated (one hopes) to consider the assigned readings carefully. And it is likely that laboratory settings, where there are a variety of explicit means and implicit norms encouraging participants to pay close attention to whatever project they've been assigned, emphasize the salience of this particular mode of reasoning. Laboratories, classrooms, and courtrooms are special cases where we have strong social and cultural pressure to pay attention to information. If while serving on a jury a witness upsets us, we can't simply change the channel. For the most part, however, this is an exception and not the rule. Nothing normally forces us to pay any attention to claims we'd rather not consider.

Meanwhile, evaluative motivated reasoning has several drawbacks that limit its usefulness as a means of avoiding discomfiting conclusions. First, it is cognitively taxing. It requires the subject to fully engage in the social question in order to construct a reasonable-seeming interpretation that coheres to their prior beliefs. This "requires cognitive resources to carry through."[66] Motivated reasoning is in fact positively correlated with cognitive ability—persons with more cognitive resources are better able to rationalize toward the results they want.[67] This makes it a risky proposition in situations where cognitive resources may be drained.

[65] Dan Kahan, "What 'Bodycams' Can and Can't Be Expected to Do . . . Plus Coolest Study of the Year," *Cultural Cognition Project*, December 25, 2014, http://www.culturalcognition.net/blog/2014/12/25/what-bodycams-can-and-cant-be-expected-to-do-plus-coolest-st.html.

[66] Neeru Paharia, Kathleen D. Vohs, and Rohit Deshpande, "Sweatshop Labor Is Wrong Unless the Shoes Are Cute: Cognition Can Both Help and Hurt Moral Motivated Reasoning," *Organizational Behavior & Human Decision Processes* 121, no. 1 (May 2013): 87 (finding that persons "under cognitive load were less able to endorse the use of sweatshop labor than if they were not under cognitive load").

[67] See, e.g., Dries Trippas, Simon J. Handley, and Michael F. Verde, "Fluency and Belief Bias in Deductive Reasoning: New Indices for Old Effects," *Frontiers in Psychology* 5, no. 631 (2014): 6 (finding that "higher cognitive ability . . . leads to increased motivated reasoning"); Kahan, "Motivated Numeracy," 9 (finding that scientific literacy increases the divergence in opinions over controversial scientific questions because greater facility with technical reasoning enables persons to more easily construct desirable-yet-plausible conclusions).

Second, motivated cognition isn't always reliable. Evaluative motivated reasoning is not infinitely elastic; it works only if sufficient evidence exists to support a favorable outcome: "[P]eople motivated to arrive at a particular conclusion attempt to be rational and to construct a justification of their desired conclusion that would persuade a dispassionate observer. They draw the desired conclusion only if they can muster up the evidence necessary to support it."[68] But at the outset of a conversation, the existence of such ambiguous evidence cannot be guaranteed—sometimes one's interlocutor really has the goods. In that case, a person would still be left to reckon with the dissonance.

Dismissal and ignorance circumvent these risks. One need expend no effort reasoning around a given claim, or incur any serious risk that it will prove impossible to credibly reject for nonmotivated reasons, if it is never heard or dismissed out of hand. For these reasons, it is likely that motivated cognition in its evaluative form is perhaps the barrier of last resort—it emerges in those relatively rare circumstances where we are forced to hear and substantively reckon with arguments that promote thoughts we'd rather not think.

Hence, while I certainly do not discount the importance of traditional (evaluative) motivated reasoning as a distorting feature in public deliberation, the relative attention it gets in the literature may be outsized compared to parallel processes which also enable us to avoid thinking thoughts we'd rather not think. The act of dismissal, in particular, is an underappreciated and especially nettlesome deliberative mechanic. Less straightforward than ignorance, and yet likely even more ubiquitous that evaluative motivated cognition, dismissal has several unique properties that deserve special attention in how we trace deliberation over the hard thoughts. These properties, and their pernicious effects on our deliberative practices, will be the focus on the next chapter.

[68] Kunda, "The Case for Motivated Reasoning," 482–83.

3
The Mechanisms and the Harms of Dismissal

While each of the three cognitive checkpoints identified in the previous chapter interlock to ward off unamenable claims, for the remainder of the book I primarily focus on the particular problem of dismissal. Practically speaking, dismissal impacts a wide range of potential social claims without an immediately obvious form of resolution. The fix for ignorance is relatively straightforward (if not always easy to implement): publicize the claim. Beyond that, in general a person who has successfully remained ignorant of an unamenable claim will not be in an adjudicative position with respect to it. In an informal context (e.g., participation in public debate), the act of partaking in discussion about an issue presupposes that one has at least heard of it. Likewise in a formal context (e.g., a lawsuit or official complaint), by definition once that claim has been placed on the relevant docket the first checkpoint has been overcome—the respondent is on notice that there is a claim in play and now must elect how to deal with it.

The problems posed by evaluative motivated reasoning are not as easy to resolve, but they also do not cover large swaths of deliberative activity. Outside of a few specialized social contexts—a laboratory, a jury box, a classroom—nobody can force us to actually fully deliberate on topics we'd rather dismiss. These arenas are no doubt important, but their relatively high salience probably overstates their share of actual deliberative activity. In day-to-day life, much of the important action comes when we consider which claims are worthy of deliberative attention and which are not. This determination necessarily occurs prior to having much of the substantive content that would ultimately decide whether the claim in question is true or false. Indeed, one of the more dangerous attributes of dismissal is its peculiarly self-insulating character. Unlike motivated cognition, which can be overcome given sufficiently weighty evidence, dismissal operates a step earlier in the discursive process by refusing to admit certain classes of evidence at all. Consequently, it largely lacks the boundaries of plausibility that rein in motivated cognition.

So, what are some of the tactics used to effectuate a dismissal? How, in practice, do people create justifications for not considering claims—particularly if they wish to simultaneously (a) tailor their dismissal to discomforting claims while

Deliberation, Dismissal, and Democracy. David Schraub, Oxford University Press. © Oxford University Press (2025). DOI: 10.1093/9780197816424.003.0004

(b) presenting their decisions as neutral and dispassionate? In this chapter, I look to the mechanics of dismissal and identify several strategies which facilitate dismissal as a motivated and targeted practice. Such mechanisms include *desiring disagreement*, where we intentionally *avoid* finding points of commonality or overlapping consensus in order to preserve a posture of dismissive antagonism, as well as *replacement epistemology*, where an out-group's attempted communicative meaning is substituted out and replaced for an alternative meaning that is viewed as authoritatively representing the out-group's own view. I then zero in on some of the distinctive *harms* of dismissal, both primary (in how it degrades the speaker and denies them the status of a potential conveyor of useful information) and secondary (in how it decays their capabilities to serve as an effective testifier or communicator going forward).

Desiring Disagreement

Iris Marion Young identifies the condition of reasonableness in deliberation as the characteristic of coming to dialogue with the aim—not the guarantee—of agreement.[1] On a similar note, Amy Guttmann and Dennis Thompson urge that we create "an economy of moral disagreement"—minimizing the scope of our disagreements so we can work together on other issues.[2] In both cases, the presumption is that healthy participants in dialogue should want to agree with one another to the extent possible. But sometimes this expectation is subverted: in certain dialogic contexts people seem to desire disagreement more than agreement.

To take a slightly comical example: Once, while I was teaching *Parents Involved in Community Schools v. Seattle School District No. 1* (a case involving racial integration measures in Seattle and Louisville public schools),[3] a student questioned why the plurality opinion did not discuss schools offering an "Afrocentric" curriculum as a potentially race-based, but educationally beneficial, public school program. I thought the point was interesting and noted that it was an issue Justice Clarence Thomas touched upon in his concurring opinion. The (very liberal) student was aghast to find himself on Justice Thomas's side and denied that Justice Thomas could be making a point similar to his own. I referenced the context in which Justice Thomas did make this argument; the student replied by insisting that Justice Thomas clearly could not be endorsing an Afrocentric curriculum. I proceeded to find the precise passage wherein he praises

[1] Iris Marion Young, *Inclusion and Democracy* (Oxford University Press 2000), 24–25.

[2] Amy Gutmann and Dennis Thompson, *Why Deliberative Democracy?* (Princeton University Press, 2004), 134–35.

[3] 551 U.S. 701 (2007).

the district's K–8 "African-American Academy";[4] the student exclaimed, "Well, but I'm sure he didn't *mean* it!"

At a loss, I observed that the student was expending quite a lot of effort to avoid the horrifying possible that Justice Thomas might *not* disagree with him.

Here we see the most straightforward case where someone might desire disagreement: where a particular party is so objectionable to us that any consonance between their views and our own is taken as a signal that we must have gone astray. (Consider the wince felt by vegetarians when they learn that Hitler shared their dietary restrictions.)

In the case of the vegetarian, any discomfort regarding the "agreement" with Hitler seems unwarranted: Hitler is a metonym for evil, but not because of his eating habits. But perhaps in other cases it would be proper to "desire disagreement"—if one found oneself agreeing with Hitler on the subject of the Jews, intuitively that should prompt an immediate reassessment of one's position. And if one's interlocutor displays no significant concern upon learning that their views on Jews overlap with those of the Nazis, it is reasonable to use that equanimity as an indictment.

For example, in 2014 the Vassar College chapter of Students for Justice in Palestine shared an article from the far-right racist website Occidental Quarterly regarding "Zionist internet trolls." When they were questioned on their use of the Occidental Quarterly as a source, the organization defended itself: they argued that while OQ "is a white nationalist publication, that doesn't mean everything they say is invalid" and "If the idea is alright, who cares where they [*sic*] come from?"[5] In a sense, Vassar SJP was exhibiting precisely an "economy of moral disagreement"; as they put it, "[P]roviding an article link from a white nationalist publication does not mean we support white nationalist ideology; rather, we found this particular article's description of those behind zionist [*sic*] propaganda campaigns and how they operate to be a helpful articulation of problems many organizations like us face."[6] Yet their behavior hardly is praiseworthy; if anything, it seems like they are recklessly ignoring an obvious heuristic suggesting that their instincts on antisemitism have gone badly off the rails.

So it may not be the case that it is always wrong to "desire disagreement." We should hope that our opinions on people of color should diverge sharply

[4] *Id.* at 764 (Thomas, J., concurring).

[5] Rebecca Lessee, "SJP Vassar and White Nationalism," *Mystical Politics*, May 8, 2014, https://mystical-politics.blogspot.com/2014/05/sjp-vassar-and-white-nationalism.html; Rebecca Lessee, "More from SJP Vassar—It Is 'Alright' to Republish Articles from Antisemitic White Nationalists," *Mystical Politics*, May 8, 2014, https://mystical-politics.blogspot.com/2014/05/more-from-sjp-vassar-it-is-alright-to.html.

[6] Rebecca Lessee, "Once Again: Vassar SJP and White Nationalist Publications," *Mystical Politics*, May 9, 2014, https://mystical-politics.blogspot.com/2014/05/a-reply-from-vassar-sjp-about-blogposts.html.

from those of the Klan; if we find ourselves in agreement, that is worrisome, not salutary. So what distinguishes scenarios of that ilk from the cases that Young and others have in mind?

The lens of dismissal is helpful here. Dismissal, recall, occurs when one dispenses with a proffered argument without reasoning through it. It is notable that, in the Vassar example, the student organization was well on notice regarding the Occidental Quarterly's argument. The question was not whether they should preemptively disregard a position; the question was whether the position they were actually adopting was a justifiable one.

Where dismissal works through desiring disagreement, by contrast, it typically justifies a refusal to listen or meaningfully engage. Where we are convinced that a given perspective is wholly illicit or illegitimate, we may prefer to maximize perceived disagreement with out-groups or opponents. Doing so lets us avoid reckoning with a more nuanced position that might contain arguments which exercise a genuine pull on us or force reassessment of our own stance. Consequently, the possibility that an argument might be one we *agree* with can, in certain circumstances, be more threatening than one which is obviously and transparently objectionable.

Desiring disagreement insists on imputing to a given political claimant views that they do not hold and views that (at least nominally) the respondent asserts they should not hold. I do not want to say that a speaker's intentions are the only thing that matters, of course. In the context of microaggressions, for example, I've argued that some statements or behaviors can be culpably negligent even if the alleged microaggressor genuinely didn't mean to communicate an offensive message.[7] But in cases of more sweeping claims about an entire political movement, it does seem like it should matter if the movement genuinely is not pursuing the alleged projects or policies that are used to justify public disdain and dismissal.

One area where this dynamic can be seen is in the claim by many White conservatives that "Black Lives Matter" is an exclusionary mantra; they contend it implies that White lives do not matter (hence the counterslogan "All Lives Matter"). Simply as a matter of language, the dispute can be understood as asking whether BLM activists mean "*Only* Black lives matter" or "Black lives matter *too*" (with an emphasis on how this seemingly obvious proposition has been denied both de facto and intentionally in many social institutions).[8] Fortunately, BLM

[7] David Schraub, "Microaggressions as Negligence," *Journal of Social Philosophy* 56, no. 2, (2025): 282–99.

[8] Luvell Anderson characterizes these competing interpretations as the "exclusive" and "inclusive" readings of Black Lives Matter, respectively. Luvell Anderson, "Epistemic Injustice and the Philosophy of Race," in *The Routledge Handbook on Epistemic Injustice*, ed. Ian James Kidd, José Medina, and Gaile Pohlhaus Jr. (Routledge, 2017).

activists have repeatedly confirmed that they intend the latter interpretation; their goal is not to make a claim of Black supremacy but rather to demand that Black lives be included in the pantheon of lives that matter.[9]

Were they adhering to Young's norms of "reasonableness," the conservative critics would be pleased to have their worries assuaged. It would not necessarily lead to total agreement between the conservatives and the BLM activists—there might remain significant differences regarding how they view substantive cases of police misconduct or the advisability of various reform measures—but it would demonstrate an "economy of disagreement." Yet as we know, conservative critics of BLM have not been willing to concede agreement so easily—they cling fervently to an interpretation of BLM that they contend is dehumanizing to Whites even as they purport to desire nothing more than that BLM disavow such a stance (which, of course, it does).

What motivates this seemingly bizarre behavior? The answer is that by locking the debate into the question of "Do Black Lives Matter activists hate White people?" (in which they can cast BLM as extremist and unreasonable), they can avoid even engaging in the more substantive discussion on specific cases of police misconduct or reformist measures—terrain which they may find considerably more perilous. Viewing BLM as a radical anti-White insurgency allows conservative political actors to dismiss BLM easily, and so avoid considering the hard thoughts it might raise about the basic justness of the carceral and criminal law system. The desire for disagreement here becomes a mechanism for dismissal—framed in a fashion that forecloses the possibility of agreement, the Black Lives Matter campaign can be dismissed without engaging with its actual content.

Disputes relating to the Israel-Palestine conflict also often witness actors desiring disagreement. Consider a free speech controversy at the University of Minnesota Law School, involving NYU professor Moshe Halbertal. Halbertal, an eminent legal philosopher and also the author of the Israeli Defense Forces' ethics handbook, had been invited to deliver the John Dewey Lecture in the Philosophy of Law. His lecture was titled "Protecting Civilians: Moral Challenges

[9] See, e.g., Anderson, "Epistemic Injustice"; Keith Ellison, "Foreword," in Sue Bradford Edwards and Duchess Harris, *Black Lives Matter* (Abdo, 2016). Alicia Garza described the BLM movement's objective as "making all lives matter by making sure black lives matter too." Frances Wang, "Black Lives Matter Founder in Sacramento: 'Protests Make This Country Great,'" *ABC News*, September 19, 2018, https://www.abc10.com/article/news/local/sacramento/black-lives-matter-founder-in-sacramento-protests-make-this-country-great/103-596075555. The closest one finds to a contrary position comes through Ashley Atkins, who critiques the "Black Lives Matter too" formulation not because she endorses the exclusionary position (that *only* Black lives matter) but because she views the slogan as fundamentally not being addressed to White persons at all and thus not intending to say anything—positive or negative—about White lives. See Ashley Atkins, "*Black Lives Matter* or *All Lives Matter*? Color-Blindness and Epistemic Injustice," *Social Epistemology* 33, no. 1 (2019): 1–22.

of Asymmetric Warfare," and he planned to argue that professional combatants should err on the side of protecting the enemy side's civilian population, even in cases where it puts their own soldiers at heightened risk. Pro-Palestinian protesters proceeded to disrupt the speech, shouting down Halbertal and preventing him from speaking for 30 minutes. (Three protesters were eventually arrested.)[10]

The disruption was swiftly condemned by university officials. But one statement by the dean of the Law School, David Wippman, stood out. Referencing the content of Halbertal's lecture, where he would argue for heightened protection for civilian populations in the case of asymmetrical warfare, Wippman suggested that "[i]f they [the protesters] had stayed and listened, they might have actually heard something they agreed with."[11] To be clear: Wippman was unambiguous in holding that there was no right to shout down a university-sanctioned speech regardless of whether the protesters agreed with the speaker or not.[12] Nonetheless, I could not help but feel that Wippman had missed the point of the protest entirely. The protesters were not seeking to shout Halbertal down because they were afraid he'd say something that they'd find outrageous. They were shouting him down because they were afraid he'd say something that they wouldn't. That is, they were afraid he'd take a reasonable, nuanced, fine-grained position; one that would demand genuine thought and consideration—and the last thing these protesters were prepared to do was to accept that the *author of the IDF's ethics handbook* might proffer a position that demands consideration.

There's no intrinsic ideological valence to this instinct, of course. Years after the Halbertal incident at the University of Minnesota, I was giving a joint presentation at the University of Oregon on antisemitism and Islamophobia.[13] My co-presenter was Hussein Ibish, then working at the Gulf States Institute, previously a fellow with the American Task Force on Palestine. Our talk came in the midst of the Israel-Gaza war following October 7, and campus tensions were high. (The Oregon administration negotiated the end of the student pro-Palestine encampment that very weekend; a dean was texting final approvals of the deal while at dinner with Ibish and me.) In the middle of our presentation, we were disrupted by a pro-Israel heckler who demanded that Ibish disavow and

[10] Maura Lerner, "Protesters Disrupt Israeli Professor's Lecture at University of Minnesota," *Minneapolis Star Tribune*, November 4, 2015, http://www.startribune.com/protesters-disrupt-israeli-professor-s-lecture-at-university-of-minnesota/340437581/.

[11] Hannah Weikel, "Law Speaker Spurs Protest," *Minnesota Daily*, November 4, 2015, http://www.mndaily.com/article/2015/11/law-speaker-spurs-protest.

[12] David Wippman, "Halbertal Lecture Statement," November 4, 2015, https://www.law.umn.edu/sites/law.umn.edu/files/halbertal_lecture_statement.pdf.

[13] "Bridging Divides: Understanding Antisemitism and Islamophobia," University of Oregon Engagement Program on Understanding the Israel-Palestine Conflict: Educational Responses, May 22, 2024, https://international.uoregon.edu/bridging-divides-understanding-antisemitism-and-islamophobia.

condemn Hamas. While Ibish had been quite critical in his remarks about the Israeli government's conduct in Gaza and the occupation more broadly, at no point did he say anything that could be remotely construed as pro-Hamas, and in fact he has been a vocal and public critic of Hamas for many years (including following October 7).[14] But as the man was being led away by security, it occurred to me (and I said this to the audience and to the departing heckler) that the protester was not actually worried that Ibish was a Hamas sympathizer. He was worried that he wasn't—that someone who was *not* a Hamas supporter, who did *not* harbor antisemitic or genocidal intentions toward Israelis or Jews, might also proffer sharp and uncompromising criticism of the Israeli government, of the sort that this protester had in his own mind insisted was solely of the province of anti-Jewish bigots.[15] The heckler's unwarranted projection of such views onto Ibish (and his attempt to loudly drown out anything Ibish tried to say that would clarify his anti-Hamas sentiments—the very viewpoint the protester nominally *wanted* Ibish to hold) were an attempt to cleave to a position of disagreement.

A more general version of this problem occurs in divergent interpretations of the phrase "From the river to the sea, Palestine will be free." Many Jewish and pro-Israel commentators have insisted that this chant is tantamount to a call for the eradication of Israel and the expulsion or even genocide of its Jewish inhabitants.[16] Proponents of the phrase, by contrast, typically present it as advocating equal status for all inhabitants of historic Palestine.[17] One poll, taken in

[14] See Hussein Ibish, "The Palestinian People Should Be Enraged at Both Israel and Hamas," *New Republic*, November 1, 2023, https://newrepublic.com/article/176512/palestinian-people-enraged-israel-hamas; Hussein Ibish, "For Hamas, Everything Is Going According to Plan," *The Atlantic*, June 14, 2024, https://www.theatlantic.com/international/archive/2024/06/hamas-everything-going-according-plan/678690/.

[15] In 2025, Abe Silberstein made a similar argument about the New York City mayoral candidacy of Zohran Mamdani. Mamdani was a sharp critic of Israel who had been accused of antisemitism due to his past support of the Boycott, Divestment, and Sanctions campaign against Israel and his refusal to condemn the phrase "globalize the Intifada." That said, Silberstein noted that there "is no evidence Mamdani has expressed an antisemitic sentiment in his life" (notably, he had not himself ever used the phrase "globalize the Intifada," only argued that it was not an inherently antisemitic expression). Rather, Silberstein suggested, what Mamdani's critics "fear is not an antisemitic mayor, but one who will symbolize the ongoing collapse of pro-Israel hegemony in the Democratic Party, and perhaps in U.S. politics more generally." Abe Silberstein, "Why Zohran Mamdani's Candidacy for NYC Mayor Terrifies the pro-Israel Establishment," *Haaretz*, June 23, 2025, https://www.haaretz.com/opinion/2025-06-23/ty-article-opinion/.premium/why-zohran-mamdanis-candidacy-for-nyc-mayor-terrifies-the-pro-israel-establishment/00000197-9d50-df17-ab9f-9dfcef390000. To this I would add that it is in a real sense *more* threatening to Mamdani's detractors if someone with his views on Israel does *not* have a record of antisemitism than if he does.

[16] See, e.g., "US House Resolution Condemns Chant 'From the River to the Sea, Palestine Will Be Free,'" *Times of Israel*, April 17, 2024, https://www.timesofisrael.com/us-house-resolution-condemns-chant-from-the-river-to-the-sea-palestine-will-be-free/; Philip Klein, "Why 'Free Palestine from the River to the Sea' Means Genocide against Jews," *National Review*, October 25, 2023, https://www.nationalreview.com/corner/why-free-palestine-from-the-river-to-the-sea-means-genocide-against-jews/.

[17] See, e.g., Federica Marsi, "'From the River to the Sea': What Does the Palestinian Slogan Really Mean?," *Al-Jazeera*, November 2, 2023, https://www.aljazeera.com/news/2023/11/2/from-the-river-

January 2024, found that 66% of Jewish students understood "river to the sea" to mean "Palestinians should replace Israelis in the territory, even if it means the expulsion or genocide of Israeli Jews," but only 14% of Muslim students understood it the same way.[18] In fact, a plurality of Muslim respondents (42%) understood "river to the sea" to be a call that "Palestinians and Israelis should live in two separate countries, side by side"—that is, for a two-state solution (34% thought it meant that there should be one state where Palestinians and Israelis live together).[19]

That there is divergence over what "river to the sea" means is not necessarily the result of bad faith. "River to the sea" is perhaps unusually polysemous, even among contested political concepts. The aforementioned poll of student understandings found that, among all students (not just Jewish or Muslim) a plurality (31%) simply had no idea what the phrase meant, and the remainder were closely divided between viewing it as a call for genocide/expulsion (26%), a two-state solution (27%), and a one-state solution for both Jews and Palestinians alike (16%).[20] Other research has found that fewer than half of students who embraced the slogan could even identify what river and sea were being referred to.[21] And for all the fulmination on the pro-Israel right about the supposedly maximalist and eliminationist character of "river to the sea," a variation on the phrase can be found in none other than the founding platform of Israel's Likud Party, which insists that "between the Sea and the Jordan there will only be Israeli sovereignty."[22]

Still, one might think that learning that most proponents of "river to the sea" do not publicly subscribe to a violent or genocidal interpretation of the phrase would be a relief to Jewish listeners, since that possibility is nominally why they react so negatively to it in the first place. But often we see resistance to efforts to assert that "river to the sea" even *could* possibly have a non-eliminationist meaning. For example, the American Jewish Committee states that the expression is antisemitic only in those cases where it "is used with the harmful intent of implying the erasure of the State of Israel, ethnic cleansing of Jews from the

to-the-sea-what-does-the-palestinian-slogan-really-mean (quoting Nimer Sultany as identifying the call as "the need for equality for all inhabitants of historic Palestine"); Ben Burgis, "'From the River to the Sea' Is a Call for Democracy and Equality," *Jacobin*, November 9, 2023, https://jacobin.com/2023/11/from-the-river-to-the-sea-palestine-equality-one-state-rashida-tlaib-censure.

[18] Robert A. Pape, "Understanding Campus Fears after October 7 and How to Reduce Them," *Chicago Project on Security and Threats*, March 2024, https://d3qi0qp55mx5f5.cloudfront.net/cpost/i/docs/CPOST_Understanding_Campus_Fears_-_Report.pdf.

[19] *Id.* Just 12% and 11% of Jewish students thought that the phrase meant support for a two-state or one-state solution, respectively. *Id.*

[20] *Id.*

[21] Ron Hassner, "From Which River to Which Sea?," *Wall Street Journal*, December 6, 2023.

[22] Rashid Khalidi, "It's Time to Confront Israel's Version of 'From the River to the Sea,'" *The Nation*, November 22, 2023, https://www.thenation.com/article/world/its-time-to-confront-israels-version-of-from-the-river-to-the-sea/.

land, or simply as harassment of Jews in any other part of the world," while acknowledging that not all usages have such intent and that there is no antisemitism where it is used to call for the establishment of a Palestinian state or to insist that "all people of Palestinian heritage, wherever they reside, have their rights, culture, and freedoms honored."[23] Contrast that to the Anti-Defamation League, which asserts flatly that "river to the sea" is "an antisemitic slogan" and "hateful phrase" that "is fundamentally a call for a Palestinian state extending from the Jordan River to the Mediterranean Sea . . . which would mean the dismantling of the Jewish state . . . including through the removal of Jews from their ancestral homeland."[24] The former identifies the circumstances through which "river to the sea" can operate in antisemitic fashion, while expressly acknowledging live circumstances where it is not. The latter insists on an essentialist reading of the phrase as solely and exclusively carrying an antisemitic meaning, while leaving no room for alternative articulations.

Of course, in some circumstances people simply might not believe a professed disavowal of violent or genocidal intent. And even where such assertions were believed, we should not overstate the impact of the ensuing "agreement." There is still plenty of potential for (genuine, undesired) disagreement regarding, for example, a one- versus two-state solution, or the contours of what "equality" means in a future political arrangement, or on more specific issues like a "right of return" or on security guarantees for Jewish or Palestinian residents. But it seems clear that for some, like the ADL, who insist that "river to the sea" "fundamentally" means only its most extreme and hostile possible interpretation, part of the motivation is precisely to short-circuit genuine deliberation over these reasonable areas of dispute and controversy by bootstrapping them onto unreasonable and abhorrent demands of political annihilation. Much like the heckler at Oregon, the last thing the ADL wants is to grapple with the possibility that someone chanting "From the river to the sea, Palestine will be free" might *not* be committed to Israel's utter eradication and the removal of its Jewish residents, because then the ADL might be compelled to give their challenges and criticisms serious consideration in a way one can legitimately refuse to do for a genocidaire. The two-step move—demanding disavowal of an eliminationist position but also refusing to accept any such disavowals as authentic—permits a more sweeping dismissal of pro-Palestinian advocacy that in many (though not all) cases is genuinely compatible with the putative demands of their pro-Israel counterparts recognizing the equal standing and legitimacy of a Jewish presence in the land.

[23] American Jewish Committee, "Translate Hate: 'From the River to the Sea,'" accessed April 29, 2025, https://www.ajc.org/translatehate/From-the-River-to-the-Sea.

[24] Anti-Defamation League, "Slogan: "From the River to the Sea Palestine Will Be Free," October 26, 2023, https://www.adl.org/resources/backgrounder/slogan-river-sea-palestine-will-be-free.

Without belaboring the point, the term "Zionism" also exhibits similar properties where the polysemous quality of the word can be exploited to maintain desired disagreements. "Zionism" means different things to different people, ranging from simple support for Jews' right of self-determination to carte blanche support for any and all Israeli policies to entrench anti-Palestinian discrimination and dispossession. This ambiguity can be leveraged such that a person who identifies as "Zionist" insofar as they support Jewish self-determination, but who also holds a genuine and credible commitment to Palestinian equality and independence, can be indicted as a full-throated defender of permanent occupation or anti-Palestinian subjugation because that is asserted to be intrinsic to the identity of a Zionist.[25] So, for example, the *Berkeley Journal of Gender, Law & Justice*, as part of a bylaw amendment pledging not to invite speakers who "have expressed and continued to hold views or host/sponsor/promote events in support of Zionism," acknowledged that Zionism "has many strains historically" but insisted that "the Zionism that took hold and stands today is a settler-colonial movement" that, "in practice, has resulted in massacres of Palestinian people and the systematic separation of Palestinians from their homes, land, and each other."[26] Of course, such crimes have absolutely occurred under a Zionist banner, just as "river to the sea" politics have taken eliminationist forms. But there are many Jews who identify as Zionist who are loud and vocal critics of Israel's predations upon the Palestinian people and who see no conflict between those positions. Ironically (or not), it is these persons who are *most* likely to be practically excluded by the *Journal*'s amendment, precisely because they *don't* actually disagree with the *Journal*'s opposition to anti-Palestinian dispossession, and that lack of disagreement in turn makes their other potential critiques of the *Journal*'s political positions harder to dismiss. Much like the insistence that "river to the sea" can only be a call for eliminationist violence, the insistence that a "Zionist" can only be one supportive of anti-Palestinian massacres functions primarily as a way of maintaining a disagreement that enables dismissal of "Zionist" individuals whose positions would normally demand greater and more serious consideration.

[25] See David Schraub, "Does Anti-Zionism=Antisemitism?," *Third Narrative*, September 13, 2023, https://thirdnarrative.org/does-anti-zionismantisemitism/. As I observe in that article, the maneuver can also run in the opposite direction—persons who don't identify with "Zionism," insofar as they perceive it as embodying a specific form of Greater Israel territorial maximalism, can be treated as if they reject Jewish self-determination even if they disavow the latter position. In this way, many critics of Israel whose actual, specific criticisms are nominally "in bounds" vis-à-vis what Zionists claim are the acceptable contours of criticism of Israel can nonetheless be dismissed as illegitimate.

[26] Third Party Motion to Intervene filed by Adam Lerman, Berkeley Law Jewish Students for Justice in Palestine (BLJ4P) et al., *Louis Brandeis Ctr. v. Regents of the Univ. of Cal.*, 23-cv-06133 (filed Aug. 19, 2024 N.D. Cal.), Exhibit F. Some of this language is taken from the anti-Zionist organization Jewish Voice for Peace, "Our Approach to Zionism," accessed April 29, 2025, https://www.jewishvoiceforpeace.org/resource/zionism/.

Replacement Epistemology

A related but potentially even more extreme mechanism for dismissal is one I term "replacement epistemology." Replacement epistemology describes a state of affairs whereby certain social movements or groups find their attempted communicative meaning systematically hollowed out and replaced by a different message more easily digestible to empowered groups. The term intentionally evokes the concept of "replacement *theology*" (also known as supersessionism): the belief that Christianity has "superseded" Jewishness and taken Judaism's place as holder of covenantal status.[27] Importantly, replacement theology is more than a declaration that Christianity is a rival to Judaism or even superior to Judaism. What makes replacement theology distinct is that it holds itself out as an authoritative pronouncement of *Jewish* history as much as of Christian history. It erases the Jew by claiming to speak in a Jewish voice—a voice which (unsurprisingly) ends up validating Christian theological claims.

Supersessionism "describes a situation where one entity, by virtue of its supposed superiority, comes to occupy a position that previously belonged to another, the displaced group becoming outmoded or obsolete in the process. The term thus properly applies to a completed process of replacement."[28] Christian supersessionists take Jewish texts and ascribe meanings to them that they claim are not just Christian interpretations but in fact the proper *Jewish* meanings as well. In circumstances where Christians are dominant over Jews, these meanings—including the belief that they are *Jewish* meanings—will be generally socially accepted.[29] Christians are thus validated in speaking not only on their own behalf but also on behalf of others. Christians are presumed more capable and more authoritative in speaking about Jews than are Jews.

Replacement epistemology, then, describes a state of affairs where an actor is capable of (being perceived as) authentically presenting the perspective of the other without the other's input and frequently in defiance of the other's true opinions. The speaker thus replaces the subject's perspective with their own, but in a way which still is publicly perceived to be emerging from the other—as when Christian articulations of what Jewishness *means* are given greater social weight and are more decisively taken to establish "actual" Jewish ideologies, beliefs, or practices than are "counter-"articulations made by Jews

[27] See, e.g., Michael J. Vlach, "Various Forms of Replacement Theology," *Master's Seminary Journal* 20, no. 1 (2009): 57–69.

[28] Terence L. Donaldson, "Supersessionism in Early Christianity," *Canadian Society of Biblical Studies Bulletin* 69 (2009): 9.

[29] Richard L. Rubenstein, *After Auschwitz: History, Theology, and Contemporary Judaism*, 2nd ed. (Johns Hopkins University Press, 1992), 70 (noting that "because of the overwhelming numerical and cultural predominance of Christianity as a world religion, the Christian reading of Scripture came to carry far greater weight and influence" than Jewish interpretations).

themselves. Put slightly more formally, replacement epistemology describes a situation where A's statement that "B endorses position P" *is socially understood and taken up as* "B endorses position P"—and this assessment is relatively immune to B's own (potentially contrary) statements regarding whether or not they in fact endorse P.

Importantly, replacement epistemology is more than just a matter of stereotypes or false beliefs. Any person might have certain false beliefs about how a given out-group behaves or what opinions it holds. But the locus question of replacement epistemology is whether this false belief is, on a social level, successfully imputed to the out-group itself. This is a function of power. If, as Miranda Fricker writes, "social power is a capacity we have as social agents to influence how things go in the social world,"[30] then such power is what allows the fictive or concocted epistemology to replace the original or authentic perspective. Replacement epistemology usually replaces the out-group narrative with one which is more amenable to the interests or ideologies of the powerful. Doing so both validates the dominant group's own ideology (as in Christian reinterpretations of Jewish texts to presage the coming of Jesus), as well as cancels out need for engagement with the actual out-group insofar as its positions have been effectively straw-manned and are now assumed to be "known."[31]

While united around the authoritative *replacement* of the subject's view with an alternative one posited by a dominant actor, replacement epistemology can take on several forms. The most basic occurs through *inferiorization*, where the perspective of the other is taken to be so simple or straightforward that it can simply be known without any specialized knowledge, experience, or effort—including significant knowledge of or experience with the group itself. (The famed slogan "Nothing about us without us" can be seen as a counter to this move.)[32] Orientalism can take on this character, insofar as "the Orient"—seen as primitive and basic—is thought to be completely open to Western interpretations without much role for input from the "Orientals" themselves.[33] Judaism, likewise, can be cast as a backward and primitive religion compared to a more enlightened Christianity and so can be interpreted without speaking to

[30] Miranda Fricker, *Epistemic Injustice: Power and the Ethics of Knowing* (Oxford University Press, 2007), 9.

[31] On straw man arguments, see Robert Talisse and Scott F. Aiken, "Two Forms of the Straw Man," *Argumentation* 20, no. 3 (2006): 345–52. We might say that, in part, replacement epistemology represents a systematic or totalizing iteration of the straw man argument—applying not just in the idiosyncratic case of A misrepresenting B, but where group A is able to successfully and totally renarrate B's claims.

[32] See James I. Charlton, *Nothing about Us without Us: Disability, Oppression and Empowerment* (University of California Press, 1998).

[33] See Ramón Grosfoguel, "Epistemic Islamophobia and Colonial Social Sciences," *Human Architecture* 8, no. 2 (2010): 29–38.

Jews; ditto Black culture cast as pathological but otherwise uninteresting and unproductive.

A more aggressive form of replacement epistemology is *possessory*: a perceived entitlement over the other that is so complete that the claimant believes they can (and are understood to be able to) overwrite the other's perspective with their own. Possessory replacement epistemology can be very literal in the case of, for example, slave ownership, where the owner's declaration of what the slave wants or what is good for the slave will be understood as taking precedence over even seemingly direct contrary statements from the enslaved person himself or herself. Kate Manne draws a parallel in the rhetoric that frequently accompanies sexual assault, where the assailant may declare what his victim "actually" is thinking and have that declaration be taken up and viewed as authoritative by essential interpreters, such as police or the courts. Sexual assault, Manne observes, often "involves not just overriding the victim's will, but mentally rewriting it. ('You like that, don't you.' A fake question)."[34] Rae Langton accordingly describes a form of silencing available to those with power: allowing marginalized subjects to speak but "stop[ping] that speech from counting as an action. More precisely, stop[ping] it from counting as the action it was intended to be."[35]

Finally, replacement epistemology can be *assimilationist* in character, whereby the perspective of the other is recast as "our" perspective, so we already know it simply by knowing ourselves. This aptly characterizes the problem with speaking of a "Judeo-Christian" ethos or tradition; such a framing (as will be explored in more detail below) typically enables Christians to assume they know Jewish positions because they know Christian vantages. However, this form of replacement epistemology also may pose special danger for progressive *critiques* of dominant cultural groupings whose outlook and positions are presented as ubiquitous and therefore effectively "known" by out-groups. When certain minorities are constructed as part of an elite such that their views are presumptively already accounted for in dominant institutions (media, politics, and so on), it can take this turn. Consider James Baldwin's declaration in his famous essay "Negroes Are Anti-Semitic Because They're Anti-White" that "Jewish history, whether or not one can say it is honored, is certainly known."[36] Why *should* we think Jewish history is "certainly known"? What generates this confidence? The most likely answer is that "Jewish history" is viewed as having been successfully assimilated into the dominant "Christian history" (note how the appellation "Judeo-Christian" assists in this move), and so, to the extent the latter

[34] Kate Manne, *Down Girl: The Logic of Misogyny* (Oxford University Press, 2017), 207.

[35] Rae Langton, "Speech Acts and Unspeakable Acts," *Philosophy & Public Affairs* 22, no. 4 (Autumn 1993): 299.

[36] James Baldwin, "Negroes Are Anti-Semitic Because They're Anti-White," *New York Times*, April 9, 1967.

is "certainly known," the former is too. And like all other forms of replacement epistemology, this presumption of already possessed knowledge can facilitate dismissal when the relevant out-group attempts to insist that they do have a distinct and alternative perspective that still needs airing—as when a Jewish feminist recounted being dismissed at a conference because "Jewish women are just White middle-class women," and consequently "[t]here is nothing that differentiates them from the ruling majority. There is no reason to treat them as a specialized minority or to devote any of our time to their particular experience."[37]

From a dialogic vantage, replacement epistemology can be particularly dangerous because it *presents its targets as speaking*, perhaps even quoting some of their words or nodding at some of their texts,[38] while actually obscuring or silencing their ability to contribute to discourse as equals. It claims to engage in deliberation, but one side is effectively sock-puppeted, trapped inside a set of social meanings that it did not accede to and may well fervently deny. When operative, replacement epistemology acts to block marginalized groups from effectively communicating not just any knowledge but knowledge of the most intimate kind: that which writes out their collective understandings and narratives as a community. Unsurprisingly, Christian relations with Jews often take on the character of replacement epistemology, but this pattern can be found in other hierarchical social engagements as well.

In the context of Jewish-Christian relations, sometimes replacement epistemology occurs in a straightforwardly offensive fashion, when Christian actors simply assert the ability to declare what or who is or is not Jewish. "Jews for Jesus" is a prominent example—an attempt by Christian actors to redraw the communal borders of Jewishness to their tastes. A popular podcast, *A Jew and a Gentile Discuss*, provides an even more direct example: it holds itself out as presenting a dialogue between Jews and Christians, which would be perfectly laudatory except that the two participants—the Gentile and the "Jew"—"both believe in Jesus."[39] The goal is clearly to present a Christian speaker as a valid and authentic exponent of Jewishness; to the extent the gambit is successful, it is

[37] Quoted in Marc Dollinger, *Black Power, Jewish Politics: Reinventing the Alliance in the 1960s* (Brandeis University Press, 2018), 130.

[38] While not precisely on this point, Rachel McKinney's discussion of "extracted speech" is nonetheless illustrative: "

> Yet our speech can also be (as the phrase goes) *used against us*. Our interlocutors can get us to do things with our words that we otherwise would not: to speak because it is our only option, to produce words on the basis of fear and deception, to express things without deciding to do so. . . . Rather than choosing whether, how, and what to say, our speech is—in a sense—chosen for us.

" Rachel Ann McKinney, "Extracted Speech," *Social Theory & Practice* 42, no. 2 (2016): 260.

[39] "A Jew and a Gentile Discuss" available at https://podcasts.apple.com/us/podcast/a-jew-and-a-gentile-discuss/id1529172889.

a clear example of replacement epistemology. (Indeed, it is at least a close cousin of replacement theology in its original sense.)

This sort of maneuver appears in political discourse as well.[40] Rudy Giuliani, for instance, notoriously declared himself (a practicing Catholic) to be "more of a Jew" than the liberal political figure (and Holocaust survivor) George Soros. Giuliani's criteria for Jewishness were given in strikingly Christian terms: among the reasons Giuliani gives for his "more Jewish" status is that Soros "doesn't go to church."[41] Of course, Soros *is* Jewish, and remains Jewish no matter how infrequently he attends "church" (or synagogue). But Giuliani's comments bank on the notions (a) that, specifically, a largely Christian audience will understand religious affiliation through a primarily Christian frame and (b) that, generally, a largely Christian audience will credit a fellow Christian speaker as capable of speaking authoritatively about the boundaries of Jewish peoplehood. To the extent Giuliani's gambit is successful even in the face of actual Jewish testimony to the contrary, it is a clear illustration of replacement epistemology in practice.

The problem of replacement epistemology cannot, however, be limited to such stark and in some ways superficial examples. While to some extent any religion with claims to universality is necessarily rivalrous with other religious groups, Christianity's origin as an outgrowth of Judaism makes the relationship between the two especially fraught. Christianity shares—and thereby lays claim to—key texts in Jewish religious belief, particularly the Tanakh (or, as Christians dub it, the Old Testament).[42] Christian interpretations of these shared texts are perpetually at risk of being undermined by Jewish articulations which are, of course, disinclined to view various biblical passages or stories as presaging the arrival of Christ. And the fact that Judaism did not wither away and agreeably assimilate into Christianity is, in addition to a point of vulnerability, a source of ongoing embarrassment for Christianity.

The problem, as Daniel Boyarin observes, is that "Christianity is for Paul and all of his followers simply the correct understanding of Torah."[43] This belief is unsettled any time Jews today are acknowledged to have any, much less an

[40] For more sustained discussion, see David Schraub, "Liberal Jews and Religious Liberty," *New York University Law Review* 98, no. 5 (2023): 1609–18.

[41] Aviya Kushner, "News Flash for Rudy Giuliani: Jews Don't Go to Church," *Forward*, December 23, 2019, https://forward.com/culture/437197/news-flash-for-rudy-giuliani-jews-dont-go-to-church/.

[42] A term which, itself, both assumes the Christian position that there is a *New* Testament that stands as a partner to the "Old" one and at least arguably implies that this New Testament is superior as a revision, updating, or advancement upon the old version. See J. Jonathan Schraub, "For the Sin We Have Committed by Theological Rationalizations: Rescuing Job from Normative Religion," *Soundings* 86, nos. 3–4 (Fall–Winter 2003): 456n2.

[43] Daniel Boyarin, "The Subversion of the Jews: Moses's Veil and the Hermeneutics of Suppression," *Diacritics* 23, no. 2 (1993): 35.

authoritative, claim on the ongoing meaning of what Jewishness is. Marianne Moyaert puts the dilemma well:

> For most of Christian history, the Church seemed to believe that Judaism, because it "failed" to recognize Jesus as the prophesied Messiah, lost its reason for existence. Moreover, the general assumption was that Judaism, after the destruction of the Second Temple by the Romans and the expulsion from Jerusalem, had come to an end. It still existed, but no longer developed. These theological assumptions made it difficult, if not impossible, for the Church to recognize Judaism as a vibrant tradition, with its own symbolic practices and textual hermeneutics. Judaism *after the coming of Christ* (and the destruction of the Temple) was viewed as an anachronism. There was no provision within Christianity to reckon with further developments within living Judaism.[44]

Christian actors have employed a variety of strategies to address the stubborn fact of ongoing Jewish existence. But while these tactics vary in the degree of overt hostility they express toward actual Jews, they frequently unite around a firm belief that Christians are, more so than the Jews, ultimately entitled to declare what Jewishness is. On one end of the spectrum, some Christian thinkers have been unapologetic in insisting that contemporary Jews are simply irrelevant as claimants to Jewish heritage. Supersessionism, which holds that the covenant which God had made with the Jewish people has been permanently and irrevocably transferred over to the Church, proclaims what it takes to be a brute truth, that after Christ "God is done with the Jews."[45] What Jews have done after the death and resurrection of Christ is nothing more than false prophecy. Yet even though God may be done with the Jews, the Church is not: it still needs Jews *historically* to serve as the wellspring for the contemporary Church which will come to replace them.[46] Insofar as living Jews are unlikely to accede quietly to this reformulation, they represent a significant threat to the Christian narrative. And so replacement theology requires an epistemic replacement as well, where Christian articulations of Jewish history supersede those of Jews.[47]

Under this view, it becomes almost impossible for Christian actors to conceive of a live and evolving Jewish tradition. Moyaert offers up the example of some orthodox Christians who have begun celebrating Passover Seders as a putative window into the life of Jesus. These adaptations—which usually closely

[44] Marianne Moyaert, "Christianizing Judaism? On the Problem of Christian Seder Meals," in *Is There a Judeo-Christian Tradition?*, ed. Emmanuel Nathan and Anya Topolski (de Gruyter, 2016), 137–63, 145–55.

[45] Loraine Boettner, *The Millennium* (Presbyterian & Reformed, 1957), 89–90.

[46] Bruce K. Waltke, "Kingdom Promises as Spiritual," in *Continuity and Discontinuity: Perspectives on the Relationship between the Old and New Testaments*, ed. John S. Feinberg (Crossway, 1988), 274.

[47] See Rubenstein, *After Auschwitz*, 70.

mimic contemporary Orthodox Jewish traditions—assume "that *today's Jewish tradition is more or less the same as that to which Jesus adhered*," which in turn depends upon the view "that Judaism is an almost ahistoric tradition frozen in time."[48] Every development in Jewish history over the past 2,000 years, from the fall of the Temple to the writing and codification of the Talmud to the Inquisition, pogroms, and the Holocaust is assumed to have had no practical impact on Jewish practice observed today (hence why the practice observed today can be taken to accurately reflect something Jesus would have experienced millennia ago).[49] Christian Seders are, Moyaert concludes, a "form of trespassing: they take and redefine a ritual practice that belongs to the heart of the religious life of Jewish tradition, which they have oppressed for centuries. Once again Christians are in control: a Jewish ritual is used to enhance Christian tradition without much concern for what that ritual means for Jewish communities today. Since Jews are typically not present during such Christians Seders, once again Christians are writing Jews out of their own story."[50]

The Christian who observes a Seder as a way of celebrating Jesus's life fossilizes Jewish history and thereby dramatically rewrites it. Yet the very point of conducting a Christian Seder is to stake a claim that this fossilized, historically static telling is, in fact, properly Jewish. And the larger binary, where Christians represent progress and Jews represent dated tradition, is sufficiently rooted in Western thought to jump beyond its theological boundaries. As Ethan Katz and Ari Joskowicz observe, "[T]he idea that a forward-looking Christianity had superseded an archaic Judaism established patterns of thinking about time and meaning in history that shaped notions of progress among religious, non-religious, and anti-religious thinkers alike."[51]

Certainly not all Christian writers have sought to erase contemporary Judaism in so stark a fashion. Yet even efforts at fostering egalitarian inclusion of Jews have often, in practice, replicated the logic of replacement epistemology. The (in)famous term "Judeo-Christian" is illustrative. It surged in popularity in the mid-20th century as a means of reacting against exclusionary and antisemitic politics (not just in Nazi Germany but in the United States as well), attempting to replace a posture of oppositional antagonism with one that emphasized commonality and unity between Judaism and Christianity.[52] Yet as many have remarked, there is a dark undertone to the purported "synthesis" represented

[48] Moyaert, "Christianizing Judaism?," 155.
[49] *Id.*
[50] *Id.* at 156–57.
[51] Ari Joskowicz and Ethan B. Katz, "Introduction: Rethinking Jews and Secularism," in *Secularism in Question: Jews and Judaism in Modern Times*, ed. Ari Joskowicz and Ethan B. Katz (University of Pennsylvania Press, 2015), 2.
[52] See Mark Silk, "Notes on the Judeo-Christian Tradition," *American Quarterly* 36, no. 1 (Spring 1984): 65–85.

in this term: only one side of the hyphen "is meant to be fully overcome, and only one has living representatives whose refusal to disappear seems to challenge the triumphant claims of synthesis itself."[53] "Judeo-Christian," I've argued elsewhere, effectively erases Jews because the presumption is that the proposed "commonality" between the two faiths occurs entirely on Christian terms. To illustrate, "first ask what is considered the 'traditional Judeo-Christian view' on abortion or the death penalty; then ask which specifically Jewish sources and texts are typically used to arrive at that answer."[54] Most Americans would draw a blank, because most immediately understand "Judeo-Christian" to mean Christian. It does not even occur to them that Jewish texts or sources *could* have a different vantage than that of their Christian colleagues (a differentiation which would in any event shatter the stipulated unity that Judeo-Christian relies upon). The result of "Judeo-Christian" is to facilitate the *dismissal* of distinctively Jewish articulations of social, political, or religious values insofar as they conflict with what is thought to be authoritatively known about analogous "Judeo-Christian" (read: Christian) values.

Replacement epistemology can also be observed in the racial context. We already mentioned how the meaning of Black Lives Matter can be altered by White discussants to carry a different and in many ways contrary meaning to that intended by the African American activists propagating the campaign. To the extent that these alterations succeed in becoming the *authoritative* meaning of "Black Lives Matter" in a given social context—that is, where a given set of listeners accepts that this is the meaning of Black Lives Matter *to its Black proponents*, regardless of what Black BLM activists themselves say—then we have an example of replacement epistemology. A similar practice can be seen in public discussions of "critical race theory," which also finds itself ascribed increasingly outlandish or absurd political positions.[55] Not only do these ascriptions typically fail to engage in any meaningful way with primary-source critical race

[53] David Nirenberg, *Anti-Judaism: The Western Tradition* (W. W. Norton, 2013), 570.

[54] David Schraub, "White Jews: An Intersectional Approach," *Association for Jewish Studies Review* 43, no. 2 (November 2019): 397.

[55] See, e.g., David Bernstein, Nicole Levitt, and Daniel Newman, "Critical Social Justice Ideology and Antisemitism: Assessment and Strategy," Jewish Institute for Liberal Values, September 1, 2021, https://45557309.fs1.hubspotusercontent-na1.net/hubfs/45557309/Whitepapers/Whitepaper-%20How%20Critical%20Social%20Justice%20Ideology%20Fuels%20Antisemitism.pdf. The JILV's white paper associates "Critical Social Justice" (within which it includes "critical race theory" and "intersectionality") with a variety of extreme and antisemitic positions, such as promoting an "erasure of Jewish identity." In making these claims, however, the white paper cites virtually no examples of actual critical race theory scholarship and almost entirely ignores CRT-influenced work which, far from erasing Jewish identity, operates from a self-consciously Jewish standpoint. For examples, see Schraub, "White Jews"; Daniel Ian Rubin, "HebCrit: A New Dimension of Critical Race Theory," *Social Identities* 26, no. 4 (2020): 499–514; Marla Brettschneider, *Jewish Feminism and Intersectionality* (SUNY Press, 2016); Deborah C. Malamud, "The Jew Taboo: Jewish Difference and the Affirmative Action Debate," *Ohio State Law Journal* 59, no. 3 (1998): 915–70.

theory materials,[56] but they are stubbornly immune to *correction* by critical race theorists themselves even as they present themselves and in many contexts are accepted as authoritative pronouncements of what critical race theory means.[57] Indeed, Christopher Rufo, a leading activist against critical race theory, openly bragged about engaging in this tactic. "We have successfully frozen their brand—'critical race theory'—into the public conversation and are steadily driving up negative perceptions. We will eventually turn it toxic, as we put all of the various cultural insanities under that brand category," Rufo wrote. "The goal is to have the public read something crazy in the newspaper and immediately think 'critical race theory.' We have decodified the term and will recodify it to annex the entire range of cultural constructions that are unpopular with Americans."[58]

A final example returns us to the *Parents Involved* case, and in particular the competing understandings between Chief Justice John Roberts's plurality, and dissents by Justices John Paul Stevens and Stephen Breyer, regarding the meaning of *Brown v. Board of Education*. *Parents Involved* concerned voluntary, race-conscious measures to ensure public K–12 schools in Seattle and Louisville were racially integrated.[59] It thus brought to the fore two distinct conceptions regarding what civil rights advocates were pursuing in the *Brown* litigation: racial integration (in which case the measures by these municipalities carried forward *Brown*'s legacy) or color-blindness (in which case they thwarted it).[60] Chief Justice Roberts, for his part, cited portions of the plaintiff's argument in *Brown* that pointed to a color-blind approach, writing that "it was that position that prevailed in this Court."[61] The problem for the chief justice is that many of the *Brown* lawyers were still alive when *Parents Involved* was decided, and they made it clear in no uncertain terms that he had misapprehended the legal and

[56] For overviews, see Richard Delgado and Jean Stefancic, *Critical Race Theory: An Introduction*, 3rd ed. (NYU Press, 2017); Kimberle Crenshaw, Neil Gotanda, Gary Peller, and Kendall Thomas, eds., *Critical Race Theory: The Key Writings That Formed the Movement* (New Press, 1996).

[57] See Rachel Hatzipanagos, "What the Founders of Critical Race Theory Have to Say about the Conservative Attacks," *Washington Post*, July 22, 2021, https://www.washingtonpost.com/nation/2021/07/22/critical-race-theory-founders/.

[58] Quoted in Laura Meckler and Josh Dawsey, "Republicans, Spurred by an Unlikely Figure, See Political Promise in Targeting Critical Race Theory," *Washington Post*, June 21, 2021, https://www.washingtonpost.com/education/2021/06/19/critical-race-theory-rufo-republicans/.

[59] See David Schraub, "Sticky Slopes," *California Law Review* 101, no. 5 (2013): 1278–79, for discussion.

[60] The struggle over the meaning of *Brown* is a recurrent theme in scholarship about racial equality and the Fourteenth Amendment. See, e.g., Pamela S. Karlan, "What Can *Brown*® Do for You? Neutral Principles and the Struggle over the Equal Protection Clause," *Duke Law Journal* 58, no. 6 (2009): 1049–69; Mark Tushnet, "Public Law Litigation and the Ambiguities of *Brown*," *Fordham Law Review* 61, no. 1 (1992): 23–28; William Van Alystene, "Rites of Passage: Race, the Supreme Court, and the Constitution," *University of Chicago Law Review* 46, no. 4 (Summer 1979): 775–810.

[61] *Parents Involved*, 551 U.S. at 747.

moral position they had advanced.[62] "Robert Carter, whose argument before the Brown court was stated to have 'no ambiguity' by Chief Justice Roberts, said '[i]t's to stand that argument on its head to use race the way they use it now.' Jack Greenberg called the plurality opinion 'preposterous,' while William T. Coleman, Jr., said it was '100 percent wrong.'"[63]

The problem is not, to be clear, that Chief Justice Roberts (or anyone else) is forbidden from holding a different view regarding racial equality or racial integration than that promoted by the litigators and activists who spearheaded *Brown*. The problem is that Chief Justice Roberts and his allies have effectively *replaced* the meaning of *Brown* with one he prefers, and attributed authorship of that meaning not to himself but to the desegregation campaign of the civil rights movement. In the annals of the law, and in the eyes of many Americans, *Brown*'s meaning is what Chief Justice Roberts says it means, and the robustness of that meaning is relatively immune from challenge by the individuals who actually brought *Brown* into existence.

"We do not really associate with each other," wrote W. E. B. Du Bois, "we associate with our ideas of each other, and few people have either the ability or courage to question their own ideas."[64] If Du Bois is right (and, e.g., White people do not "associate with" Black people but rather with their "ideas" of Black people), then the ability to colonize out-group voices so their speech is no longer theirs can long serve to insulate dominant social institutions from meaningful challenge. Here replacement epistemology shows its force as a key element of Charles W. Mills's "racial contract." Part of the racial contract, Mills argues, is an epistemological "agreement to *mis*interpret the world. One has to learn to see the world wrongly, but with the assurance that this set of mistaken perceptions will be validated."[65] This, Lorraine Cole suggests, "serves to filter out empirical evidence that would unsettle or counter any suspicion that these fundamental beliefs might indeed be held together by webs of distortion and error—of epistemically careless, irresponsible knowledge construction."[66] Through replacement epistemology we can maintain indefinitely an image which justifies a failure to engage with ideologies or interest groups that we fear will be challenging. Sometimes (as in the BLM case) this can manifest as

[62] See Adam Liptak, "The Same Words, but Differing Views," *New York Times*, June 29, 2007), A24.

[63] Schraub, "Sticky Slopes," 1279 (quoting Liptak, "The Same Words"). Thurgood Marshall had passed away by that point, but he too was quite unambiguous in rejecting the pure color-blind approach promoted in *Parents Involved*, expressly endorsing race-conscious integration and affirmative action programs in *University of California v. Bakke*. Regents of Univ. of Cal. v. Bakke, 438 U.S. 265, 387 (1978) (Marshall, J., concurring and dissenting).

[64] W. E. B. Du Bois, *Darkwater: Voices from Within the Veil* (1920; Humanity, 2003), 159.

[65] Charles W. Mills, *The Racial Contract* (Cornell University Press, 1997), 18.

[66] Lorraine Cole, "The Power of Ignorance," in *Race and Epistemologies of Ignorance*, ed. Shannon Sullivan and Nancy Tuana (SUNY Press, 2007), 214.

forcing disagreement to present one's interlocutors as unreasonable, outlandish, or otherwise extreme. At other points (in some Jewish-Christian interactions, particularly those which proceed through a "Judeo-Christian" frame) it can occur through fictive consonance—masking genuine differences and using an imposed harmony to make the very idea of a challenge seem fanciful, obstinate, or agitating. In either case, the effect is to preserve preexisting ideological commitments and shield them from effective challenge. Unsurprisingly, then, these fortifying tactics are most often deployed when the commitments in question are deeply felt or passionately held.

The Harms of Dismissal

In addition to suppressing consideration of important social issues, dismissal often comes attached to some particularly pernicious dignitary harms. Neither ignorance nor evaluative motivated reasoning makes explicit any negative attitudes about the person whose allegations are going unheeded. But dismissal is often different. In order to reject a known claim *prior* to substantive evaluation, dismissal frequently requires explicit negative assertions regarding the claimant—that they are uncredible, untrustworthy, paranoid, or delusional.[67] Consider a case of dismissal which relies on the "poisoning the well" fallacy, whereby a person's group membership makes them and their claims inherently untrustworthy.[68] This rejoinder blocks the consideration of any assertion that could be made, "no matter how good it is, or how much it [is] based on good evidence."[69] One often sees, consequently, stereotypes that target the supposed unreliability of a group—as in cunning Jews or unsophisticated African Americans—all of which can buttress the decision to dismiss.

This, of course, is a dignitary harm all on its own—it undermines a person's status as a "knower," the sort of person who can possess and transmit useful knowledge, which is an inherent wrong.[70] But it comes attached to further secondary wrongs. Dismissal necessarily impacts the "epistemic confidence" of the targeted group, whose instincts regarding their own experience are taken to be

[67] See Kate Abramson, "Turning Up the Lights on Gaslighting," *Philosophical Perspectives* 28, no. 1 (2014): 5 ("[I]t's important to consider the variety of ways . . . women are dismissed—e.g. 'too sensitive,' 'paranoid,' 'crazy,' 'prude' or the peculiarly existentialist dismissal of 'bad faith.'"). It is, again, not the case that *every* form of dismissal relies on those sorts of malign stereotypes. (Return again to the "drooling imbecile" example.) But certainly it is a regular enough feature of our discourse to be familiar and worrisome.

[68] See D. N. Walton, "Poisoning the Well," *Argumentation* 20, no. 3 (2006): 275 (describing, as the paradigmatic case of the fallacy, the claim by Charles Kingsley that Cardinal Newman's claims "were not to be trusted" because, as a Catholic, Newman's first loyalty was not to the truth).

[69] *Id.* at 276.

[70] Fricker, *Epistemic Injustice*, 44.

so transparently ludicrous that they need not even be given a hearing. "When you find yourself in a situation in which you seem to be the only one to feel the dissonance between received understanding and your own intimated sense of a given experience, it tends to knock your faith in your own ability to make sense of the world."[71] Importantly, the rhetoric that supports dismissal typically goes beyond alleging that the target is simply "wrong or mistaken." Rather, it presents her as "being in no condition to judge whether she is wrong or mistaken. The accusations are about the target's basic rational competence—her ability to get facts right, to deliberate, her basic evaluative competencies and ability to react appropriately: her independent standing as a deliberator and moral agent."[72] At the extreme, this message can be so internalized that the target entirely loses confidence that her felt experiences or instincts bear any correlation to an objective reality, and so she refrains from articulating them altogether. At this stage, dismissal can loop back around into ignorance—if a targeted group does not believe that its thoughts (or particular categories of thoughts) are rational ones worthy of being aired in the public sphere, it is unlikely to present them in the first place.

Indeed, dismissal is dangerous precisely because of how easily it can move "up the ladder" to exacerbate the problem of ignorance. In the previous chapter, I identified two mechanisms through which ignorance can self-replicate—that is, how the relative dearth of claims making a given assertion renders it less likely that such claims will be aired in the future. The first, associated with Fricker, is the idea of a hermeneutical injustice—the maldistribution of interpretative resources which make it harder for out-groups to describe their situations in recognizable and socially compelling ways. The second, elucidated by Elisabeth Noelle-Neumann, is the "spiral of silence," where people are more comfortable expressing common views and more reticent to express rare ones. Dismissal can feed into both mechanisms. The rhetoric of dismissal tends to present the interpretive frames proffered by the claimant as illegitimate and the testimonial offerings of the claimant as irrational. The former contributes to the hermeneutical gap by limiting the array of social presentations seen as valid; the latter promotes the spiral of silence by converting an unpopular opinion into a wholesale indictment of the speaker's deliberative capacity.

[71] *Id.* at 163. *See also* Elisabeth Noelle-Neumann, "The Spiral of Silence: A Theory of Public Opinion," *Journal of Communication* 24, no. 2 (1974), 44 (contending that when a particular opinion seems to be rare, adherents will find themselves uncertain and may become reticent to express their views; "the more this appears to be so, the more uncertain he will become of himself, and the less he will be inclined to express his opinion").

[72] Abramson, "Turning Up the Lights," 8. Abramson and Fricker both recount a passage in Simone de Beauvoir's diary where, after a long-ranging discussion with Jean-Paul Sartre, she was left so dispirited in her reasoning that she wrote, "I'm no longer sure what I think, or even if I think at all." *Id.* at 4; Fricker, *Epistemic Injustice*, 50.

It is important to note that dismissal is a problem separate from whether the underlying claim ultimately has merit. Of course, dismissal entails declining to substantively address an extant claim, and that implies that certain claims that should be ratified will instead be ignored. But even if a given claim should—after due consideration—be rejected, it would still be problematic if the claimant was in fact never given the opportunity to receive such consideration.[73] Much of the public outrage over the Trayvon Martin killing, for example, arose not only because of the actual death of a young Black teenager but because the police initially did not arrest his shooter, instead seeming to instantly credit George Zimmerman's claim of self-defense.[74] Even if one thinks that the evidence that was ultimately produced was insufficient to prove Zimmerman guilty beyond a reasonable doubt, the initial failure to seriously investigate it as a potential homicide—to effectively dismiss the possibility that it was a murder—is hard to square with any commitment to epistemic equality and is a wrong in itself. A significant motivator of the Black Lives Matter movement, it seems, is not about the specific outcomes of individual cases but rather a more general sense that allegations of violence against Black persons are systematically dismissed as valid candidates for investigation. Though writing decades prior to the development of Black Lives Matter as a mantra, Patricia Williams encapsulates this point well when she described "[t]he black experience of anonymity, the estrangement of being without a name," as being "beyond the dimension of any consideration at all."[75]

The confidence that one's contributions to the debate are given due consideration, even if the outcome is unfavorable, matters. Tom Tyler's work on "procedural justice" amasses powerful evidence that people place considerable independent weight on the knowledge that their voices were heard, even where they know they did not affect the ultimate conclusion.[76] It follows that people will

[73] See Jane McConkey, "Knowledge and Acknowledgment: 'Epistemic Injustice' as a Problem of Recognition," *Politics* 24, no. 3 (2004): 201 (distinguishing between whether a person "was a victim of racism" and the separate harm of lacking "the rhetorical space to have [one's] claims appreciated or properly assessed"); Laurence Tribe, *American Constitutional Law* (Foundation, 1978), 503 ("Both the right to be heard from, and the right to be told why, are analytically distinct from the right to secure a different outcome."); Alon Harel and Tsvi Kahana, "The Easy Core Case for Judicial Review," *Journal of Legal Analysis* 2, no. 1 (2010): 238–39 (articulating the right of a judicial hearing that is "valued independently of the merit of the decision likely to be generated at the end of this process").

[74] See, e.g., Cynthia Lee, "Making Race Salient: Trayvon Martin and Implicit Bias in a Not Yet Post-Racial Society," *North Carolina Law Review* 91, no. 5 (2013): 1558 (noting that "[t]he failure of the Sanford police department to arrest Zimmerman" after he asserted he acted in self-defense "created a firestorm of protests").

[75] Patricia J. Williams, "Alchemical Notes: Reconstructing Ideals from Deconstructed Rights," *Harvard Civil Rights–Civil Liberties Law Review* 22, no. 2 (1987): 414.

[76] See, e.g., Tom R. Tyler, *Why People Obey the Law* (Princeton University Press, 2006), 149 (finding that people do not need to know that their contribution affected the outcome for them to consider the outcome legitimate, but they do need to know that their contribution was considered).

experience an injustice when their attempts to enter into social conversation are systematically rebuffed, and they do not conflate this treatment with considered disagreement regarding the merits of their position even though the tangible outcomes might be identical. There is, in other words, a significant and morally salient distinction between rejecting a claim because after serious consideration we conclude it is untenable, and rejecting a claim because we conclude the person bringing it simply isn't worthy of our attention (even if the underlying facts of the claim are the same). Dismissal implicates the latter set of concerns; the problem of dismissal is not that of ill-formed or even biased appraisal of the merits of a given controversy, but the failure to even acknowledge the controversy as a legitimate entrant into public conversation.

The ideal theory response to dismissal might seem to be a demand that all claims in all contexts be given full, fair, and charitable review. Unfortunately, we do not live in an ideal world, and in particular we lack the surfeit of deliberative resources that would allow us to give every single proffered claim this sort of full hearing.[77] What are our deliberative obligations given these limitations?

Most obviously, those claims that are left aside due to the inability to devote proper attention to them still cannot be justly rejected. We can only (and should only) reserve judgment on them until such time as they are able to be given their due consideration. This may mean that judgment on certain claims is deferred more or less indefinitely; this is an injustice, but a lesser one (and a more unavoidable one) than outright rejecting them without providing reasoned argument.

More concretely, recognizing the particular biases in dismissal suggests that we should expend considerable effort in ensuring that the claims that we do consider come from a diverse and representative cross-sample of the community. Recall that the wrong of both dismissal and ignorance is less the inescapable fact that not every claim will be considered and more the maldistribution of deliberative expenditures to favor the sorts of claims which are amenable to dominant social groups. Moreover, precisely because some forms of dismissal are both inevitable and ubiquitous, it can be difficult for those afflicted by *wrongful* dismissal to identify with confidence even to themselves—let alone to convince external observers—that theirs is a case of the morally pernicious type.

[77] See Mark E. Warren, "Deliberative Democracy and Authority," *American Political Science Review* 90, no. 1 (1996): 57–58 (noting that there will always be limits on the amount of time and attention persons can devote to particular issues); José Medina, *The Epistemology of Resistance: Gender and Racial Oppression, Epistemic Injustice, and Resistant Imaginations* (Oxford University Press, 2012), 33 ("[O]nly a superhuman knower could be always ready to embark on every possible discovery journey that comes her way.").

In a related context, Laurence Thomas observes that there are "a thousand and one ways" one can communicate to an interlocutor that they are of lesser value: "One may listen inattentively, or interrupt frequently, or not directly respond to what the person actually says, or not respond with the seriousness that is appropriate to the person concerned." Yet "[w]e often do not realize that we are" engaging in this sort of behavior, "because communicating positive and negative expectations with regard to others is a natural part of life" and because the putative markers (inattentiveness, dismissiveness) can and often are fairly attributable to causes having nothing to do with any actual or intended denigration of value.[78] This ambiguity "can easily create an internal sense of paranoia and second-guessing (Am I being oversensitive? Did it really happen that way?) that will inevitably be exacerbated by the lack of any 'smoking gun' evidence."[79] In the context of dismissal, the very fact that (wrongful, unjustified, biased) dismissal often looks observationally equivalent to (reasonable, ordinary, unremarkable) satisficing—simply choosing to stop a conversation at the point where one reasonably concludes (as in the "drooling imbecile" case) that investing additional time into consideration is unlikely to yield a deliberatively productive outcome—is part of its danger. Deliberative scarcity can justify not considering every claim in the aggregate, but it cannot justify the motivational slant that makes dismissal so dangerous—and so appealing.

One hint that we are in the realm of wrongful dismissal rather than reasonable satisficing is if our conversational cutoffs disproportionately act to short-circuit deliberative offerings made by members of marginalized communities. After all, it is hard to imagine a (morally justifiable) basis for assuming that claims emanating from those sources are *systematically* more worthy of rightful dismissal. Consequently, political deliberation should take special attention to ensure that the perspectives of marginalized individuals are given an opportunity to voice their claims.[80] As Fricker observes, the key virtue that needs to be brought to bear

[78] Laurence M. Thomas, "Moral Deference," in *Theorizing Multiculturalism*, ed. Cynthia Willet (Blackwell, 1998), 366.

[79] David Schraub and Joel Sati, "Epistemic Injustice in Collecting and Appraising Evidence," in *The Routledge Handbook of the Philosophy of Evidence*, ed. Maria Lasonen-Aarnio and Clayton Littlejohn (Taylor & Francis, 2024), 224. See Saba Fatima. "On the Edge of Knowing: Microaggression and Epistemic Uncertainty as a Woman of Color," in *Surviving Sexism in Academia: Feminist Strategies for Leadership*, ed. Kirsti Cole and Holly Hassel (Routledge, 2017), 147–57.

[80] *See* Young, *Inclusion and Democracy*, 136–46. Young's analysis of the concept of "perspective," which focuses on the fact that people are "differently positioned" and therefore "have different experience, history, and social knowledge derived from that positioning" (*id.* at 136), is informative. Particularly relevant is her observation that perspective places the focus on what helps create the set of questions and assumptions from which we begin to reason, rather than the specific content that we ultimately arrive at once the deliberative process concludes. *Id.* at 137–39.

to correct testimonial injustices is the possession of "reflexive critical awareness of the likely presence of prejudice."[81] We should, in other words, be especially on alert in circumstances where it seems more likely that prejudice, implicit bias, hermeneutical gaps, or other like malfunctions are in play and are the tail wagging the dismissal dog. A prominent arena where these factors seem likely to be in play is when claims of discrimination are dismissed via the general declaration that they are leveled in bad faith.

[81] Fricker, *Epistemic Injustice*, 91 ("When the hearer suspects prejudice in her credibility judgment . . . she should shift intellectual gear out of spontaneous, unreflective mode and into active critical reflection in order to identify how far the suspected prejudice has influenced her judgment.").

4

Playing with Cards

Discrimination Claims and the Charge of Bad Faith

An African American alleging he was racially profiled at a department store is told he is "playing the race card."[1] A woman objecting to a culture of sexual harassment in the tech industry is dismissed as covering up for her own lack of drive and ambition. A Jew who expresses concern about antisemitism at her university is told she is only interested in shielding Israel from criticism. Refrains such as these are routine responses to members of marginalized groups claiming bias, harassment, or discrimination.[2] The presumption that underlies this response is that the paradigmatic claim of discrimination is made in bad faith. It is not motivated by a credible (or perhaps even sincere) belief that unfair or unequal treatment has occurred but is merely a ploy designed to harness the widespread commitment to oppose such injustice. The "card" metaphor is evocative: it connotes a strategic gambit that one deploys to win a game rather than an honest and organic attempt to advance discussion.

The "bad faith" charge is an allegation that the discrimination claimant[3] knows or should have known that her claim is baseless. This response has proven to be an exceptionally effective way to shut down public discussion of discrimination claims, no matter what their substance. By presenting the paradigmatic discrimination claim as a baseless one, the bad faith response justifies dismissing these claims as part of a pattern or practice of illegitimate claims which need not occupy our attention.

[1] A prior version of this chapter was published as David Schraub, "Playing with Cards: Discrimination Claims and the Charge of Bad Faith," *Social Theory & Practice* 42, no. 2 (2016): 285–303.

[2] Once again, I group together this entire cluster of wrongs—including individual discriminatory acts as well as contentions of structural oppression—under the general moniker "discrimination." While there are important differences between these types of wrongs, the "bad faith" response reacts to all of them similarly (and often affirmatively collapses the distinctions between them). I am, however, using "discrimination" in its "moralized" rather than "descriptive" form—to connote a form of wrongful behavior. See Deborah Hellman, *When Is Discrimination Wrong?* (Harvard University Press, 2008), 13.

[3] For clarity, I refer to persons alleging discrimination as "claimants" and those making the bad faith charge in response "respondents." The respondent may, but need not, be the person who is the subject of the discrimination claim.

Deliberation, Dismissal, and Democracy. David Schraub, Oxford University Press. © Oxford University Press (2025). DOI: 10.1093/9780197816424.003.0005

Obviously, the manner in which the bad faith charge is forwarded varies depending on the situation. Still, there is a pattern to the way this charge is often forwarded, consisting of five steps:

(1) A declaration that the card has been played.
(2) A contention that the "card" is part of a pattern of *generally* suspect discrimination claims being made.
(3) An affirmation that, theoretically, illegitimate discrimination exists and should be combated.
(4) A claim that making bad faith charges of discrimination has chilling effects on discourse and hurts efforts to fight "real" instances of discrimination.
(5) An assertion that the pattern of false claims, coupled with the need for caution around discrimination allegations, is sufficient to dispose of the extant claim.

I don't claim that each of these five elements will be explicitly referenced in any discrimination response that appears to include a charge of bad faith. I do suggest that these elements represent key components of this response, and that the power of this response as a tool for dismissing discrimination stems from each of these elements having considerable (if pernicious) popular resonance.

In the previous two chapters, I gave a full accounting of the concept of "dismissal": the act of dispensing with a proffered claim *prior* to substantive consideration of its merits. As applied to claims of discrimination, the charge of bad faith will serve as a keynote example of how dismissal impedes consideration of a quintessential hard thought. Replying to claims of discrimination by dismissing them as offered in bad faith takes an important claim, one that should occupy our attention as citizens concerned about fair and egalitarian treatment, and removes it from the domain of acceptable public discourse.

One reason why it is important to consider the dismissal of discrimination claims is that, frequently, claims of discrimination are alleged to be a *form* of dismissal. Many advocates of "free speech culture" (or concurrent critics of "cancel culture") allege that widespread claims that various social beliefs or practices are discriminatory are a mechanism through which freewheeling speech and debate are chilled. Through this pattern, "free speech" and "antidiscrimination" commitments are presented as antagonists. I don't dispute that it is possible for people to wield a discrimination claim as a means of evading an uncomfortable thought. But frequently, it is the dismissal of discrimination claims that is the more powerful and more prominent mechanism for evading the hard thoughts. Those who extol the virtues of free speech culture, and of deliberating even over uncomfortable propositions, should be more attentive to their own discomfort over pondering potential complicity in discriminatory behavior. More often than not, "the 'race card,' is typically trumped by the 'race-card card.'"[4]

Discrimination claimants have lacked a cohesive theory about the bad faith response and therefore have struggled to articulate why their claims do not merit this prima facie dismissal in the deliberative context. This chapter fills that gap in three ways. First, it provides an account of the assumptions and characteristics which reflect how the response is deployed in practice. Second, it identifies how the bad faith response interacts with discriminatory attitudes and occupies an important niche in the *psychological* rationalization of ongoing discriminatory practices. Third, it identifies the wrongs the bad faith charge imposes upon discrimination claimants, obstructing our ability to effectively respond to injustice and degrading their equal participation in political and social discourse.

The Card in Play

The core of the bad faith response is the contention that discrimination claims should *generally* be viewed with suspicion. In this way, the response can be seen as a special form of Miranda Fricker's larger concept of testimonial injustice: "The basic idea [of testimonial injustice] is that a speaker suffers . . . if prejudice on the hearer's part causes him to give the speaker less credibility than he would otherwise have given."[5] Fricker's "central case" of testimonial injustice occurs when there exists *systematic* prejudice on the basis of one's identity that consistently yields this credibility deficit.[6] This maps well onto the generalized belief that discrimination claims are leveled opportunistically and therefore should be appropriately discounted. The context of discrimination claims sharply compounds the testimonial injustice, however, because it is self-insulating—prejudice yields the injustice and simultaneously wards off complaints aimed at attacking the prejudice.

That the bad faith response relies upon prejudicial outlooks is illustrated by the fact that, for the most part, the bad faith claim is not keyed to the claimant's specific history. Rather, it is asserted to be a common feature of discourse by members of his or her social class (women, African Americans, Jews, etc.). Consider two brief examples. Anita Sarkeesian's series "Tropes versus Women in Video Games" contended that many prominent video games were replete with sexist themes and practices. Sarkeesian's criticisms were met with a torrent of

[4] Jon Hanson and Kathleen Hanson, "The Blame Frame: Justifying (Racial) Injustice in America," *Harvard Civil Rights–Civil Liberties Law Review* 41, no. 2 (2006): 471.

[5] See Miranda Fricker, *Epistemic Injustice: Power and the Ethics of Knowing* (Oxford University Press, 2007), 4.

[6] *See id.* at 28.

abusive threats and calls for violence. But in addressing these issues, video game columnist Ryan Carroll asserted that any claim of sexism was merely an "'I win' button" and "a way to shut out opposing viewpoints."[7] Likewise, critic Howard Jacobson alleged that Caryl Churchill's play *Seven Jewish Children* was antisemitic: he argued the play presented Jews as conspiratorial and deceitful, trafficked in the blood libel by casting Jews as reveling in the blood of non-Jewish children, and played upon old-school antisemitic interpretations of the concept of "chosen." Churchill dismissed Jacobson's arguments by calling such contentions "the usual tactic" and suggested that Jacobson purposefully elided the distinction between criticism of Israel and antisemitism.[8] In asserting this type of cynical opportunism, neither Churchill nor Carroll cite any specific practices by Jacobson or Sarkeesian. The allegation is rather that antisemitism claimants (Jews) or sexism claimants (women) as a whole illicitly register these charges. The self-insulating nature of the response is also evident: if Jacobson or Sarkeesian argued that Churchill's or Carroll's argument reflected ingrained prejudice, it could be dismissed for the same reason as the original critique.

The key element of the bad faith response is not just that it allows the claim to be dismissed, but that it can be dismissed *prior to* significant substantive engagement in the merits of the claim. This obviates the need for any sustained look into the particular controversy at hand. It is the move of first resort—not a conclusion drawn from careful consideration of the evidence[9] but rather a presumption drawn from one's view of the paradigm case of discrimination claims. It is only upon adopting the view that these claims are *systematically* groundless that one can plausibly infer that the next claim will be false as well. The bad faith response isn't troubling because discrimination claims are never made in bad faith; it is troubling because it is relied on as a first-cut response that presents

[7] Ryan Carroll, "'Gamergate' Is an Accountability Problem, Not a Sexism One," *ModVive*, September 1, 2014, https://web.archive.org/web/20140903171324/http://www.modvive.com/2014/09/01/gamergate-accountability-problem-sexism-one/.

[8] Caryl Churchill, "My Play Is Not Anti-Semitic," *The Independent*, February 21, 2009, http://www.independent.co.uk/voices/letters/letters-jacobson-on-gaza-1628191.html (responding to Howard Jacobson, "Let's See the 'Criticism' of Israel for What It Really Is," *The Independent*, February 18, 2009, http://www.independent.co.uk/voices/commentators/howard-jacobson/howard-jacobson-letrsquos-see-the-criticism-of-israel-for-what-it-really-is-1624827.html).

[9] To be clear, it is possible to make a warranted assertion of bad faith. But the evidence supporting such an assertion would almost certainly come after substantive investigation, the avoidance of which is a prime motivator behind the response. This also distinguishes the "card" case from circumstances where a *particular* speaker with a *particular* known history of peddling falsehoods or smears is discredited on that basis. So, for example, one could argue that the Trump administration's putative opposition to campus antisemitism is in bad faith by citing its pretextual character vis-à-vis the administration's general hostility to academia, as well as the long history of Trump and his allies propagating (right-wing) antisemitic activity. But that argument is tied to specific actions taken by the Trump administration; it is difficult to imagine a circumstance where such a history could be imputed to an entire identity group.

marginalized persons as inherently untrustworthy, incredible, or lacking in basic understanding regarding the true meaning of discrimination.

The assertion that members of marginalized groups routinely level groundless charges of discrimination relies on seemingly obvious prejudicial foundations. Yet there is a peculiar Janus face to this mode of argument. Even as they assert systematic bad faith across the entire class of racism, sexism, antisemitism, or other like charges, respondents will nearly invariably couple their case with the counterintuitive assertion that these forms of discrimination are severe moral failings. Discrimination is a serious wrongdoing, not to be taken lightly. Both Carroll and Churchill are well aware of, and condemn, certain instances of sexism and antisemitism (respectively). In his book *The Race Card*, Stanford Law professor Richard Thompson Ford argues that we should be vigilant against "opportunistic" accusations of racism precisely because such claims "undermine popular support for racial justice"—a project Ford clearly believes has considerably more work ahead of it.[10]

On its face, this affirmation is strange. Intuitively, it would seem easier to dismiss discrimination claims if they were seen as no big deal and if the consequences of a false negative were viewed as minimal. Yet respondents seem adamant that they do take discrimination seriously even in the course of urging systematic dismissal of actual extant claims. And they often explicitly connect this concern with their decision to dismiss—doing so, they argue, ensures that we take "real" discrimination claims (whatever those might be) seriously. That the argument for regularly dismissing actual discrimination claims is paired with vigorous affirmation of the grievous wrong discrimination represents suggests something deeper is at work. The following section situates these affirmations and the bad faith response generally as part of a larger practice that reduces the perceived conflict between liberal egalitarian ideals and ongoing prejudicial beliefs and behaviors.

Bad Faith and the Aversive Racist: Commonality versus Condemnation

Noting the mechanics of the bad faith response does not explain *why* it works or, perhaps more accurately, why the bad faith allegation is so ubiquitous as a response to discrimination claims. I suggest that the bad faith response does important work in allowing public commitments to equal treatment to coexist with private (or subconscious) animus. The key to the riddle lies in the

[10] Richard Thompson Ford, *The Race Card: How Bluffing about Bias Makes Race Relations Worse* (Picador, 2009), 339.

professed belief that the theoretical type of discrimination at issue (racism, sexism, antisemitism, etc.) is a serious breach of ethical conduct.

The primary theoretical model which explores the concurrent possession of conscious egalitarian commitments alongside continuing subconscious prejudice is John Dovidio and Samuel Gaertner's concept of "aversive racism."[11] Aversive racists abjure overt antipathy or hostility toward racial out-groups—the traditional "dominative" form of racism that characterizes Nazis, the Klan, and Jim Crow. They affirm noble ideals of racial egalitarianism and fair treatment. Nonetheless, they retain "some negative feelings toward or beliefs about [racial minorities], of which they are unaware or which they try to dissociate from their nonprejudiced self-images."[12] Consequently, these people display aversion—not outright hatred—to people of color, while also being averse to suggestions that they are in fact prejudiced (charges which conflict with their egalitarian self-image).[13] Aversive racist behavior seeks to reduce the dissonance between subconscious prejudices and conscious egalitarian commitments.

Typically, aversive racists are said to act on their subconscious prejudices only in cases of ambiguity—where there is a credible, nonprejudiced rationale for engaging in hostile or discriminatory treatment.[14] Hence, the aversive racist will behave in a discriminatory fashion only in circumstances where it would not be obvious (to themselves and to others) that their behavior is motivated by prejudice. The act of robustly condemning discrimination helps create this ambiguity—it makes it harder to conclude that the actor is such a discriminator. Obviously, part of this effect is simply a function of the declaration, and indeed there is considerable evidence that persons given the opportunity to affirm their opposition to discrimination will be more likely to indulge in discriminatory practices—the pronouncement having given them a "moral credential" which blunts otherwise credible inferences of prejudice.[15] But there are more subtle forces at work. Presenting "discrimination"—as a concept—as a serious wrong

[11] See, e.g., John F. Dovidio and Samuel L. Gaertner, "Aversive Racism," *Advances in Experimental Social Psychology* 36 (2004): 1–52 [Dovidio and Gaertner, "Aversive Racism"]; John F. Dovidio and Samuel L. Gaertner, "Aversive Racism and Selection Decisions: 1989 and 1999," *Psychological Science* 11, no. 4 (2009): 315–19 [Dovidio and Gaertner, "Selection Decisions"]; Samuel L. Gaertner and John F. Dovidio, "The Aversive Form of Racism," in *Prejudice, Discrimination, and Racism*, ed. John F. Dovidio and Samuel L. Gaertner (Academic Press, 1986), 61–89. Name notwithstanding, Dovidio and Gaertner have affirmed that their theory is not limited solely to the racial context ("Aversive Racism," 3).

[12] Dovidio and Gaertner, "Aversive Racism," 4.

[13] *Id.*

[14] Dovidio and Gaertner, "Selection Decisions," 315 ("Because aversive racists consciously recognize and endorse egalitarian values, they will not discriminate in situations in which they recognize that discrimination would be obvious to others and themselves.... However, because aversive racists do possess negative feelings, often unconsciously, discrimination occurs when bias is not obvious or can be rationalized on the basis of some factor other than race.").

[15] *See generally* Benoît Monin and Dale T. Miller, "Moral Credentials and the Expression of Prejudice," *Journal of Personality & Social Psychology* 81, no. 1 (2001): 33–43.

simultaneously constructs it as rare, aberrant, and therefore unlikely to apply to anything but the most vicious cases of obvious antipathy.

In other work, I have hypothesized that there is an inverse relationship between how people perceive the severity of an ambiguous norm and how they perceive its scope.[16] The more morally serious a norm (and therefore also its breach) is taken to be, the narrower the range of behavior that will be seen to be encompassed under the norm's ambit. There are several reasons why this might be the case. In general, people tend to believe in a "just world," wherein for the most part people play fairly and get what they deserve.[17] Consequently, they are likely to be resistant to the notion that significant moral wrongdoings are commonplace, which would imply widespread and systematic injustice. More concretely, people have a very obvious rationale for narrowly interpreting what constitutes a severe moral breach: the alternative risks encompassing their own behavior.[18] Not wanting to be viewed as moral monsters, people naturally will be suspicious of ethical reasoning that risks placing them in such a category. Moreover, this theory is bidirectional: persons won't view common behavior as constituting a severe moral breach, and they will view wide application of a normative rule as diminishing the seriousness of its content. Ford registers this concern in stark terms: "The good-natured humanitarian who listens attentively to the first claim of social injustice will become an impatient curmudgeon after multiple similar admonishments.... The growing number of social groups making claims to civil rights protection threatens the political and practical viability of civil rights for those who need them the most."[19] Elevating the moral seriousness of a given norm perversely acts to *limit* the range of behavior the norm can constrain.

This "sticky slope" effect illuminates why respondents are so anxious to elevate the moral seriousness of discrimination as a concept: doing so sharply decreases the likelihood that the particular behavior they are defending will be perceived as falling within its ambit.[20] Promoting, in the abstract, harsh moral condemnation

[16] See David Schraub, "Sticky Slopes," *California Law Review* 101, no. 5 (2013): 1300–1301.

[17] See Melvin J. Lerner and Dale T. Miller, "Just World Research and the Attribution Process: Looking Back and Ahead," *Psychological Bulletin* 85, no. 5 (1978): 1031–32; Hanson and Hanson, "Blame Frame," 419–20.

[18] Taunya Lovell Banks, "Exploring White Resistance to Racial Reconciliation in the United States," *Rutgers Law Review* 55, no. 4 (2003): 948 ("[A] person who believes that racism is wrong will have trouble admitting that her own acts, though not motivated by racial hatred normally attributed to Klansmen or Nazis, can still be classified as racist."); Hanson and Hanson, "Blame Frame," 446 ("Because 'racists' are people with ugly prejudices or malignant dispositions, most of us do not perceive ourselves to be racists—indeed, we abhor such people; by adopting [a narrow] definition, we comfort ourselves with the assurance that we are not among them.").

[19] Ford, *Race Card*, 176.

[20] Cf. Schraub, *Sticky Slopes*, 1313 (asserting that one risk of sticky slopes is that they may "block changes without [decision-makers] ever having to directly address the substantive merits of the claim").

of bigoted, prejudiced, or discriminatory practices insulates concrete examples from critical examination—it will be seen as overkill to view them as exemplars of something as extreme as *discrimination*. Sociologist David Hirsh recounts an illustrative conversation with a Dutch friend regarding *Seven Jewish Children*: "I asked if she had judged that the play was antisemitic. She looked concerned and surprised and told me that in the Netherlands one would not characterise such a play as antisemitic. After the Holocaust the word 'antisemitic' was too strong, she explained."[21] Antisemitism is defined in terms of the Holocaust, one of the greatest atrocities of the 20th century in which millions were killed. *Seven Jewish Children*, which is not responsible for even a single measly murder, thus cannot rightfully be mentioned in the same breath as antisemitism. Teun A. van Dijk found similar reproaches against the use of the term "racism" in Western political debates. The term is effectively off-limits because it is "by definition too strong, if only because the present situation cannot be compared to the monstrosities of the Nazis."[22] In this way, elevating the seriousness of antisemitism, racism, or sexism acts to shield from consideration all but the most overt and vicious instances of the wrong.[23] The impact of this rhetorical turnabout is impressive indeed—the act of dismissing discrimination becomes a mechanism for performing one's commitment to taking discrimination seriously; the act of claiming discrimination is demonstrative that one has little concern for "real" racism, sexism, or antisemitism.

It is no accident, then, that the bad faith charge almost always constructs the claim in question as of a very particular sort: overt, conscious antipathy toward the target group. This stands in contrast to other potential understandings of discrimination, such as the presence of unconscious prejudice, disparate impact against vulnerable populations, or a cultural meaning of inferiority. Discrimination claims which rest on these alternative understandings are not just rejected; they're scarcely even recognized. For example, many articulations of the concept of microaggressions self-consciously do not posit that the microaggressor harbors intentional animus toward their target. (For instance, in other work I have argued that many microaggressions are better thought of as instances of negligence.)[24] Yet critics of the concept of microaggressions often

[21] David Hirsh, "Struggles over the Boundaries of Legitimate Discourse: Antizionism, Bad-Faith Allegations and the Livingstone Formulation," in *Global Anti-Semitism: A Crisis of Modernity*, vol. 5: *Reflections*, ed. Charles Asher Small (ISGAP, 2013): 89.

[22] Teun A. van Dijk, "Denying Racism: Elite Discourse and Racism," *Racism and Migration in Western Europe*, ed. John Solomos and John Wrench (Berg, 1993), 191.

[23] Hirsh, "Struggles over the Boundaries," 89 ("[T]he concept *antisemitic* could not be used in a civilised rational or analytic discussion about Churchill's play because it was too big and too powerful. It could not be used as a scalpel, to dissect a text; it was a nuclear bomb.").

[24] David Schraub, "Microaggressions as Negligence," *Journal of Social Philosophy* 56, no. 2 (2023): 282–99.

dismiss the term precisely on the grounds that it putatively alleges bad intent without sufficient evidence—precisely the sort of claim proponents of the concept say they're abjuring.[25] Here, too, we see an example of the "replacement epistemology" discussed in the previous chapter—those who speak of microaggressions are viewed as making claims of conscious intentional bias, even over their express disavowals, because their critics have successfully made such a claim the authoritative understanding of what a microaggression is.

More broadly, it is clear that conscious intentionality is for many a functional prerequisite before any claim of racism, sexism, or other like claims will be taken seriously—hence the appeal of stock responses like "That's not what I meant," "You're taking me out of context," or "It was just a joke." And because actual conscious intent to wound is nearly impossible to prove, this requirement erases all but the most outrageous instances of discriminatory practice. Racism becomes restricted only to extreme hate or violence,[26] antisemitism the domain of "nobody except a crazed Nazi."[27]

Given these considerations, the appeal of the "bad faith" defense to the aversive racist is evident. Most obviously, it presents a "neutral" reason for rejecting the possibility of discrimination. The reason is "neutral" both in the sense that making a claim in bad faith is wrong no matter who the claimant is, and in the sense that it is socially coded as a normal and legitimate response to discrimination claims that is not inconsistent with a sincere belief in egalitarianism. Indeed, this response allows one to perform an outward commitment to egalitarianism in the course of rejecting consideration of the concrete case before them. Stating that one's interlocutor is "playing the race card" (or analogous assertions applied against other groups) perversely draws much of its power from accepting the importance of egalitarian principles. The aggressive response to claims of racism necessarily recognizes the moral gravity of such charges and the implied ethical obligation to be responsive toward them, and as noted proponents of the "race card" trope typically couple their arguments with sweeping statements affirming the seriousness with which they take racism and racial discrimination. They often assert that the "race card" is dangerous because it minimizes the significance of some unidentified core of "real racism" or (ironically enough) causes people to fail to take claims of racism seriously because of the supposed glut of false accusations.

[25] See Scott O. Lilienfeld, "Through a Glass, Darkly: Microaggressions and Psychological Science," *Perspectives on Psychological Science* 12, no. 1 (2017): 178–80; Scott O. Lilienfeld, "Microaggression Research and Application: Clarifications, Corrections, and Common Ground," *Perspectives on Psychological Science* 15, no. 1 (2020): 27–37.

[26] Banks, "Exploring White Resistance," 948.

[27] Hirsh, "Struggles over the Boundaries," 91 (responding to a union's proposed definition of antisemitism restricted to "hostility towards Jews as Jews").

Equally important, the bad faith response heads off potentially dissonant argumentation that might force the aversive racist (or others whose opinions the aversive racist respects) to seriously account for the possibility of prejudice. The only thing better than ambiguity, for the aversive racist, is certainty that prejudice will not be taken seriously as an explanatory factor for one's behavior. Viewed in isolation, it would be difficult to determine in advance whether a claimant's charge of discrimination has merit until after significant investigation and inquiry (at which point we might as well play the analysis out to its end, rather than making an inferential judgment based on the credibility of the claimant). But creating an understanding of discrimination claims as *systematically* erroneous or false justifies refraining from even entertaining the claim in the first instance. The "bad faith" charge preemptively boxes out such claims as outside the bounds of legitimate discourse, and thereby dissipates the risk that information that "proves" discrimination will come to light.

The conscious, intentionalist model of understanding "discrimination" is of great use to the respondent in this endeavor. In addition to elevating the severity of the wrong (deliberate attempts to hurt others are generally viewed as more serious than thoughtless participation in damaging institutions), it shifts the terrain of the debate to one where the respondent is in an epistemically privileged position. Persons accused of biased conduct can examine their own mind, adjudge themselves to be innocent, and thus justify brushing off the claim as patently frivolous.[28] Third-party observers who may have harbored comparable beliefs or taken actions similar to those claimed to be discriminatory can do the same; unless they are willing to self-identify as bigoted, they will be reticent to infer discriminatory animus in another based on evidence that would also self-indict. At this stage, the status of the initial claim starts to look insupportable, even outrageous. What possible basis could the accuser have for claiming any insight (much less superior insight) into the minds of those they assert practice discrimination?

Indeed, thinking in terms of the bad faith response helps further illuminate the lay appeal of the simplistic, intentionalist-only account of discrimination. Lay theories of discrimination "tend to be constructed in ways that allow [people] to maintain a safe distance from any appearance of personal bias."[29] Persons who can credibly claim not to possess conscious biases have a vested interest

[28] See *id.* ("Antiracists who are accused of antisemitism . . . find it easier to look within themselves and to find they are not intentionally antisemitic, indeed they are opponents of antisemitism. Intimate access to the object of inquiry yields an apparently clear result and seems to make it unnecessary for the antiracist to look any further at how contemporary antisemitism actually functions independently of the will of the particular social agent.").

[29] Samuel R. Sommers and Michael I. Norton, "Lay Theories about White Racists: What Constitutes Racism (and What Doesn't)," *Group Process & Intergroup Relations* 9, no. 1 (2006): 119.

in the conversation ending there, and so the intentionalist model of bias has the straightforward "benefit" of being a relatively narrow account of discrimination that encompasses only a few extreme behaviors or beliefs. But it also has a secondary effect of placing the relevant facts about the discrimination claim in the minds of the respondent, enabling such claims to be dismissed without a significant investment of time. It is easy to dismiss an allegation of discrimination as made in bad faith if discrimination is purely a function of conscious intent. But if discrimination is defined more broadly—for example, accounting for structural barriers faced by marginalized groups or with attention to the "cultural meaning"[30] of a given claim as perceived in surrounding society—then accurately reckoning with a discrimination claim seems to require deeper analysis (and, more important, analysis of facts that are not primarily in the mind of the respondent). In short, adopting a more robust theory of discrimination does not just implicate a wider range of behavior as potentially discriminatory; it also removes some of the epistemic controls respondents possess over the nature of the debate when it is cast in intentionalist terms. To the extent that people value the ability to quickly dispense with uncomfortable discrimination claims, it is obvious why that trade-off would be unappealing.

The Bad Faith Charge as a Testimonial Injustice

The prior sections have identified examples and general characteristics of the bad faith response and provided a theory explaining its utility and appeal for members of the dominant classes seeking to preserve both a credible commitment to egalitarian ideals alongside significant subconscious prejudice. Unsurprisingly, these "benefits" come with real costs to the victims whose discrimination claims are cavalierly dismissed. Both the practical impact of this response as well as the political and social presumptions which prop it up assist in the project of domination.

Return to the understanding of power given by Carol Gilligan. Power means "you can opt not to listen. And you do so with impunity."[31] The ability to dismiss discrimination claims by contending they are made in bad faith is a concrete exercise of this form of power. The universal availability of the bad faith response

[30] See Charles Lawrence III, "The Id, the Ego, and Equal Protection: Reckoning with Unconscious Racism," *Stanford Law Review* 39, no. 2 (1989): 345–46 (inquiring whether the challenged conduct "conveys a symbolic message to which the culture attaches racial significance").

[31] "Feminist Discourse, Moral Values, and the Law—A Conversation: The 1984 James McCormick Mitchell Lecture," *Buffalo Law Review* 34, no. 1 (1985): 62 (Isabel Marcus and Paul J. Spiegelman, moderators; Ellen C. DuBois, Mary C. Dunlap, Carol J. Gilligan, Catherine A. MacKinnon, and Carrie J. Menkel-Meadow, conversants).

means one can always "opt not to listen" and there will be no consequences—material or psychological—for the declination. By contrast, the consequences of the bad faith response with respect to those making the initial claim are quite significant: the response obstructs—even obliterates—the ability to effectively challenge discrimination. "Denials challenge the very legitimacy of anti-racist analysis, and thus are part of the politics of ethnic management: As long as a problem is being denied in the first place, the critics are ridiculed, marginalised, or delegitimated: denials debilitate resistance."[32] The most straightforward harm of the bad faith response, of course, is simply that it assists in preserving and perpetuating continued unjust structures of domination.

Who we opt to listen to in large part defines who we consider to be our moral and political equals.[33] To begin, who we decide to listen to channels how we make collective decisions regarding what we conceptualize to be social problems and our strategies for resolving them. Ideally, these decisions should be made "under conditions of equality and mutual respect" where "all the affected perspectives have a voice."[34] By contrast, where certain groups' contributions to this conversation are preemptively dismissed, it is quite likely that their discrete needs and concerns will be systematically unaddressed. But there is a further harm in the bad faith charge, related again to Fricker's idea of testimonial injustice. Testimonial injustice harms people in their capacity as knowers.[35] As Fricker observes, this would always be problematic—to be degraded as a knower is to be degraded as a human, for one's ability to know is a defining feature of one's status as a human.[36] The decision to systematically dismiss certain classes of claimant as lacking credibility necessarily places them as lesser members of the political community.

In the discrimination context these harms combine to devastating effect, because the particular arena in which the claimant is deemed especially *un*credible is precisely their ability to identify and contest unjust differential treatment. The injustice here has the peculiarly dangerous function of insulating itself from critical engagement—the act of protesting against it reifies the credibility gap. It is thus no wonder that so many prominent negative stereotypes

[32] van Dijk, "Denying Racism," 181.

[33] See Brandon Morgan-Olsen, "A Duty to Listen: Epistemic Obligations and Public Deliberation," *Social Theory and Practice* 39, no. 2 (2013): 188 ("[T]o fail to listen fair-mindedly in the public square . . . represent[s] a failure to acknowledge another's status as citizen.").

[34] Iris Marion Young, *Intersecting Voices: Dilemmas of Gender, Political Philosophy, and Policy* (Princeton University Press, 1997), 59.

[35] Fricker, *Epistemic Injustice*, 44.

[36] See *id.*

key in on the supposed unreliability of the targeted group—devious and conspiring Jews, irrational and emotional women, simple and unsophisticated Blacks.[37] If the best way to correct prejudices against marginalized others is in their ability to effectively communicate a countervailing narrative of their own experience,[38] testimonial injustice guards against even that personal, direct challenge to the maintenance of prejudiced beliefs.

As a means of regulating and redirecting the effective participation of marginalized persons in public deliberation, the bad faith response has a clear connection to more traditional forms of "hate speech" (cross-burnings, Klan rallies, and the like). One of the most important goals of hate speech is "to intimidate targeted groups from participating in the deliberative process."[39] A direct way of accomplishing this is overt threats of violence or explicit statements of degradation toward the out-group. But as we've seen, the bad faith charge yields similar results while still superficially remaining within and citing the values of free and open political discussion. This parallels the distinction between dominative and aversive racism noted above. While both preserve preexisting hierarchies and result in unjust discrimination against marginalized persons, the latter does so in a much more subtle fashion that preserves its practitioners' self-conception as fair-minded and egalitarian.

The effect of all of this is to preserve the ability of the dominant class to maintain a hegemonic interpretation of others' experiences. Christine Littleton describes the feminist method as starting "with the very radical act of taking women seriously, believing that what we say about ourselves and our experience is important and valid, even when (or perhaps especially when) it has little or no relationship to what has been or is being said *about* us."[40] The bad faith

[37] See Linda Martin Alcoff, "On Judging Epistemic Credibility," in *Engendering Rationalities*, ed. Nancy Tuana and Sandra Morgan (SUNY Press, 2001), 61 ("Peasants, slaves, women, children, Jews, and many other nonelites were said to be liars or simply incapable of distinguishing justified beliefs from falsehoods. Women were too irrational, peasants too ignorant, children too immature, and Jews too cunning.").

[38] See, e.g., Fricker, *Epistemic Injustice*, 41 ("I think this possibility of a subject's unprejudiced perception of another human being winning out against his prejudiced beliefs is crucially important for our understanding of how social change is possible, including the social change involved in reforming our patterns of credibility judgment."); Young, *Intersecting Voices*, 45 ("[T]he only correction to . . . misrepresentation of the standpoint of others is their ability to tell me that I am wrong about them."); David Schraub, "Racism as Subjectification," *Berkeley Journal of African-American Law & Policy* 17, no. 1 (2016): 28 ("[B]ecause nothing can replace the voice of the Other in deliberative discourse, their presence is an indispensable part of the democratic project.").

[39] Alexander Tsesis, "Dignity and Speech: The Regulation of Hate Speech in a Democracy," *Wake Forest Law Review* 44, no. 2 (2009): 499.

[40] Christine A. Littleton, "Feminist Jurisprudence: The Difference Method Makes," *Stanford Law Review* 41, no. 3 (1989): 764. *See also, e.g.*, George Yancy, "Introduction: Fragments of a Social Ontology of Whiteness," in *What White Looks Like: African American Philosophers on the* Whiteness *Question*, ed. George Yancy (Routledge, 2004), 12 ("[W]hiteness admits of no ignorance vis-à-vis the black. Hence, there is no need for white silence, a moment of quietude that encourages listening to the black."); Richard L. Rubenstein, *After Auschwitz: History, Theology, and Contemporary Judaism*,

response inverts this paradigm; the life of women is whatever men conceptualize it to be. The same goes for Blacks and Whites or Jews and Gentiles. Functionally, this also acts to deny that members of these groups have any special insight into the nature of their own oppression. The respondent instead tacitly asserts his or her own superior ("objective") vantage on the question. Particularly for persons who share the respondent's privileged social position, this is a desirable entitlement.[41] For members of the marginalized group, by contrast, the results are less sanguine: they are taken to be either pathological liars or delusional about their own experiences.

Objections

I have sought to explain the function—and the harm—of using the charge of bad faith as a means of dismissing discrimination claims. The implied obligation, then, is that when encountering a discrimination claim we should take it seriously. While we are not obliged to ultimately agree or accede to every discrimination claim we face, we should not preemptively dismiss them prior to giving them full and fair consideration.[42]

The most obvious objection to this principle is tackling what appears to be one of its foundations: that discrimination claims are *not* for the most part false, bad faith, or opportunistic. Yet even if we believed the opposite, it would not necessarily follow that the bad faith response is appropriate. Even if most discrimination claims are groundless, prior to examination it would be at most an inference to say that the claim at hand is as well. Valid claims inevitably will be scooped up and tarred as illegitimate without ever receiving due examination. Giving discrimination claimants full and fair consideration—ensuring that we do not miss the few genuine cases—may trump whatever gains we might experience from preemptive dismissal. After all, bad faith claims presumably

2nd ed. (Johns Hopkins University Press, 1992), 70 (arguing that Christians have long claimed, as against Jews, a superior vantage point on the meaning of Judaism).

[41] *See, e.g.*, Naomi Scheman, "Feminist Epistemology," *Metaphilosophy* 26, no. 3 (1995): 184 ("[T]here are good reasons, from the perspectives of privilege, for dismissing as unreliable the perspectives of those in subordinated positions: from such perspectives are frequently revealed truths damaging to the maintenance of their subordination."); Schraub, *Sticky Slopes*, 1304 ("Because a legitimating ideology helps resolve the cognitive dissonance latent between our desire to see ourselves as just and the reality of injustice, buying into these ideological justifications is to the advantage of privileged persons.").

[42] *See* David Hirsh, "Accusations of Malicious Intent in Debates about the Palestine-Israel Conflict and about Anti-Semitism: The Livingstone Formulation, 'Playing the Antisemitism Card' and Contesting the Boundaries of Antiracist Discourse," *Transversal* 1 (2010): 47–48 (distinguishing between "those who are accused of employing antisemitic discourse and who respond in a measured and rational way to such accusations in a good faith effort to relate to the concern, and to refute it," and those who refuse outright "to engage with the issue of anti-Semitism").

would not survive an honest, critical, engaged inquiry into the possibility of prejudice or bias.

Moreover, the self-insulating character of the bad faith charge should give us considerable pause regarding how reliable our intuitions regarding discrimination claims might be. The belief that discrimination claims are generally groundless may well have been arrived at precisely because we still possess these discriminatory impulses. Without some guarantee that discrimination claims will receive reasonable consideration, there is no way to ratify the legitimacy of the bad faith belief. And proponents of the bad faith response face a further difficulty in that they seem to take inconsistent approaches in how they appraise the intentions of discrimination claimants and respondents. For the respondent, epistemic humility and a presumption of good faith are paramount. Even where there might be some markers suggesting malice or very real deleterious impacts on a vulnerable community, absent extraordinary evidence we should be reluctant to ascribe bad motives to potentially innocent behavior. In contrast, the bad faith charge depends on precisely such an ascription of malign motivation to claimants. Instead of humility and charity, the minds of the marginalized are taken to be transparent and suffused with opportunism. Given the widespread disagreement over the meaning of discrimination and the inability to confidently assess the motives of discrimination claimants, our intuitions about how regularly discrimination claims are made in bad faith can be given only so much influence over how we treat individual claims and claimants.

To be sure, none of this denies that there are circumstances where it is perfectly reasonable to contend that a given discrimination claim is being made in bad faith. We might fully and charitably explore the allegation and, in doing so, discover that it is obviously unsupported by facts known to the claimant or inconsistent with principles supposedly acknowledged by the claimant. Such a conclusion, however, would differ substantially from the sort of problematic bad faith response I indict, precisely because it would be tied to specific shortcomings of the particular claim (or, perhaps, specific behaviors of the claimant); it could not rely on a *general* assertion that claims of this sort lack credibility. Perhaps more important, in nearly all cases such a conclusion could only be arrived at following considerable investigation into the claim itself; it could not be deployed as the tactic "of first resort" and thus could not have the deleterious effects of suppressing discourse into the merits of the allegation.[43]

[43] The prime exception might be a situation where an individual person has, time and again, shown a propensity to make frivolous allegations. It is clear, though, that one must tread very carefully in relying on such an assessment. The pattern would have to be specific to the person (rather than stemming from affiliation with a specific group), and we would have to have confidence that our assessments of the prior allegations which allegedly constitute the pattern of frivolity was not itself biased, or did not rely on the problematic tropes of bad faith articulated above.

It is worth considering, however, what benefit this sort of (accurate, justified) bad faith allegation would then carry. After all, much of the evidence that would tend to support an inference of bad faith would be the same evidence that would refute the claim on the merits. Once one can address and reject the claim on its substance, it is unclear what additional benefit is derived from adding a bad faith allegation on top. While such a contention would not be unjust in these circumstances, it also would not be a terribly important element of the discussion. And so it makes sense that bad faith responses are not typically put forward to gild the lily of a well-constructed substantive refutation, but rather as responses of first resort designed to elide substantive discussion (and to suggest that future claims of a similar sort can likewise be summarily dismissed).

Outside direct challenges to the premise, perhaps the most frequent objection leveled by defenders of the bad faith retort is that being forced to address issues of prejudice has a chilling effect on discourse. Discrimination claims supposedly prevent important issues from being debated openly. Carroll, continuing with the "card" metaphor, described sexism claims as a "trump."[44] Stephen Walt and John J. Mearsheimer make the same allegation with respect to antisemitism; they refer to it as "the great silencer" surrounding debates over Israel.[45] This argument often dovetails with the declarations regarding the moral seriousness the respondent ascribes to discrimination claims—it is *because* they are so important that raising them supposedly blots out the ability to have a dispassionate, objective discussion. As Hirsh puts it, when claims of discrimination are characterized as "nuclear bombs"—attributed the rhetorical impact of nuclear weaponry—then they cannot actually be deployed. Doing so "would not only destroy the object of inquiry but also the whole discursive space."[46]

Unfortunately, the bad faith charge relies on premises incompatible with a true desire for open dialogue. For political communication to proceed in any meaningful fashion, there must be the "*expectation*—however counter-factual—that one's interlocutor will speak sincerely, truthfully, openly, and uncoercively."[47] The bad faith charge, of course, denies all of these premises—it is precisely an allegation that the claimant is engaging in a deceptive, malicious, and opportunistic game designed to browbeat her interlocutor into agreement. And

[44] See Carroll, "Gamergate."

[45] John J. Mearsheimer and Stephen M. Walt, *The Israel Lobby and U.S. Foreign Policy* (Farrar, Straus & Giroux, 2007), 191–96. To the extent Mearsheimer and Walt's position is that the antisemitism argument is made in good faith but is simply wrong on its merits, but that addressing it nonetheless is a distraction to their preferred agenda item, they stand on even weaker ground. There is no entitlement to be able to evade reasonable, good faith objections to one's claims simply because it may turn out, after investigation, that the claims do not hold water. (Of course, how would we know that they don't hold water unless they are investigated!)

[46] Hirsh, "Struggles over the Boundaries," 89.

[47] Noelle McAfee, *Habermas, Kristeva, and Citizenship* (Cornell University Press, 2000), 25.

contrary to the respondents' allegation, this same sin is not (or at least not necessarily) fairly attributed to those who claim discrimination. A claim of racism, sexism, or antisemitism need not come attached to any assertion of insincerity or bad faith. This is because the contours of discrimination are not exhausted by the intentions of the speaker. It is a perfectly valid discursive request to interrogate potential injustices lurking within positions honestly taken and passionately felt. To reduce such inquiry to a mere search for hidden motivations is to dramatically circumscribe justice-talk generally.

Moreover, whether or not discrimination claims descriptively "chill" discourse, it is inaccurate to place blame on the claimant. It is not the discrimination claimant who wants conversation to stop; she merely wants another element (the possibility of discrimination) added to the discussion. In the racism context, Julie Suk notes the function of the "'race card' card," where "in response to the slightest allusion to racism, past or present, the speaker is accused of playing the race card, and this new allegation is used to deflect attention away from legitimate complaints of racial injustice."[48] It is the bad faith response—and the respondents' concurrent refusal to carry the conversation forward unless the discrimination claim is dropped—that stifles open conversation.

The argument that discrimination claims chill discourse is thus better understood as a perceived entitlement to not have to discuss issues of discrimination. Instead of opening conversational opportunities, it places artificial borders on legitimate discourse in ways that can render the ensuing discussion stilted, even nonsensical. Anyone who has ever taught a class that considers affirmative action has encountered that student who is very interested in having a discussion regarding racial preferences but is exceptionally aggrieved at being asked to talk about racism while he's at it. The absurdity of this position is obvious: while there are indeed important questions regarding the efficacy, implementation, and legitimacy of affirmative action programs, to discuss these issues while ignoring racism is an exercise in gibberish. What the student desires is not an open conversation but "a coerced agreement . . . that concedes the key intellectual contest."[49]

In fairness, my contention that discrimination claims are better understood as entries into a conversation rather than "conversation stoppers" does impose certain obligations on those who proffer the discrimination claim: namely, they have to accept that their allegation cannot, simply by raw fact of invocation, suffice to end the conversation. It is sometimes asserted that discrimination claimants do in fact want to claim this awesome power—for example, some

[48] Julie C. Suk, "Race without Cards," *Stanford Journal Civil Rights & Civil Liberties* 5, no. 1 (2009): 117 (reviewing Ford, *Race Card*).

[49] Jerome McCristal Culp Jr., "To the Bone: Race and White Privilege," *Minnesota Law Review* 83, no. 6 (1999): 1641.

allege that the #MeToo mantra "Believe women" translates to a demand that any and all allegations of sexual assault be instantly and incontestably credited without any further investigation.[50] If this was the demand, it could not be sustained. Yet purveyors of this slogan have emphatically rejected this interpretation. Tarana Burke, one of the leaders of the #MeToo movement, has explicitly said, "[W]hen we say we believe survivors, it's *not* believe them without investigation."[51] The goal of the slogan is not to end a conversation but to make sure it begins, and begins on a footing which does not take as a presupposition that women regularly lie about sexual assault.[52] It surely is possible to find individuals who deploy slogans like "Believe women" and consider it to mean that all discussion must cease. But as a description of the overall landscape, this objection reeks of being a straw man.

Finally, it is possible to reject the obligation to take seriously all discrimination claims in order to triage scarce deliberative resources.[53] There are reasons to be cautious of this argument, however. It is true that deliberative resources are limited, but it is also true that any robust theory of deliberation will often require holding multiple thoughts at the same time. Clearly, decisions regarding the allocation of deliberative resources can mask substantive preferences—permitting discussion of certain (amiable) claims while warding off uncomfortable or undesirable presentations. The fact that deliberative resources *are* genuinely scarce makes it particularly valuable as a neutral rationale for dismissing particular clusters of information the listener would rather not risk hearing. Similar to the "bad faith" response itself, the "limited resources" objection allows entire categories of potentially dissonant information to be excluded from the conversation while not obviously running afoul of norms of equal treatment.

Nonetheless, the scarce resources objection cannot be entirely ignored on its merits. But it does seem only tangentially related to the *bad faith* response specifically. If the problem is purely one of limited time and energy, then our refusal to consider certain discrimination claims should not require degrading

[50] See, e.g., Dan Subotnik, "Why Not Believe Women in Sexual Assault Cases? An Engagement with Professors Tuerkheimer, Colb, and Many Others," *Touro Law Review* 34, no. 4 (2018): 995–1024.

[51] Quoted in Lesley Wexler, "#MeToo and Procedural Justice," *Richmond Public Interest Law Journal* 22, no. 2 (2019): 20 (emphasis added).

[52] In Anglo-American law, this had indeed been the more or less official legal starting point for "investigating" rape accusations for centuries, dating back to Matthew Hale's infamous comment that rape "is an accusation easily to be made and hard to be proved, and harder to be defended by the party accused, though never so innocent." See Laurie Edelstein, "An Accusation Easily to Be Made? Rape and Malicious Prosecution in Eighteenth-Century England," *American Journal of Legal History* 42, no. 4 (October 1998): 351–90.

[53] See Mark E. Warren, "Deliberative Democracy and Authority," *American Political Science Review* 90, no. 1 (1996): 57–58.

the claimant by accusing them of rendering the charge in bad faith.[54] They have every right to have their claim considered; it is an unfortunate limitation of resources that prevents us from giving their allegation the attention it deserves. To the extent that the bad faith response is rendered in such circumstances, it resonates strongly with the "just world" literature discussed above.[55] The key study grounding that literature found that when persons were unable to rectify an injustice, they would simply reimagine the victims as deserving of their plight (rather than concede the existence of an unavoidable injustice).[56] Similarly, instead of conceding the unfairness (inevitable, perhaps, but still unfair) of disregarding potentially valid claims, constructing the allegations as likely made in bad faith acts as a salve—confirming that no injustice occurred and that the dismissed claimants deserved to be ignored.

A more powerful version of the scarce deliberative resources objection, however, points specifically to discrimination claims that appear obviously groundless but nonetheless occupy disproportionate public attention.[57] The most striking example of the problem might be a "men's rights activist" who insists that "men are the real oppressed group in society." Technically a claim of systematic sexism, it appears under the argument made above that this is an assertion which must be given serious attention even if all we really want to do is roll our eyes. In a sense, this provides a stronger example of the objection addressed above—that certain types of discrimination claims really *are* leveled in bad faith and are worthy of preemptive dismissal.

The most obvious limiting principle, then, is that our obligation to take seriously discrimination claims should be limited to those which sound from actually extant oppressed groups (which men are not). While initially attractive, this solution relies on a very shaky presupposition—that our prediscursive intuitions on which groups are and are not oppressed are reliable. Unfortunately, there is no reason to believe that our naïve views on this issue are not infected by the same biases and prejudices that prop up discriminatory systems more generally. "The ability to name oppressions," Jessica Greenebaum observes, "is a mode of power and those who produce these categories occupy a position of power."[58] Indeed, many groups—Jews, for example—are oppressed by stereotypes that

[54] See Fricker, *Epistemic Injustice*, 172 (noting that in "contexts where there is not sufficient time" to attend to a claim, the virtuous response would be "*reserving* judgment" on the claim's merits).

[55] *See* text surrounding note 17.

[56] *See* Hanson and Hanson, "Blame Frame," 419.

[57] Jeremy Engels makes an interesting argument about the role of a "victimage ritual" wherein a population that is not, in fact, marginalized is kept "weak and in need of leadership by keeping them perpetually hostile at their purported victimizers." Jeremy Engels, "The Politics of Resentment and the Tyranny of the Minority: Rethinking Victimage for Resentful Times," *Rhetoric Society Quarterly* 40, no. 4 (2010): 305.

[58] Jessica Greenebaum, "Placing Jewish Women into the Intersectionality of Race, Class and Gender," *Race, Gender & Class* 6, no. 4 (1999): 42.

present them as controlling, world-dominating figures.[59] Such stereotypes make it particularly difficult to conceptualize the targeted groups as oppressed and thus create a significant loophole for dismissing their discrimination claims.

A slightly more expansive approach would require serious engagement with discrimination claims from *historically* oppressed groups (i.e., groups which—whatever their position in society now—have at some point in the past been subordinated within a given society or culture). Even those who contend that racism is over or that Jews are now a privileged group or that women have attained total equality usually will concede that this was not always the case. The debate is not whether the group has been oppressed but whether it still is (or is in the relevant context). The fact of the historical oppression makes it reasonable to believe that the oppression is ongoing—at least reasonable enough to demand that we actually follow through and investigate the claim.

Nonetheless, this response is unsatisfactory as well. For one, while it may have validity as against structural oppression claims, it is less useful in individual cases (e.g., employment discrimination claims), which are less likely to rely on generalizations about a group's social position and more on idiosyncratic and situation-specific facts. And even on its own terms, it may be overly optimistic regarding which groups we consider to be "historically" oppressed (for the same reason we can't be confident about the groups we consider *currently* oppressed). Ultimately, it may be that we do have to take seriously even many discrimination claims that seem patently frivolous on their face. Given the serious consequences that false negatives pose for the entire democratic project and our inability to have confidence in our prediscursive intuitions regarding the social position of differentiated groups, the desire to dismiss such claims must yield. We can take solace, however, in the fact that (if we're right) the results of our investigation should confirm the initial instinct.[60]

***

The bad faith charge occupies a central niche in public debates regarding discrimination. Its role is not a salutary one. The bad faith response manages the delicate task of affirming one's personal status as an egalitarian while minimizing the threat that one will have to take concrete (even painful) steps to confront inegalitarian injustice. At the same time, it seizes control from marginalized persons their interpretation of their own experiences and forces them to accept

[59] See David Schraub, "White Jews: An Intersectional Approach," *Association for Jewish Studies Review* 43, no. 2 (November 2019): 390–92.

[60] We can also take solace in the possibility that, as noted above, where a particular agent (as opposed to a large identity group as a whole) repeatedly makes discrimination claims that, after full investigation, turn out to be frivolous, we could be justified in dismissing future discrimination claims alleging similar predicates as likely made in bad faith.

both the majoritarian interpretation of prejudice as well as the majority actor's self-definition as unprejudiced. Perhaps most important, the bad faith response is a keystone example of the perils of dismissal. It is a means by which discrimination claims can be rejected without being considered on their merits. In this way, the response insulates itself—as well as the surrounding structure of discrimination—from critical review.

In addressing the bad faith charge, this chapter has concentrated on the harms done by not listening and by refusing consideration in the context of an especially pressing moral issue—that of discrimination. In this, it is in accord with the broader theme of the book thus far, where listening has almost always been presented as inherently desirable and virtuous. The next two chapters stretch out to consider the dilemma of dismissal more broadly. Chapter 5 returns to the idea of consideration, leveraging John Stuart Mill to provide an ethos of listening that can help resolve prominent (and sometimes seemingly intractable) debates over speech and censorship in the press and on college campuses. Chapter 6, by contrast, seeks to arrest some of the enthusiasm for listening and consideration by exploring circumstances where it is important not to listen—or perhaps more accurately, important to affirm the *right* and *capacity* to not listen. Not listening, it turns out, is also an important component of human autonomy and freedom, one which can easily be overlooked if one is too fervent in viewing listening as the paramount deliberative virtue.

5
Listening, to Mill

The need to truly consider challenging or difficult claims—and the concurrent worry that we are too quick to dismiss them—feeds into a larger public conversation about "free speech." Worries about "cancel culture," "censorship," "epistemic closure," and the like speak to a broader public concern about whether and how we as a society confront thoughts or questions that we would rather avoid. We all know, at some level, that we should not enclose ourselves in ideological bubbles where we speak and listen only to those who already agree with us. We also know that we make decisions every day about what newspapers to read, what blogs to peruse, what shows to watch, and what conversations to have—and in making those choices, we inevitably make substantive appraisals of what speech is worthy of our attention and what is not. When we decide to cancel our subscription to a magazine because the views it publishes strike us as outlandish, preposterous, or hateful, we could be engaging in meritorious judgment that the periodical is unworthy of our patronage (no magazine is *entitled* to its readership), or we could be further sequestering ourselves from viewpoints which challenge and provoke us. How can we tell the difference?

Everyone faces a form of this dilemma to some degree, but certain people whose job entails soliciting, promoting, or otherwise amplifying particular speech—editors, publishers, teachers—confront it in an especially stark way. An editor deciding whether to drop a controversial columnist, for instance, is torn between the instinct that part of her job is to expose her readers to controversial commentary they might not otherwise encounter, regardless of whether she or they agree with the content, and the fact that another part of her job is to engage in quality control, weeding out speakers and ideas whose content does not merit the platform of her publication. Accepting the former role comes with accusations that one is running a publication that is a haven for trolls and shock jocks, provocateurs for their own sake. The latter role risks claims that one is censorial and illiberal, suppressing unconventional or unpopular views to preserve one's own sense of comfort. Inevitably, editors and professionals in similar roles will be buffeted by accusations that they are failing in either direction or both.

In its political valence, at least, speech matters because it is the vector by which we hash out controversial issues without resorting to violence or unreflective atomistic preferences. Even more than the electoral process, public conversation and debate is the primary arena we have for engaging in such consideration.

Deliberation, Dismissal, and Democracy. David Schraub, Oxford University Press. © Oxford University Press (2025). DOI: 10.1093/9780197816424.003.0006

Unlike "the privacy and anonymity of the ballot box," where "we have no chance to review our own judgments against what others have to say," the purpose of public argument is precisely to at least provide the opportunity to "revise and reconsider our positions."[1]

Dismissal is, first and foremost, a legal term, and it is if anything a cliché to make an intervention into debates over free speech via a legal metaphor. After all, it is common—bordering on typical—to cast problems surrounding free speech in juridical terms. Free speech is threatened when a government—or a similar authoritative actor[2]—formally obstructs speech. As Cass Sunstein puts it, under the most common conception the principle of free speech is nothing more than a prohibition on "government from 'censoring' speech of which it disapproves."[3] So long as there is no *juridical* ban on the speech, the fact that *in practice* certain speech is discouraged—or mocked or scorned or simply ignored—is not a violation of free speech. Indeed, it represents free speech as it should function: the give and take of competing views, a marketplace where some ideas turn out to be winners and others lose out. John Stuart Mill's *On Liberty* is frequently cited as the proof text for this understanding of free speech, though, as we'll see, he does not at all restrict himself to legal strictures.[4]

How, if at all, can we understand the value and limits of free speech outside cases of de jure action? In this chapter, I provide a reading of Mill's *On Liberty* that gives special attention to the importance of *listening*, rather than *speaking*, in order to develop a more robust understanding of free speech that can capture cases beyond juridical censorship. Drawing on Mill, I distinguish between two registers of free speech: a deliberative register and a regulative register. The deliberative register emphasizes a set of values good citizens are meant to practice: virtues such as open inquiry, hearing diverse viewpoints, and being willing to consider challenging claims—these track Mill along the dimension of *private practice*. The regulative register, by contrast, is almost orthogonal to the deliberative dimension: it focuses on how we decide what we will *decline* to consider, what doesn't get published, and what gets ignored. This register reflects Mill along the axis of *political (and jurisprudential) governance*. These two registers

[1] Anne Phillips, *The Politics of Presence* (Oxford University Press, 1995), 150; see also Fred O. Smith Jr., "Due Process, Republicanism, and Direct Democracy," *New York University Law Review* 89, no. 2 (2014): 611–13.

[2] I am thinking here of private universities, which—though lacking formal governmental power—act in a quasi-governmental capacity insofar as they are empowered to promulgate regulations restricting speech by students, professors, or other campus actors.

[3] Cass R. Sunstein, *#Republic: Divided Democracy in the Age of Social Media* (Princeton University Press, 2017), 34.

[4] John Stuart Mill, *On Liberty* (1859), ed. Elizabeth Rapaport (Hackett, 1978). The association of the "marketplace of ideas" metaphor with Mill—who does not use the phrase—is controversial, particularly depending on how one understands the "market" to operate. See Jill Gordon, "John Stuart Mill and the 'Marketplace of Ideas,'" *Social Theory & Practice* 23, no. 2 (Summer 1997): 235–49.

are mostly harmonious from the perspective of liberal governance and jurisprudence, where they coalesce into a familiar liberal posture opposing censorship or de jure restraints on speech. But once translated to the private sphere, these two conceptions of free speech become far more antagonistic to one another. Many pressing public controversies which do not significantly implicate the government's authority or desire to censor speech are exceptionally nettlesome because they bring the private-sphere tension of these two registers to the fore.

One particularly high-profile contemporary problem that helps illustrate the difficulties but also the promise of this framework is student activism that, in protesting various invited speakers or faculty arguments, is said to be antipathic to free speech on campus. Perhaps unsurprisingly, the conflicting tendencies of the deliberative and regulative registers generate widely divergent (and often internally inconsistent) accounts of who is and is not acting in opposition to free speech as a value. Frequently, the decisive factor is not an objective accounting of particular conduct but instead one of power—persons in power can effectively refuse to listen to speech even as they claim to be protecting free speech values. When persons lower in the relevant hierarchy adapt a similar approach, however, they are condemned for their censorial instincts. And while hypocrisy is a two-way street, the inconsistency in these appraisals suggests the need for a more nuanced approach to how values of free speech and open inquiry should be pursued, one which ultimately dispenses with the notion that open listening is always and at all times a paramount value—an assumption I will examine further in the following chapter.

Mill's Duty to Listen

Much of the dominant liberal attitude toward speech issues in America today owes at least a perceived intellectual debt to John Stuart Mill. But while it is primarily cited today—in popular if not academic reference—as a defense of free speech as against official censorship, *On Liberty* was at least as concerned with the threats posed to open dialogue that emerge from private society and prevailing social norms. As Dan Threet observes, Mill seeks to delineate "the proper limits of the authority of *society* over individuals, not just the authority of the state."[5] Indeed, the freedom from governmental censorship is in many ways Mill's easy case—it is relatively straightforward, if not entirely cost-free, to impose a rule against juridical interference with the expression or publication

[5] Dan Threet, "Mill's Social Pressure Puzzle," *Social Theory and Practice* 44, no. 4 (October 2018): 565–66. See Mill, *On Liberty*, 73.

of ideas, no matter how offensive or controversial.[6] But Mill emphasizes that "[p]rotection . . . against the tyranny of the magistrate is not enough." In addition to freedom from official censorship, "there needs protection also against the tyranny of the prevailing opinion and feeling, against the tendency of society to impose, by other means than civil penalties, its own ideas and practices as rules of conduct on those who dissent from them."[7]

In fact, Mill goes so far as to suggest that informal social tyranny is perhaps more dangerous than the expressly juridical kind, "since, though not usually upheld by such extreme penalties, it leaves fewer means of escape, penetrating much more deeply into the details of life, and enslaving the soul itself."[8] This is what Mill strikingly refers to as the "despotism of custom,"[9] and in articulating the harm principle[10] he actually places the "moral coercion of public opinion" on the same terrain as "physical force in the form of legal penalties."[11] Both represent forms of societal "compulsion and control," and therefore both are subject to the rules of the harm principle.[12]

Mill's concern with nonjuridical barriers to the free flow of ideas is sometimes overlooked. Robert Post, for example, cites the passage where Mill warns against the "tyranny of the prevailing opinion" but immediately uses it to pivot back to the need for state neutrality with respect to the sources that enable public opinion to form—a noble goal, perhaps, but not what Mill is concerned with when he expressly speaks of problems *aside* from civil penalties.[13] Even though careful readers of Mill are by no means unaware that his focus is not on legal proscriptions, there does appear to be (certainly in the American context) a gravitational pull which seemingly tugs even prudent commentators back toward making a jurisprudential point. For Mill's part, however, he is quite clear in informing his reader that where "society is itself the tyrant, its means of tyrannizing are not restricted to the acts which it may do by the hands of its political functionaries."[14] And particularly once we leave the domain of repressive political functionaries, the problems Mill identifies have less to do with our freedom to speak, and more

[6] Jeremy Waldron baldly states, "Law is actually the secondary subject matter of *On Liberty*." See Jeremy Waldron, "Mill as a Critic of Culture and Society," in *On Liberty*, ed. David Bromwich and George Kateb (Yale University Press, 2003), 225.

[7] Mill, *On Liberty*, 4.

[8] *Id.*

[9] *Id.* at 67.

[10] Among the more famous arguments in *On Liberty*, the "harm principle" is the idea that interference with personal liberty is only justified in order to prevent harm to others. *Id.* at 9

[11] *Id.*

[12] *Id.*

[13] Robert C. Post, *Democracy, Expertise, and Academic Freedom: A First Amendment Jurisprudence for the Modern State* (Yale University Press, 2012), 28.

[14] Mill, *On Liberty*, 4.

to do with debilitating those practices of listening which are essential to effective social and civic participation

Consider one of the primary villains of *On Liberty*: "custom." On this subject, Mill is withering in his critique: "The human faculties of perception, judgment, discriminative feeling, mental activity, and even moral preference are exercised only in making a choice. He who does anything because it is the custom makes no choice."[15] The need to "gain . . . practice . . . in discerning or in desiring what is best"[16] is presented as something one gets via interaction with diverse others—or put differently, it is not by one's own speech but by encountering the (varied) speech of others by which one is truly enabled to choose a path of life that is authentic to oneself.

To be sure, obedience to custom also could be thought to represent a form of listening—one can follow the instincts of the masses only if one knows what they are doing, after all. But Mill certainly does not view this as truly listening—if by that one means open-minded but ultimately self-directed consideration of one's own position. The person who follows custom does not "choose what is customary in preference to what suits their own inclination," rather, "[i]t does not occur to them to have any inclination except for what is customary."[17] For this, a person "has no need of any other faculty than the ape-like one of imitation."[18]

Crucially, then, Mill's account of freedom of speech—though surely concerned with a person's individualized and authentic self-development—still is inherently located in a deeply social context meant to be characterized by mutual aid and benefit. Self-development is not something that occurs in monastic contemplation; to the contrary, "Millian autonomous agents generally are deeply immersed in communities and intimate relations with others. What distinguishes the autonomous agent from the other-determined agent is that the former makes her own choices at the conclusion of the dialogue—albeit with due concern for the welfare of significant others."[19]

Mill's main attack on and critique of slavish adherence to custom solely because it is custom is introduced via a series of quotes from Wilhelm von Humboldt conjoining individualism and social diversity—the object "toward which every human being must ceaselessly direct his efforts, and on which especially those who design to influence their fellow men must ever keep their eyes."[20] Mill concedes that this high regard for individualism may be unusual;[21] nonetheless,

[15] *Id.* at 56.
[16] *Id.*
[17] *Id.* at 58.
[18] *Id.* at 56.
[19] Wendy Donner, "Mill on Individuality," in *A Companion to Mill*, ed. Christopher Macleod and Dale E. Miller (Wiley, 2016), 429.
[20] Mill, *On Liberty*, 55 (quoting von Humboldt's *The Sphere and Duties of Government*).
[21] *Id.*

Wendy Donner suggests, good Millian subjects are those who "see themselves as being enhanced and enriched by the diversity they encounter every day, rather than feeling threatened by others' individuality and difference."[22] An individual free thinker, Mill writes, is "more valuable to himself, and is therefore, capable of being more valuable to others. There is a greater fullness of life about his own existence, and when there is more life in the units there is more in the mass which is composed of them."[23] Donner thus contends that for Mill, "[t]he spirit of free inquiry in the interest of truth and authenticity call upon this full hearted open dialogue with others, before we make our choices. The benefits of this dynamic and dialogical exchange go in both directions."[24]

Where *On Liberty* is primarily read as a reference to the *freedom to speak*, it can thus unfortunately occlude the great importance Mill places on how we *listen to speech*. Persistently, Mill frames the utility of his arguments in favor of freedom of thought and freedom of speech not in terms of the liberty accorded to the speaker but of the intellectual benefits to the community of listeners. Suppressing an opinion hurts "those who dissent from the opinion, still more than those who hold it."[25] It either deprives them of the opportunity to exchange "error for truth," or they lose the ability to clarify the rightness of their own views through its "collision with error."[26] An opinion which is not "fully, frequently, and fearlessly discussed . . . will be held as a dead dogma, not a living truth."[27] "He who knows only his own side of the case knows little of that."[28] These are all benefits that accrue on the listening, not speaking, side of the equation.[29]

Indeed, Mill sometimes presents the speakers' liberty side of the equation in strikingly instrumental terms. The reason arguments must be made by the persons who believe them (as opposed to "teachers, presented as they state them") is defended not by reference to the free speech interest of the speaker but because the latter actors will inevitably not present the case in its "most plausible and persuasive form."[30] He goes as far as to lament the progressive disappearance of even concededly wrong opinions (the "gradual narrowing of the bounds of diversity of opinion") as a loss—while he recognizes that it is an inevitable product of

[22] Donner, "Mill on Individuality," 430.
[23] Mill, *On Liberty*, 60.
[24] Donner, "Mill on Individuality," 429.
[25] *Id.* at 16.
[26] *Id.*
[27] *Id.* at 34. Mill carries this point forward in his concern that persons who have ceased to critically consider Christianity will inevitably practice it simply by "look[ing] round for Mr. A and B to direct them how far to go in obeying Christ." *Id.* at 40.
[28] *Id.* at 35.
[29] In his highly Millian exegesis of the First Amendment, Alexander Meiklejohn comes to a similar conclusion: when it comes to free speech's relationship to enabling political self-government, "the point of ultimate interest is not the words of the speakers, but the minds of the hearers." Alexander Meiklejohn, *Free Speech and Its Relation to Self-*Government (Harper & Bros., 1948), 25.
[30] Mill, *On Liberty*, 35.

the progressive march toward truth: "I confess I should like to see the teachers of mankind endeavoring to provide a substitute for it."[31] And Mill's disdain for the "princes . . . who are accustomed to unlimited deference" and therefore are not habituated to considering challenging perspectives[32] confirms that he thinks it important to inculcate certain virtues as listeners—the utility he perceives in free expression does not manifest if dissident voices are "free" only to shout into a crowd wearing ideological earplugs.

Giving primacy to listening, rather than speaking, also ameliorates (although it does not eradicate) a long-standing puzzle in *On Liberty*: the fact that free individual speech reacting to the speech or conduct of others can and often will exert the sort of informal social pressure that is grist for the "despotism of custom."[33] On the speaking side, it is difficult to reconcile the acknowledged barriers social pressure can exert on the free expression and development of others with the fact that expressing public revulsion is itself often a manifestation of such free speech rights.[34] Reorienting the analysis toward listening does not fully resolve this tension, but it does dissipate it insofar as it is more amenable to asking that citizens adopt *dispositions* toward the speech of others that are more accepting and tolerant of dissident others—if not of their conclusions, then at least of their facial legitimacy as entrants into social conversation. The fact that Mill's account of listening is especially *poorly* structured so as to fit into an account of "rights" is here an advantage: we cannot but also need not develop strict rules regarding when one must listen to others; what we can do is promote a "liberal ethic" wherein good Millian subjects are predisposed to relate to conversational interlocutors in a manner that is designed to minimize undue social coercion.[35] One important upshot of this approach is that it relocates how we appraise the possibility of assessing legal consequences to violations of the Millian ethos. In many cases, even some stipulated violations of the relevant liberal ethos should nonetheless be regarded as (for lack of a better term) "nonjusticiable," in that they must be immune from any *official* adjudication that generates legal consequences.

We saw this issue recently emerge in the context of investigations by the first Trump administration into several universities' Middle Eastern studies programs, which were alleged to be failing to fulfill their obligation of presenting "diverse" viewpoints (as apparently required by federal law as a condition of their funding).[36] Stipulating for the sake of argument that these programs have been

[31] *Id.* at 42.
[32] *Id.* at 17.
[33] See Threet, "Social Pressure Puzzle," 559.
[34] See Waldron, "Mill as a Critic," 231.
[35] See *id.* at 240.
[36] Jackson Richman, "US Education Department to Investigate Anti-Semitic Event Sponsored by Duke-UNC," *JNS*, June 17, 2019, https://www.jns.org/us-education-department-to-investigate-anti-semitic-event-sponsored-by-duke-unc.

inappropriately stilted in their intellectual offerings, it nonetheless seems deeply troublesome that a governmental regulator be given the authority to declare an academic program's academic offerings insufficiently "diverse." Yet resisting the government's authority to engage in this sort of inquiry does not and should not mean abandoning the notion that greater intellectual heterodoxy is a good to be pursued.

Framed in terms of speakers' rights, one faces a seemingly irreconcilable conflict between the government's right to choose what it funds and a speaker's right to teach or do research on what they believe. If that is the frame, potentially the most intuitive resolution is that the speakers are free to teach whatever they want and the government is free not to provide them any funding—a resolution that would essentially obliterate the idea of academic freedom outright in the context of public schooling and public education (and, given the ubiquity of government grants in the education sector generally, would sharply circumscribe it in private schools as well).[37] But the reorientation toward listening, and toward cultivating a *disposition* toward hearing from a wide range of viewpoints, provides a more tractable accounting of the situation. The problem (if there is one) in Middle Eastern studies associations is less that researchers are given too much freedom to decide what positions they will assert and more that they may be too unwilling to listen and consider competing paradigms or frameworks (and so, for example, do not invite proponents of said competing theories to conferences or lectures). Yet even the most strident proponent of government intervention in this field (at least, not counting those who are motivated solely by a desire to crush academic inquiry outright) might blanch at asserting the state's prerogative to dictate who or what an academic *listens* to. The remedy, if there is one, can come only from within—a reformation centered around the cultivation of a different set of values in the academic's position as a listener rather than a speaker.

Mill's arguments in terms of our obligations as listeners thus serve as a useful countertheme to his more commonly presented stance on our rights as speakers. The concept of moral coercion gets at one important element of these obligations; it casts its eye upon certain types of private responses to speech which do not purport to prohibit the speech in question but still treat it in ways that seem not to reflect an honest effort to engage with the substance of an opposing view. We all know of persons who deploy heckling, derision, or dismissal in lieu of

[37] This, of course, has become exceptionally evident in the second Trump administration's sweeping attempts withhold federal grant money as leverage to compel private universities, such as Harvard and Columbia, to abandon diversity initiatives, crack down on campus protests, and adopt controversial measures putatively combating antisemitism. See Michael Casey, "Trump Administration Freezes $2.2 billion in Grants to Harvard over Campus Activism," *Associated Press*, April 15, 2025, https://apnews.com/article/harvard-trump-administration-federal-cuts-antisemitism-0a1fb70a2c1055bda7c4c5a5c476e18d.

considering a proffered argument on its merits. Often they seek to promote the sense that the argument in question should not be part of legitimate or civilized discourse—it is "beyond the pale" or so transparently ludicrous that it should not occupy more than a trivial, if any, amount of our attention as deliberators. It is easy to see how this behavior is incompatible with genuinely open-minded self-development, and Mill is accordingly contemptuous of persons who recognize their fallibility in the abstract but in concrete cases refuse to give a hearing to competing views.[38]

But it is equally easy to see how the cure might be worse than the disease. Mill knows he is playing a delicate game: shortly after embedding "moral coercion" into the harm principle, he clarifies that even when one's interlocutor is harming no one (or no one but himself), there may remain "good reasons for remonstrating with him, or reasoning with him, or persuading him, or entreating him."[39] When do such "remonstrations" cross over into impermissible "moral coercion"? After all, as Jeremy Waldron notes, it is not necessarily clear where "vigorous debate leaves off and inappropriate social pressure begins."[40] Unsurprisingly, on this point the lines Mill proceeds to draw are exceptionally fine: we may express "distaste" or "stand aloof" from the person but cannot "make his life uncomfortable"; we may "pity" or even "dislike" him but not subject him to "anger" or "resentment"; we may try to show "him how he may avoid or cure the evils his conduct tends to bring upon him," but "the worst we shall think ourselves justified in doing is leaving him alone."[41]

At this point, "civility" is often suggested as a means of distinguishing between speech which is truly deliberation-inducing and that which is primarily silencing. Mill explicitly considers and rejects the idea that "free expression of all opinions should be permitted on condition that the manner be temperate, and do not pass the bounds of fair discussion."[42] As Mill observes, a host of obstacles both practical and conceptual rise to block any effective usage of civility as even a tool for moral culpability, let alone legal liability. First, it's difficult to identify "where those supposed bounds [of civility] are to be placed; for if the test be offense to those whose opinions are attacked," offense is often taken in any case where the speaker lands a true or telling blow.[43] Second, Mill notes that even clear violations of the rules of fair argument—things like sophistry, misrepresentation, or suppression of relevant facts—unfortunately often make appearances

[38] See Mill, *On Liberty*, 17.
[39] *Id.* at 9.
[40] Waldron, "Mill as a Critic," 233.
[41] Mill, *On Liberty*, 77.
[42] *Id.* at 50.
[43] *Id.* at 50–51.

even among speakers arguing in good faith.[44] And third, there is an asymmetry in how the demand for civility is typically employed—it is often demanded of those challenging prevailing opinion, even as invective, sarcasm, and the like are often cheered when deployed against the ideological minority.[45]

There are additional reasons why incivility may, at least some of the time and in certain circumstances, advance important deliberative goals. Derek Edyvane argues for the positive democratic importance of certain forms of incivility—the intentional flouting of civility norms (norms generally recognized as valid) for the purpose of registering a political point. Incivility can serve as a means of *compelling* a response and recognition in circumstances where powerful persons often are capable of otherwise ignoring the underlying claim.[46] This is often a feature of protests, which frequently (though not always) gain their power from flouting the normal rules of civil interaction (a sit-in, for instance, flouts the basic—and normally quite reasonable—norm that one not obstruct another's use of a public space). Marilyn Frye levels a similar defense of angry speech: "[A]nger implies a claim to domain—a claim that one is a being whose purposes and activities require and create a web of objects, spaces, attitudes and interests that is worthy of respect, and that the topic of anger is a matter rightly within that web."[47] Finally, there is the risk that certain kinds of claims might be deemed "uncivil" no matter how they are framed. Claims of discrimination are often treated as falling in this category—the mere act of raising the issue, no matter how it is couched or how gentle the rhetoric, is viewed as per se uncivil. I explored this dynamic in more detail in Chapter 4; Robyn DiAngelo's influential book *White Fragility* also sounds in this theme.[48] As DiAngelo puts it, the "cardinal rule" governing discourse about racism directed at White people is simple: "Do not give me feedback on my racism under any circumstances."[49]

Yet it is fair to say that Mill's discussion of incivility pushes him against his fundamental problem: he knows that even "counterspeech" can have a functionally censorial effect, but he also knows that any standard he provides for delegitimizing particular types of speech will inevitably be deployed against outlying opinions and used to entrench the position of already dominant views.

[44] *Id.* at 51.

[45] *Id.*

[46] See Derek Edyvane, "Incivility as Dissent," *Political Studies* 68, no. 1 (2020): 93–109.

[47] Marilyn Frye, *The Politics of Reality: Essays in Feminist Theory* (Crossing Press, 1983), 87.

[48] Robyn DiAngelo, *White Fragility: Why It's So Hard for White People to Talk about Racism* (Beacon, 2018).

[49] *Id.* at 123. Emily Beausoleil makes a related point when she says that among socially advantaged groups "even minor concession can feel like victimization." Emily Beausoleil, "Listening Obliquely: Listening as Norm and Strategy for Structural Justice," *Contemporary Political Theory* 20, no. 1 (2020): 24.

I suggest an alternative way of understanding "moral coercion": it represents those modes of "discourse" which do not accept all participants as contributors to the space of reasons. Persuasion—an option Mill always leaves open even when the harm principle is not violated—requires respect for one's interlocutor as the sort of person who is both (a) amenable to reasons (they can be swayed by argument) and (b) capable of persuading back (they may have arguments worth listening to). "Arguments" that reject *these* premises—that portray the target as having no valid contributions to the dialogue and someone who must be browbeaten into submission—are the ones Mill finds most problematic. Some forms of incivility seem at odds with this standard (recall the "you drooling imbecile" example). But not at all are, as when allegedly uncivil actions are used to force consideration of arguments or communities that have been wrongfully dismissed.[50] And tying moral coercion to a rejection of an interlocutor's status as one capable of giving and receiving reasons tracks nicely with Mill's objection to appeals to custom—it does not sufficiently value persons in their capacity as choosers, as individuals who can discern between diverse options and come to their own conclusions about the good.

Consider in this light Mill's statement that "the worst we shall think ourselves justified in doing [to the dissident who is not harming others] is leaving him alone." While Mill clearly does think there are *unjustified* things we could do to him that are worse still, there is a sense in which one can read this passage literally. The Mill who praises a vision of human life as "rich, diversified, and animating"—and who presents this richness as rendering a person not just "more valuable to himself" but also "capable of being more valuable to others"—is presenting the value of open dialogue in terms of the benefits that we get from listening and experiencing the views of others.[51] The man who is left alone—isolated from the currents of persuasion and debate, pruned from the glorious multibranched tree of human diversity—would be a deeply tragic figure. The person who was too quick to pronounce the exile—to deem her neighbor outside the realm of those worth persuading or being persuaded by—would be engaging in a grievous wrong (to herself and to her target).

Why does this matter? For one, once Mill's concerns leave the realm of juridical censorship and enter the terrain of "prevailing opinion and feeling," many of the seemingly straightforward applications of his arguments become considerably more complex to operationalize in practice. It is easy to craft a rule prohibiting government from blocking publication of a book based on its

[50] Note that this does suggest that even potentially warranted incivility can be justified only in a relatively temporary and provisional way. It may be justifiable as a means of prompting consideration from recalcitrant interlocutors, but once they do enter the space of reasoning they must be permitted to express their own opinions (including objections and reservations) on equal terms.

[51] Mill, *On Liberty*, 60.

offensive content. It is impossible to craft a rule prohibiting publishers from declining to publish a book based on similar reasoning. Indeed, one substantial purpose behind requiring the government to step out of the space of approving or disapproving works of literature, politics, or other expressions is precisely to enable these judgments to occur freely in the private sphere.[52]

The impossibility of a pure posture of neutrality becomes even clearer upon redirecting our attention from speaking to listening. Here, in particular, the encroachment of Mill onto purely private action—and what could be more "private," more insulated from direct legislative prescription, than whether we listen to and "take up" a proffered argument?—clearly must stretch beyond the thin juridical indifference of the anticensorship position. If people are to avoid becoming like the spoiled princes, then certain specific *virtues* must be cultivated, governing how people respond to speech that can be both freely made and freely ignored. These include attributes like curiosity, intellectual humility, and open-mindedness—the ordinary virtues[53] of democratic citizenship that mediate everyday political interaction alongside more extraordinary requests for sacrifice, bravery, and national solidarity that might be demanded in times of crisis. Max Weber thus identifies "the first task of a competent teacher" as teaching his or her "students to acknowledge *inconvenient* facts.... [the] facts that are *inconvenient* for their own personal political views."[54] Writing in 1943, Sidney Hook thus explicitly combined the classic marketplace-of-ideas metaphor with language suggesting the importance of certain deliberative *dispositions* as comprising the core of proper liberalism: "liberalism as an intellectual temper, as faith in intelligence, as a tradition of the free market in the world of ideas."[55]

Free Speech beyond the Juridical: The Campus Case

In terms of official judicial doctrine, at least, America has perhaps never lived in a more speech-protective moment. On matters ranging from campaign finance to hate speech, courts have staked out a virtually absolutist pro-speech position

[52] See Franciska A. Coleman, "They Should Be Fired: The Social Regulation of Free Speech in the U.S.," *First Amendment Law Review* 16, no. 1 (2017): 3 (arguing that "the First Amendment [reflects] a choice of social regulation over legal regulation"); David Schraub, "They Managed a Protest: Prohibitory, Ethical, and Prudential Policing of Academic Speech," *Brigham Young University Law Review* 50, no. 3 (2024): 658 ("[T]o a large extent the liberal neutrality stance" limiting the ability to officially prohibit certain speech "claims its power precisely because it *shifts* the substantive position-taking into the ethical/prudential domains.").

[53] Cf. Judith Shklar, *Ordinary Vices* (Harvard University Press, 1984).

[54] Max Weber, "Science as a Vocation," in *The Vocation Lectures*, ed. David Owen and Tracy B. Strong, trans. Rodney Livingstone (Hackett, 2004), 22. Weber helpfully adds, "Such extremely inconvenient facts exist for every political position, including my own." *Id.*

[55] Sidney Hook, "The New Failure of Nerve," *Partisan Review* 10, no. 1 (1943): 3.

which does not seem in any danger of ebbing in the near future. Indeed, many commentators have articulated significant worries about the First Amendment creeping forward to colonize other domains. The specter of "First Amendment Lochnerism,"[56] where nearly all government regulation is recast as a constraint on "speech" and is accordingly suspect, looms over much of the contemporary progressive political project.

Yet outside the courtroom, it does not seem as if we believe we live in a paradise of unconstrained discourse. Partially, this is because as of 2025 certain free speech principles many had taken for granted now are being flouted in increasingly brazen fashion. The Trump administration's full-scale attack on public and private universities, threatening billions of dollars in civil penalties and withheld funding for those campuses which do not bend to the government's will, represent a threat to free speech that is simultaneously simple and existential. As of this writing, lower courts have blocked some of the worst injustices, but the legal terrain remains uncertain and the mere threat of government force has cowed many universities into preemptive submission.

But even before the recent resurgence of brazen de jure attacks on free speech, it was still quite common to hear complaints about threats to free speech that emanated from unofficial sources. Complaints about "political correctness," trigger warnings, safe spaces, microaggressions, and epistemic closure (to name a few) were ubiquitous features of our political debates. People complain about being "chilled" from expressing unpopular views or of being "silenced" when they challenge dominant shibboleths. We frequently speak of "censorship" or "silencing" or "chilling" in cases where the state, or other holders of juridical or quasi-juridical power, remains neutral.

Nowhere does the conceptual drift of free speech loom larger than in debates over speech on campus. In this context, Amy Gutmann argues:

> The controversy on college campuses over racist, ethnic, sexist, homophobic, and other forms of offensive speech directed against members of disadvantaged groups exemplifies the need for a shared moral vocabulary that is richer than our rights to free speech. Suppose one grants that members of a university community should have the right to express racist, anti-Semitic, sexist, and homophobic views provided they do not threaten anyone. What is left to say about the racist, anti-Semitic, sexist, and homophobic remarks that have become increasingly common on college campuses? Nothing, if our shared moral vocabulary is limited to the right of free speech.[57]

[56] For a collection of sources using this term, see Amanda Shanor, "First Amendment Coverage," *New York University Law Review* 93, no. 2 (May 2018): 331n57.

[57] Amy Gutmann, "Introduction," in Charles Taylor, *Multiculturalism: Examining the Politics of Difference* (Princeton University Press, 1994), 21–22.

It may seem quaint to revisit these older campus speech controversies at a time when the aforementioned official, juridical threats to campus speech have reasserted themselves in terrifying fashion. But I believe these questions remain pertinent even today, if for no other reason than that the older demands to craft a "free speech culture" paradoxically helped germinate the anti-speech extremism that characterizes the present moment. After all, in its first term the Trump administration signed an executive order hinging federal funding of universities on their willingness to defend free speech and "foster environments that promote open, intellectually engaging, and diverse debate" on campus.[58] This somewhat brief conservative flirtation with free speech absolutism rapidly collapsed in the face of concerted efforts by the political right to begin censoring certain concepts, such as critical race theory and "woke" ideologies, that were said to be offensive in their own right.[59] But there may be lessons to learn in how they and we made the journey.

Moreover, as crucial as it is to unite against the legal assault on academic autonomy and independence, academics in exercising that autonomy and independence have an indefeasible obligation to consider how to cultivate and preserve a healthy intellectual environment on campus. After all, perhaps no place is thought to better embody the problem of "hard thoughts" than the university. The university's very mission is to bring together a diverse body of students and faculty to engage in robust inquiry and criticism. It would be a sad commentary on universities as knowledge producers if they were impotent to tackle the "hard thoughts" that seem in most pressing need of rigorous, sustained, and fearless investigation.

In many cases, even when public reactions to controversial speech appear to stop short of calling for official, juridical censorship, it is clear that certain forms of what initially appear to be nothing but speech are at least perceived as in fact threatening open dialogue. In turn, liberal theorists have thus always recognized that "free speech" is a concept that depends on significant investment by private actors; it cannot survive solely via the promise of governmental noninterference. State neutrality may be a necessary condition for free speech to exist, but it cannot be sufficient. The bedrock commitment to juridical free speech

[58] Executive Order 13864, "Executive Order on Improving Free Inquiry, Transparency, and Accountability at Colleges and Universities," March 21, 2019, https://www.presidency.ucsb.edu/documents/executive-order-13864-improving-free-inquiry-transparency-and-accountability-colleges-and.

[59] Florida Governor Ron DeSantis's "Stop WOKE Act" was a prominent example. *See, e.g.*, Sydney Bishop, Denise Royal, and Carlos Suarez, "Judge Permanently Blocks Part of Florida's 'Stop WOKE Act,'" CNN, July 29, 2024, https://www.cnn.com/2024/07/29/us/florida-ron-desantis-stop-woke-act-part-overturned/index.html. As others have noted, that this resurgence of explicit de jure censorship has been "enacted in the name of free speech and/or academic freedom" is a cruel irony indeed. Joan Wallach Scott, "Academic Freedom and the Politics of the University," *Journal of Free Speech Law* 5, no. 2 (2024): 312.

is no doubt important, and indeed its importance has been underscored in the breach. But formal free speech protections are not alone sufficient to craft the sort of deliberative community we should aspire to, inside or outside of campus.

The dust-up over the infamous "Yale Halloween costume" case, which led to the eventual resignation of Yale dorm associate master Erika Christakis, provides a well-publicized example. Christakis—who as associate master of a residential house was charged with creating an open and welcoming environment for Yale undergraduates under her charge—had written skeptically of a Yale administrator's suggestion that students refrain from wearing potentially offensive Halloween costumes. Students reacted with outrage, insisting that Christakis had failed grievously in her duty as associate master by underselling the genuine harms caused by racist or bigoted costumes. In turn, many commentators excoriated the students, insisting that they were "snowflakes" who were seeking to extirpate any form of deviation from a narrow progressive orthodoxy.[60]

The Yale case received significant national attention, but it is important to stress that these debates do not carry an intrinsic partisan valence. In 2019, a controversy erupted at Stanford regarding the circulation of cartoons by left-wing Jewish artist Eli Valley. A conservative (also Jewish) student—signal-boosted by *New York Times* columnist Bari Weiss—contended that Valley's artwork was replete with "Nazi imagery," "depict[ing] Jews and Jewish rituals in the most grotesque of terms; yellow stars, concentration camp uniforms, blood libels and the reliable hooked noses."[61] The left-wing Jewish group which had distributed Valley's cartoons (in advance of co-sponsoring his visit to campus) apologized for not giving the cartoons proper contextual grounding but denied that Valley or his work was antisemitic and insisted that Valley's contribution was important as part of a burgeoning "conversation" and "dialogue" and was thereby

[60] There was voluminous commentary on this controversy and its wake. For a sampling, see Conor Friedersdorf, "The New Intolerance of Student Activism," *The Atlantic*, November 9, 2015, https://www.theatlantic.com/politics/archive/2015/11/the-new-intolerance-of-student-activism-at-yale/414810/; Daniel W. Drezner, "A Clash between Administrators and Students at Yale Went Viral. Why That Is Unfortunate for All Concerned," *Washington Post*, November 9, 2015, https://www.washingtonpost.com/posteverything/wp/2015/11/09/a-clash-between-administrators-and-students-at-yale-went-viral-why-that-is-unfortunate-for-all-concerned/; Jelani Cobb, "Race and the Free Speech Diversion," *New Yorker*, November 10, 2015, https://www.newyorker.com/news/news-desk/race-and-the-free-speech-diversion; Jim Sleeper, "The Truth about the 'Campus Free Speech' Crusade and Its Myths That Won't Die," *Salon*, March 31, 2019, https://www.salon.com/2019/03/31/the-truth-about-the-campus-free-speech-panic-a-myth-that-wont-die/.

[61] Ari Hoffman, "A Disgrace in the Valley—Co-Sponsoring Anti-Semitism at Stanford," *Stanford Daily*, May 6, 2019, https://www.stanforddaily.com/2019/05/06/op-ed-a-disgrace-in-the-valley-co-sponsoring-anti-semitism-at-stanford/; Bari Weiss, tweet, May 7, 2019, 10:47 a.m., https://x.com/bariweiss/status/1125789271959277569.

essential to protect "even if that [the conversation Valley provokes] makes us uncomfortable."[62]

Many commentators, noting Weiss's profile as a sharp critic of allegedly censorial instincts emanating from oversensitive students on campus, claimed hypocrisy—suggesting that in the case of anti-Israel speech she was apparently quite keen on student activism designed to chill or suppress controversial views.[63] Defenders of Weiss's position rejoined that they were not advocating censoring Valley—in the form of any sort of institutional prohibition on hosting him—they were only claiming that the decision to invite him was a "bad choice" and the student group which did so should reconsider it.[64] This generated the reply that, in other circumstances, Weiss would certainly view attempts to pressure student groups to rescind a speaker's invitation on the grounds of "offense" as an illicit form of chilling speech.

Here, the progressives cited the value of discomfort and potential alienation, against conservatives asserting certain forms of expression to be threatening or hostile.[65] In other cases, the postures flip: Williams College has a club named "Uncomfortable Learning" designed to bring to campus "controversial" speakers (here, generally meaning speakers controversial to the campus's progressive majority); they have had at least one speaking invitation (to right-wing author John Derbyshire) canceled by the college administration on the grounds that

[62] Emily Wilder and Esther Tsvayg, "Stanford Jewish Voice for Peace's Statement on Eli Valley Art Exhibition," *Stanford Daily*, May 6, 2019, https://www.stanforddaily.com/2019/05/06/op-ed-stanford-jewish-voice-for-peaces-statement-on-eli-valley-art-exhibition/.

[63] See, e.g., Jeet Heer, tweet, May 7, 2019, 2:26 p.m., https://x.com/HeerJeet/status/1125844399747788800; Parker Molloy, "Free Speech Enthusiast Matt Yglesias Refers to Book Bans as 'Identity Politics for Librarians,'" *Present Age*, February 9, 2023, https://www.readtpa.com/p/free-speech-enthusiast-matt-yglesias.

[64] See, e.g., Jonathan Chait, tweet, May 7, 2019, 1:52 p.m., https://x.com/jonathanchait/status/1125835769095045121; Ari Hoffman, tweet, May 7, 2019, 2:40 p.m., https://x.com/AriHoffmanWrite/status/1125847893972111360. Weiss retweeted both of these posts.

[65] Consider also the challenge Open Hillel (now known as Judaism on Our Own Terms) has made against Hillel International's "standards of partnership." The partnership guidelines preclude Hillel chapters from collaborating with organizations or speakers who "[d]eny the right of Israel to exist as a Jewish and democratic state with secure and recognized borders; [d]elegitimize, demonize, or apply a double standard to Israel; [s]upport boycott of, divestment from, or sanctions against the State of Israel; or [e]xhibit a pattern of disruptive behavior towards campus events or guest speakers or foster an atmosphere of incivility." Hillel International, "Hillel Israel Guidelines," https://www.hillel.org/israel-guidelines/. Open Hillel objected to these standards in principle, instead urging "commitment to the Jewish values of open discussion and debate" and insisting "that free discourse, even on difficult subjects, is essential in the context of an educational institution and a democratic society." Quoted in Kenneth S. Stern, *The Conflict over the Conflict: The Israel/Palestine Campus Debate* (University of Toronto Press, 2020), 147. In this debate, Hillel can be seen as representing the "safe space" position, offering itself as an oasis of refuge where Jews (or at least a majority of Jews) can retreat secure in the knowledge that certain issues will not be litigated, while Open Hillel presses for freewheeling inquiry and debate across all collegiate fora, even where it is perceived as uncomfortable, "triggering," or marginalizing.

Derbyshire engages in "hate speech."[66] Considering all these cases together, it may be there is little more to say than to take note of the dueling allegations of hypocrisy. In the right circumstances, both liberals and conservatives can either insist on the need to challenge and provoke or to dig in on the importance of avoiding threat and offense.

Yet it is worth asking how, exactly, free speech values are at stake in these campus debates. At first blush, after all, it might seem that labeling these matters a free speech problem is simply confused. Specifically, it mistakenly identifies *counterspeech* as a form of *censorship*. In the Halloween costume controversy, for instance, the most straightforward way of tracing the controversy is as a simple progression of speech and counterspeech. First, Yale administrators *said* (without requiring) that students should refrain from wearing offensive Halloween costumes. Then Christakis *said* that students should not rely on the administration to police such choices and should develop thicker skins against what she considered the relatively petty insult of an offensive Halloween costume. In response, many students then *said* Christakis's comments were themselves hurtful and insensitive, understating the harms of these costumes, and that her remarks were not in keeping with the role of a dorm master. Finally, many commenters interceded to *say* that the Yale students were oversensitive and unreasonable in their reaction to Christakis.

Strikingly, virtually every entry in this script was characterized by its opponents as at least a cousin of, if not the same as, censorship and speech suppression. The initial message delivered by the Yale administrators was alleged to squelch those who wanted to wear racy or potentially politically insensitive costumes (even though it solely asked for students to exercise their own prudent judgment and never threatened any formal administrative sanctions). Christakis's remarks were alleged to be silencing to minority or marginalized communities that did not feel as if the issue of insensitive Halloween costumes was minor or not worth administrative notice, even though she (quite clearly) lacked the ability to end that conversation. Student protests against Christakis in turn were claimed to be silencing her, and external commentary on the protests was argued to be an attempt to chill the protests. There was little effort to provide any conceptual justification as to why one class of speech was truly speech and the other thinly disguised censorship.[67]

[66] See Alex Morey, "Williams College Bars 'Uncomfortable Learning' Speaker from Campus, Declares 'Hate Speech' Too Uncomfortable," Foundation for Individual Rights in Education, February 18, 2016, https://www.thefire.org/williams-college-bars-uncomfortable-learning-speaker-from-campus-declares-hate-speech-too-uncomfortable/.

[67] Ken White's "Doctrine of the Preferred First Speaker" identifies a fallacy whereby the first person to enter an argument occupies a privileged position such that harsh counterspeech to his or her claim is labeled censorship rather than counterspeech. Hence, if Jane writes a column alleging that kids these days are oversensitive and shouldn't hassle people on their choice of Halloween costumes,

At one level, of course, the critics are absolutely right in identifying a desire—on both sides of the Yale controversy—to see certain speech "silenced." The more left-of-center participants hoped that certain expressions—initially wearing stereotypical Halloween costumes, later polemics suggesting that concerns about these costumes were overwrought—would dissipate and eventually disappear. The more right-of-center participants likewise wanted other expression—what they took to be histrionic reactions to a mere costume or to discussions about the role of university administrators in addressing costume etiquette—likewise to fade.

Indeed, were either side successful in "silencing" the speech of other, they might argue that it represented a deliberative success story. A significant feature of the marketplace-of-ideas metaphor, for example, is the belief that, eventually, false or bad ideas will be displaced by true or better ones.[68] This displacement occurs not through the heavy hand of governmental censorship but rather through the mechanisms of speech itself. Many people used to argue that the Earth is flat. Now few do, not because the position has been banned but because we voluntarily came to the consensus that such a view is unsupportable. Any remaining outliers will likely find themselves subjected to cruel mockery. Many people used to argue that slavery is just. Now far fewer do, and again, not because the position has been banned. We came to the consensus that such a view was morally abhorrent; persons who hold it are subject to scorn and condemnation. Were we in a polity where this was not the case—where there was not just the formal permissibility of advocating these views but where they were taken seriously as important questions demanding deep and penetrating public engagement in perpetuity—that would be a sign not of a healthy deliberative sphere but of a stagnant one. A deliberative community that cannot at any stage of progression distinguish and eventually weed out bad or malicious ideas is fundamentally malformed.[69]

and Mark replies that Jane is a crude bigot, Mark will be said to be censoring Jane. But if instead Mark got off the blocks first with a column saying that the continued prevalence of certain Halloween costumes is proof of publicly acceptable bigotry, and Jane retorts that Mark is a Millennial snowflake who needs to learn to keep his sense of perspective, then Jane will be accused of silencing Mark. See Ken White, "Ten Points about Speech, Ducks, and Flights to Africa," *Popehat*, December 21, 2013, https://www.popehat.com/2013/12/21/ten-points-about-speech-ducks-and-flights-to-africa/.

[68] Though whether a "market" in ideas would actually necessarily lead to the triumph of "true or better" ideas is dubious—this is one of the primary critiques of the "marketplace of ideas" metaphor. See Gordon, "Marketplace of Ideas"; Robert Sparrow and Robert E. Goodin, "The Competition of Ideas: Market or Garden?," *Critical Review of International Social and Political Philosophy* 4, no. 2 (2001): 45–58. Nonetheless, the point is that eventual displacement of bad ideas by better ideas is viewed as a general desideratum of organized discursive practice.

[69] Though consider again Mill's lament about the gradual "narrowing" of public opinion.

Under this view, the Yale Halloween controversy presented no free speech issue at all. Both sides of the debate spoke out and exercised their right to freedom of speech, and to the extent one side prevailed in silencing the other, that is not a free speech violation but rather the desired terminus of how open debate is supposed to end. This outlook appears to offer a neat resolution to a host of controversies often cast in the language of free speech, one that returns to its perceived juridical roots. On the jurisprudential approach, all we must do is check to see if there is any governmental (or quasi-governmental) attempt to ban speech. Since the answer is no, the free speech inquiry is done—now all that is left to do is retreat and observe whose speech-silencing desires, if any, prevail.[70]

Yet in practice this resolution seems to satisfy no one. Certainly it does not account for the near-universal sense that censorship or free speech was indeed at issue at Yale and Stanford.[71] At Stanford, the blowback against Valley seemed to presage a broader intolerance of sharp criticism of Israel (including by Jewish critics); an intolerance which later has been used to warrant increasingly draconian measures against pro-Palestinian speakers in campus spaces. As for Christakis, she left not just Yale but the entire state of Connecticut in the aftermath of her event; perhaps such (self-imposed) exile is in some cases a desirable outcome, but if and when that is what we want we should say so, rather than assiduously averting our eyes and evading reckoning with an actual, tangible, and very material consequence of our actions. In any event, it seems odd to "resolve" the problem by suggesting that everyone is simply making a terminological mistake. At most, the jurisprudential frame gives a dispositive answer as to a proposed juridical remedy: no campus actor can leverage governmental authority (or, perhaps, university administrative authority) to effectuate a de jure silencing.[72] But that leaves plenty of open space to consider Mill's problem of "the tyranny of the prevailing opinion."[73]

[70] Consider here the lawsuit brought by Prager University against YouTube, claiming that YouTube's demonetization of Prager University content, allegedly done on the basis of Prager University's conservative ideology, violated the First Amendment. The Ninth Circuit quickly concluded that the suit failed based on the "insurmountable barrier" that the First Amendment applies only to government actors. Prager University v. Google LLC, 951 F.3d 991, 994 (2020) (9th Cir. 2020).

[71] The incident at Williams presents a different case because there the college administration did intercede to bar a particular speech-event.

[72] David Schraub, "Academic Freedom versus Academic Legitimacy," *Florida International University Law Review* 9, no. 1 (2013): 71–72.

[73] Mill, *On Liberty*, 4.

The Deliberative and Regulative Dimensions of Free Speech

Each of the above examples showcase situations where opposing sides of a campus speech controversy both framed their activities as promoting freedom of speech, while presenting their adversaries as engaging in censorship, intolerance, or worse. How can free speech be enlisted on behalf of so many seemingly contradictory goals? Part of the confusion stems from the fact that "free speech" is a mantra addressing two very different political dimensions: one deliberative, the second regulative. The former emphasizes the importance of open inquiry, hearing diverse and divergent viewpoints, considering alternative claims, and coming to a consensus or at least a reasoned and informed appreciation of what one's colleagues and co-citizens actually think. The latter, by contrast, concerns almost the exact opposite set of considerations: how we decide what we will *decline* to consider, what doesn't get published, and what gets ignored.

For Mill, the deliberative versus regulative registers track his prescriptions for personal ethics and political liberalism, respectively—we should as a matter of individual ethics strive to be open-minded, and in our politics we should refrain from permitting government officials from deciding certain opinions or arguments are off-limits. But in fact each register speaks in both a personal and a political voice. For example, the deliberative and regulative dimensions of free speech are also related to what Sunstein labels a "political" versus "consumer" vision of sovereignty. The former is the capacity of people to self-govern via hearing and deliberating over diverse views—a *political* capacity that generates a *political* obligation to ensure that these arteries of self-government are not obstructed by censorship. The latter, by contrast, is the freedom of individuals to tailor their consumption of ideas to match their preferences—the creation of a "Daily Me" whose content precisely tracks what the individual has already decided he or she wants to hear.[74] Understanding how these registers diverge from one another can help illuminate critical tensions that appear intractable when these competing values are merged under a single banner of "free speech."

In the deliberative register, free speech means, if not agreeing with, then at least actually *listening* to challenging opinions. This is the primary dimension through which persons protesting "censorship" by private actors—through scorn, derision, disdain, loss of companionship, and so on—typically make their complaint. But while it is a popular justification for treating free speech as a virtue, it actually fits better as a plea for an ethic of *listening*.

[74] Sunstein, *#Republic*, 52–55. On the consumerist attributes of the Supreme Court's First Amendment jurisprudence, particularly in the *Citizens United* case, see Wendy Brown, *Undoing the Demos: Neoliberalism's Stealth Revolution* (Zone, 2015), 159.

Important elements of free speech doctrine are centered on this point. Consider the "public forum" doctrine—the principle that certain areas of society (e.g., parks and sidewalks) must be left open for the relatively untrammeled conveyance of ideas. Sunstein observes that this doctrine, in large part, is not just about the liberty of speakers in the abstract; it is specifically about guaranteeing speakers' access *to people*—that is, to potential listeners. Even "if many citizens would prefer to have peace and quiet, and even if it seems irritating to come across protesters and dissidents when you are simply walking to the grocery store," the public forum doctrine exists to ensure that in practice speakers of unfamiliar ideas can have their ideas heard.[75]

If the only free speech worth speaking of is the liberty of speakers, the public forum doctrine might be obsolete in the digital age, when anyone can set up a blog or make a social media post to communicate their views. Those who wish to hear the ensuing opinions can choose to do so; if nobody wants to hear them, then their purveyors will howl into a digital void. But an important feature of the public forum doctrine is that it does not simply leave matters up to individual choice—the fact that speech can be encountered in a *public forum*, often a physical public forum like a street or a park, where it is not intentionally being sought out in practice, acts to compel people to listen to ideas even if they'd rather not hear them.

As Sunstein observes, the assurance that speech will be free from restriction in a public forum makes it more likely that speakers seeking to persuade will be able to communicate their message to a *heterogeneous* public, including precisely the sorts of persons who might never otherwise encounter their particular issue area and would not think to seek it out on their own. Sunstein writes, "On your way to the office or when eating lunch in the park, you cannot easily wall yourself off from contentions or conditions that you would not have sought out in advance, or that you would have avoided if you could." Moreover, the availability of public forums ensures access to "specific people and specific institutions against which" one has a complaint. The ability to march in front of the legislature or picket a business ensures not just that "the people" generally but specific entities "cannot easily avoid hearing complaints that are directed against them."[76] The goal is not simply to respect the right of speakers to speak, but to impose limits on the power of listeners to insulate themselves from challenge.

If we think about public forums as effectuating these deliberative goals, we can also make better sense of when and why speech *can* be restricted even in those spaces. "Time, place, and manner" restrictions respect the reality that the sort of accidental, undesired, and often irritating speech one encounters in a public

[75] Sunstein, *#Republic*, 35.
[76] *Id.* at 38–39.

forum need not, and probably should not, be a 24/7 thing. We want to ensure there is *some* space for it, but we also acknowledge that individuals are entitled to have some portions of their day when they can simply go about their lives (even in public) without being bombarded with messages to consider and arguments to deliberate over.

Exceptions to the general freewheeling protections for speech in a public forum may reasonably turn on the conclusion that *this* context, specifically, is not one where it is appropriate to compel consideration of alternate (or any) views. In *Phelps-Roper v. City of Manchester*,[77] the U.S. Court of Appeals for the Eighth Circuit considered an ordinance which prohibited picketing within 300 feet of a funeral. The effective target of the ordinance was the Westboro Baptist Church, which has taken to protesting at military funerals to communicate the message "God Hates Fags" and that America will be punished for tolerating homosexuality. Offensive as that message is, under well-accepted First Amendment doctrine its grotesque character cannot subject it to sanction. And, the content of the speech aside, we might normally think that persons who are out in the community may be forced to hear such unsavory messages when they are in or adjacent to public spaces.

Nonetheless, the court upheld the anti-picketing ordinance in the particular context of a *funeral* setting. Even when it occurs in or near a public area, a funeral presents a uniquely strong example of an environment where persons are entitled to the privacy to simply grieve. Funerals are not an example of a social setting where it is important or even reasonable to expect public-goers to engage in contemplation of contested social issues.[78] While they may technically be out in public, mourners are functionally "captive to their overwhelming human need to memorialize and grieve for their dead."[79] Even if in general ensuring that members of the public face opportunities to be exposed to unexpected and challenging speech is a core ambition of a public forum, in the context of a funeral, specifically, that interest is at its nadir. But in other contexts, the importance of ensuring that members of the polity are exposed to and, at least minimally, are forced to consider even controversial and challenging viewpoints means that the Westboro Baptist Church is protected in its ability to spew its hateful rhetoric.

Here we see some of the contours of the first political dimension of free speech: when and how it encourages social deliberation. It generally seeks to encourage the cultivation of social structures which promote consideration of diverse or challenging views (hence why we strongly protect the right of

[77] 697 F.3d 678 (8th Cir. 2012) (en banc).

[78] *Id.* at 693.

[79] *Id.*, quoting Alan Brownstein and Vikram David Amar, "Death, Grief, and Freedom of Speech: Does the First Amendment Permit Protection against the Harassment and Commandeering of Funeral Mourners?," *Cardozo Law Review* De Novo 2010 (2010): 368–87, 374–75.

protesters to disturb our peaceful walks in the park), while also demarcating the limits on that ambition (explaining why we do not show similar forbearance toward the protester at the funeral).

The second dimension of free speech, however, is regulative—determining who decides what opinions or arguments are worth listening to, and by extension which ones can be justly ignored or dispensed with. Notice how this was *not* at issue in, for example, *Phelps-Roper*—nominally, the ordinance at issue there would apply regardless of what subject the picketers were promoting, from labor rights to antiracism. The justification for upholding the anti-picketing ordinance, in other words, was *not* a conclusion that the specific views the Westboro Baptist Church sought to espouse were unworthy of consideration.[80] But the reason public bodies lack the authority to make such determinations is precisely because—at least in the liberal understanding—it should be up to private actors to make such judgments for themselves. Under the regulative framework, the claims of private censorship come off as incoherent, for the people who are "suppressing" the speech are in fact doing exactly what they are entitled to do. Yet this consumerist notion of free speech, where "[e]very citizen must judge the content of speech for himself or herself," is one that "makes no mention of shared deliberation or judgment in politics."[81]

In *Rowan v. Post Office Department*, for example, the Supreme Court upheld a law allowing homeowners to remove their name from mailing lists and then compelling mailers to cease sending further mailings to the household. "To hold less," the Court asserted, "would make hardly more sense than to say that a radio or television viewer may not twist the dial to cut off an offensive or boring communication."[82] In a position that seems orthogonal to the declared virtues of listening to alternative perspectives and encountering diverse views, the Court concluded, "Nothing in the Constitution compels us to listen to or view any unwanted communication, whatever its merit."[83] This is quite different from *Phelps-Roper*, to say nothing of public forum analysis in a park. *Phelps-Roper* negotiated the question of which spaces must be kept open to deliberative exposure so that people are compelled to listen to potentially unwelcome thoughts, ultimately concluding that the specific space of a funeral was not among them. It did not, however, suggest that individuals have a special or particular entitlement to avoid the Westboro Baptist Church's message, specifically. *Rowan*, by contrast, is precisely about enabling listeners to make a judgment that certain

[80] *See* Texas v. Johnson, 491 U.S. 397, 414 (1989) ("If there is a bedrock principle underlying the First Amendment, it is that the government may not prohibit the expression of an idea simply because society finds the idea itself offensive or disagreeable.").

[81] Brown, *Undoing the Demos*, 169.

[82] 397 U.S. 728, 737 (1970).

[83] *Id.*

speakers and viewpoints are not worthy of their attention. It vindicates the right of persons to make substantive deliberative judgments that they will not engage with or consider further particular views—akin to the decision to not buy a book or subscribe to a newspaper.

Hence, in the regulative domain, free speech is paradoxically often about one's right *not* to listen, consider, evaluate, or appraise. Far from demanding that individuals consider each and every argument that comes across their path, here is where free speech suggests that the proper response to offensive expression is simply "averting [one's] eyes."[84] And in some cases, the Court has intimated, even that might not suffice as a remedy. In *FCC v. Pacifica Foundation*, the case concerning the radio broadcast of George Carlin's "seven dirty words" monologue, the Supreme Court concluded that the ability to simply "turn off the radio" upon hearing indecent words offers insufficient protection—akin to "saying that the remedy for an assault is to run away after the first blow."[85] Patrick Garry accordingly contends that the First Amendment should incorporate a "right to reject": "[A]n autonomous individual should also have the right to choose what images and ideas from the outside world to reject in the formation of one's character. Just as a person has the right to speak or be silent, so too should a listener have the right to listen or reject."[86] Leslie Gielow Jacobs moderates this view—but only partially: she contends that speakers should have "one bite" to communicate with unsolicitous listeners, but that the government can legitimately enforce an individual's desire to not receive further communication after the initial encounter.[87]

The two registers—the deliberative and the regulative—are in significant tension with one another. But encased inside the framework of the liberal public, these two distinct free speech ideals can coexist in harmony: the state is neutral as between all ideas, allowing individuals to access and subsequently accept or reject opinions at their own discretion. As a principle of public regulation, the liberal vision of free speech seeks to approximate as best as possible a set of Habermasian discursive rules: every subject is *allowed* to speak, every subject is *allowed* to introduce any assertion or express any attitude, no subject can be *prevented* from exercising such speech rights.[88] But none of these considers the corresponding ability to simply ignore or dismiss all these allowances, and so

[84] Cohen v. California, 403 U.S. 15, 21 (1971).

[85] 438 U.S. 726, 748–49 (1978).

[86] Patrick M. Garry, "The Right to Reject: The First Amendment in a Media-Drenched Society," *San Diego Law Review* 42, no. 1 (2005), 152.

[87] Leslie Gielow Jacobs, "Is There an Obligation to Listen?," *University of Michigan Journal of Law Reform* 32, no. 3 (1999): 489–543.

[88] See Jürgen Habermas, "Discourse Ethics: Notes on a Program of Philosophical Justification," in *Moral Consciousness and Communicative Action*, trans. Christian Lenhardt and Shierry Weber Nicholsen (MIT Press, 1990), 89.

in the private sphere this concurrence breaks down. Free speech in the private sphere is precisely the freedom *not* to listen; to decline to publish a book; to refuse to engage in an argument; to, in short, avert one's eyes. This freedom is simultaneously a prerequisite to political engagement—it is impossible (and perhaps undesirable) for any of us to consider every potential claim—and its greatest threat. Far more dangerous than any juridical censorship is our own propensity to exercise our right not to listen—or more broadly, consider—in ways that block or close off challenging, discomforting, or otherwise alternative points of view.

Indeed, the problem is more serious still. Ideas—to borrow Hobbes's felicitous phrasing—do not spontaneously spring up in the world "like mushrooms." They are created—and, more important, distributed—by people, people who are empowered by the private, regulative dimension of free speech to promote certain views while rejecting and suppressing others. The dissident who can vitriolically condemn the powers that be without fear of imprisonment nonetheless may have to contend with newspaper editors who have no interest in her broadsides and publishers who see no profit in her polemics. The academic who is promised protection for his unpopular research will find that academic freedom does nothing to guarantee that editors and reviewers from prestigious journals do not share the wider public's disdain. The lifeblood of open discourse runs primarily through private, not public, veins. Yet here the power to suppress alternative viewpoints is paradoxically at its apex—not as a departure from the norms of free speech but as an instantiation of it.

The tension exploded into public view when the *New York Times*, in the midst of nationwide protests against police brutality and an increasingly violent crackdown by law enforcement in response, published an article by Arkansas senator Tom Cotton urging deployment of the military against its own citizens under the title "Send in the Troops."[89] The decision to promulgate Senator Cotton's view came under withering criticism by many observers, including several *New York Times* journalists, who claimed its publication was irresponsible, unnecessary, and endangered the lives of Black reporters who would likely bear the brunt of further militarized escalation.[90] Responding to this critique, editorial page editor James Bennet defended the decision to publish on the grounds that the *Times*' sympathetic coverage (in both news and opinion) of the protests and indictment of the "systemic cruelties that led" to them, meant that they "owe[d] it to [their] readers to show them counter-arguments, particularly those made by people in

[89] Tom Cotton, "Send in the Troops," *New York Times*, June 3, 2020, https://www.nytimes.com/2020/06/03/opinion/tom-cotton-protests-military.html.

[90] *See* Oliver Darcy, "New York Times Staffers Revolt over Publication of Tom Cotton Op-Ed," CNN, June 3, 2020, https://www.cnn.com/2020/06/03/media/new-york-times-tom-cotton-op-ed/index.html.

a position to set policy."[91] Kaylee McGhee in the *Washington Examiner* likewise came to the *Times*' defense, contending that "opinions are supposed to inform, challenge, and (hopefully) persuade readers while at the same time bolstering the democratic values—the right to a free press and the necessity of democratic debate—upon which our system of governance depends. *The New York Times* opinion pages should not merely confirm their readers' worldview, nor do they exist to appease the preconceived opinions of its staffers. The op-ed page, in fact, was specifically created to offer a range of opinions that may differ from the institutional editorial position."[92]

This argument, once again, appeals to the resonant values of democratic deliberation and open-mindedness to opposing views. Put another way, the defense of the *Times*' decision to publish was predicated less on Cotton's right as a speaker (surely, a U.S. senator has plenty of vectors through which he can express his opinions) and more on facilitating the newspaper's obligation to its *readers* in their capacity as listeners. The *Times* was, in this view, engaging in the salutary act of, if not compelling, then at least encouraging its readership to take up and consider an idea that they otherwise would be far less likely to encounter, at least in an unmediated form. (The alternative venues available to Senator Cotton may not, it seems probable, overlap with those regularly read by the *New York Times* subscriber base.)

But can that suffice to justify the *Times*' decision? Laura Adkins, then the opinion editor for the Jewish Telegraphic Agency, countered this line of argument by pointing out that opinion editors have a "responsibility to commission thoughtful takes that advance the discourse—and don't actively harm others."[93] The "toughest choice," she continued, that an opinion editor has to face "is saying no to pieces that you know would be widely shared and read but ultimately harmful." But "[i]f you don't do that job, you're not worthy of curating a section."[94]

This point is important to emphasize. Clearly, it is not wrong for editors to make judgments on what articles they publish or readers to make distinctions on what journals they peruse. Such determinations represent the liberal, regulative ideal of speech functioning as intended, and even those critics who urge that we create more space for "controversial" opinions rarely wish to convert

[91] Marc Tracy, "Senator's 'Send in the Troops' Op-Ed in the Times Draws Online Ire," *New York Times*, June 3, 2020, https://www.nytimes.com/2020/06/03/business/tom-cotton-op-ed.html.

[92] Kaylee McGhee, "The New York Times Was Right to Publish Tom Cotton's Op-Ed," *Washington Examiner*, June 3, 2020, https://www.washingtonexaminer.com/opinion/the-new-york-times-was-right-to-publish-tom-cottons-op-ed.

[93] Laura E. Adkins, tweet, June 3, 2020, 7:09 p.m., https://x.com/Laura_E_Adkins/status/1268364345446187010.

[94] Laura E. Adkin, tweet, June 3, 2020, 7:18 p.m., https://x.com/Laura_E_Adkins/status/1268366400038502403.

our nation's newspapers and airwaves into an Open Mic Night. When the local paper declines to run an article by a Holocaust denier, we are quite content with the decision. It would reflect poorly on the institution if it chose otherwise; we would justifiably be concerned if the media did *not* recognize Holocaust denial as a view not worth airing. The apologia from Bennet and McGhee, focusing on hearing diverse views, is, at the very least, insufficient. It needs more to justify why *these* views, in particular, are worthy of airing. Bari Weiss, in a lengthy thread addressing the Cotton editorial controversy, accused the *Times*' in-house critics of being part of a generational war against "civil libertarianism," demanding that "safety" trump "core liberal values, like free speech."[95] Yet by the end, she lamely ended up agreeing that "it's a dodge to say 'we want a totally open marketplace of ideas!' There are limits. Obviously. The question is: does his view fall outside those limits? Maybe the answer is yes."[96] Once that concession is made, how useful is the appeal to "core liberal values, like free speech"? In the private space, a raw appeal to free speech cannot satisfy as a response.

The problem is, of course, that there are other potential opinions out there, the proponents of which also tend not to appear in mainstream print, where we are less inclined to describe the absence as a salutary exercise in editorial oversight. When papers ignore the opinions of racial, religious, or sexual minorities—or present only a nonrepresentative few prescreened for palatability[97]—this is not chalked up simply to the inevitability of having to make quality-based judgments. It presents as a form of closed-mindedness or even ideological sequestration—a serious deliberative vice.

We could frame this issue as Adkins does: one of line-drawing—the inevitable tough distinctions and judgment calls as we try to distinguish between making evaluative appraisals (good) and closing ourselves off from challenge (bad). But I want to make a related but slightly different point. Deliberative resources are scarce, and triaging is inevitable. It is always legitimate, in some form, to exclude or close off certain avenues of conversation. It would be impossible (and, I suspect, undesirable) to do otherwise.

But the very legitimacy—indeed, necessity—of making choices about allocating scarce deliberative resources makes it an attractive vector for smuggling in more illicit biases. The reason that the freedom to ignore, overlook, or otherwise dismiss hostile argumentation is so dangerous is precisely because it

[95] Bari Weiss, tweet, June 4, 2020, 12:40 p.m., https://x.com/bariweiss/status/1268628680797978625.

[96] Bari Weiss, tweet, June 4, 2020, 1:07 p.m., https://x.com/bariweiss/status/1268635549390319617.

[97] On the problem of "tokenizing" minority group members who dissent from their group's general consensus regarding matters of collective liberation, see David Schraub, "The Distinctive Political Status of Dissident Minorities," *American Political Science Review* 114, no. 4 (2020): 963–75.

seems to be the natural byproduct of unavoidable choices inherent in a modern, information-saturated society. When we *have* to ignore some things, we *predictably* choose to ignore those thoughts we'd rather not think—only now we have a neutral-sounding excuse to do so. It can be exceptionally difficult to parse when our choices regarding what thoughts to consider are based on neutral, principled, or legitimate reasons, and when they're a smokescreen for ideological self-shielding. If closing one's ears or averting one's eyes was always a morally corrupted response, it would be easy to indict. But it is precisely because ignoring or refusing to publish speech is—and is often—perfectly justified that makes it difficult to police cases where such ignorance and refusals are destructive of good deliberative practice.

And the dilemma grabs us from the other side as well: knowing that these editorial decisions—to decline to publish an article, to drop an "offensive" columnist, to withdraw from a controversial panel—can easily launder illiberal instincts, it becomes too easy to indict any or all of them as manifesting an illiberal tide. These are the concerns of "cancel culture"—the decision to cancel any speaker for any reason becomes tantamount to censorship, even though private actors can and must make decisions every day about what speech is worth platforming or paying for. Part of the confusion comes from the importation of public (legal, juridical) norms of free speech into private settings—decisions which absolutely *would* be censorship if taken by a public regulator are utterly unremarkable implemented by a private publisher. Law's effective colonization of the rhetoric of free speech makes this confusion inevitable. But there is also a more inward problem: the (reasonable) fear of being illiberal in temperament atrophies our ability to accurately judge—in ourselves or in others—whether a specific decision regarding a specific book, column, speaker, or event actually is justified as a valid substantive appraisal of the speech's worth. Instead, when faced with criticism over who to publish or platform, the appeal to (avoiding) censorship becomes the excuse of first resort. "I may not agree with everything this columnist writes," the editor explains to the aggrieved reader, "but it is important that we hear from perspectives that differ from our own and challenge or even provoke us." True enough—but this mantra, often invoked totemically any time the prospect of cancelation is placed on the table, obscures the need to actually engage in a substantive judgment: *Does* the columnist in question present a perspective that actually is worth engaging with? Government regulators, under the liberal framework, do not need to answer this question. Private actors, under this same liberal framework, cannot help but answer it yet are given very few resources to answer it justly. No wonder they mistakenly try to sit under the same tent that covers the public regulator—it allows them to avoid a question they do not know how to address.

Jacobs suggests that the "question whether there is an obligation to listen is," ultimately, "really a question about the scope of the right to free speech."[98] Clearly there is a connection, but it seems mistaken to completely render the former a subset of the latter—at least if the "right to free speech" is rendered solely in juridical (regulative) terms. The ability of the regulative register of free speech to impose an obligation to listen is extremely circumscribed, and appropriately so. But obligations can stem from domains other than law, and it is entirely reasonable to oblige persons to listen without subjecting them to legal enforcement. Indeed, articulating these obligations is perhaps most important in the context of a liberal society which abjures public speech regulation. Wendy Brown observes that this liberal framework does not intrinsically protect "ideas, deliberation, or the integrity of the democratic political sphere, but an unimpeded flow (barrage) of speech."[99] Where law drowns us in speech, the mechanisms through which we ignore speech become a critical domain to theorize. The liberal free speech framework does not abandon a regulative impulse toward speech; it merely reassigns it to the private sphere. Hence the principles of regulation that do emerge must be directed toward ordering private individuals making personal autonomous choices—a domain resistant to rights discourse but perhaps amenable to the cultivation of political virtues.

Both the problem (of ideological self-shielding) and the potential solution (of developing specific deliberative virtues—those of curiosity, open-mindedness, and willingness to at least presumptively lean in to challenging thoughts) are occluded when free speech is thought of entirely as a matter of the liberty of the speaker. From that vantage, the untrammeled freedom to *ignore* speech is not a legible concern—speakers have no right to captive audiences; it is hard to identify a cognizable harm to the *speaker* if nobody is interested in what they have to say. (Recall *Rowan*: there can be no legal right "compell[ing] us to listen to or view any unwanted communication, whatever its merit.") It becomes visible only if we orient our perspective away from *speaking* and toward *listening*.[100] I return once again to the Gilligan quote: "If you have power, you can opt not

[98] Jacobs, "Obligation to Listen," 524.

[99] Brown, *Undoing the Demos*, 160.

[100] There is perhaps a connection here to Stokely Carmichael's argument that civil rights legislation is "for white people": "I am black. I know that. I also know that while I am black I am a human being. Therefore I have the right to go into any public place. White people didn't know that. Every time I tried to go into a public place they stopped me. So some boys had to write a bill to tell that white man, 'He's a human being; don't stop him.' That bill was for the white man, not for me." At least at an epistemic level, the civil rights *claimant* does not gain or lose much—they already know of what they speak. It is the listener who stands to potentially benefit from learning something new and adjusting their posture accordingly. Stokely Carmichael, "Black Power (Berkeley Speech)," in *Ripples of Hope: Great American Civil Rights Speeches*, ed. Josh Gottheimer (Basic Civitas Books, 2003), 298.

to listen. And you do so with impunity."[101] Well prior to any juridical authority to block or censor the speech of another lies the ability to simply not listen to it. Indeed, many of the values located underneath the umbrella of free speech or open inquiry depend on the cultivation of certain virtues or orientations regarding how we process and respond to speech—our standing and behavior as listeners—just as much as our rights and freedoms as speakers.

Listening and Power

So once again it seems as if the key to the puzzle will not be found in seeking to regulate the actions of the speaker. Instead we must concentrate on what the listener is doing. The claim, to reiterate, is not that listeners are obligated to consider any and all arguments they become aware of—that would be undesirable in theory and impossible in practice. Rather, the point is that the inevitable *choices* listeners make when deciding when and what to tune out or dismiss are the most promising grounds for resolving the tensions between the regulative and deliberative ideals of free speech. "The problem," as Andrew Dobson puts it, "is not one of speaking truth to power, but of getting the powerful to listen."[102]

As Mill's reference to the princes suggests and as Gilligan makes clear, the capacity to simply not listen is directly tied to the possession of social power. A position of vulnerability makes it more likely "that one will need to attend to what others are likely to notice."[103] While marginalized persons certainly can (under the right circumstances) argue against the principles or assertions of the dominant classes, they are rarely in a position to simply wave them aside outright. It's not just because dominant discourse is ubiquitous and thus virtually inescapable, though often it is. There's a more practical imperative: to survive inside a system, one must know the rules of the system—regardless of whether one agrees with them or not, regardless if one had a hand in developing them or not, and regardless of whether they cohere to one's image of oneself or not.[104]

[101] "Feminist Discourse, Moral Values, and the Law—A Conversation: The 1984 James McCormick Mitchell Lecture," *Buffalo Law Review* 34, no. 1 (1985): 62 (Isabel Marcus and Paul J. Spiegelman, moderators; Ellen C. DuBois, Mary C. Dunlap, Carol J. Gilligan, Catherine A. MacKinnon, and Carrie Menkel-Meadow, participants).

[102] Andrew Dobson, *Listening for Democracy: Recognition, Representation, Reconciliation* (Oxford University Press, 2014), 92. *See also* Joshua Habgood-Coote, Natalie Alana Ashton, and Nadja El Kasar, "Receptive Publics," *Ergo* 11, no. 5 (2024): 113–49.

[103] Gaile Pohlhaus Jr., "Relational Knowing and Epistemic Injustice: Toward a Theory of *Willful Hermeneutical Ignorance*," *Hypatia* 27, no. 4 (2012): 721.

[104] See José Medina, *The Epistemology of Resistance: Gender and Racial Oppression, Epistemic Injustice, and Resistant Imaginations* (Oxford University Press, 2013), 44.

By contrast, persons with power can often unilaterally set the conceptual boundaries of a given conversation and thereby "preemptively silence" perspectives which might—if given due consideration—present an effective challenge.[105] Such persons "experience the current organization of society as basically satisfactory and so they accept the interpretation of reality that justifies that system of organization."[106] Alison Bailey puts the point succinctly: "[M]embers of socially dominant groups [possess] an epistemic home turf advantage."[107] Their language, their concerns, their vulnerabilities, and their priorities are the ones that set the tone for conversation.

For these reasons, those invested with social power often need not resort to administrative diktat or the policeman's baton in order to take an item off the public agenda. "Efforts to restrict allegedly malign ideologies are assumed to be a tool of the strong, but often they are a tactic of the weak—people who are *not* confident that their community will unify in agreement that the ideology is in fact oppressive."[108] Indeed, it seems likely that such explicit measures more often manifest in circumstances where power is transitioning—an old guard losing hegemonic control over the currents of discourse, or a newly empowered out-group seeking to take certain deleterious views about them and theirs and declare them now "off the table." This seems to be an apt descriptor of the dynamics leading to the congressional gag rule against considering antislavery petitions in 1836. While at one level the imposition of this rule was a clear exercise of slave power, it was simultaneously an exercise motivated and compelled by the waxing influence of the antislavery position. It was the comparative growth in abolitionist sentiment that, from the vantage point of the slaveholders, necessitated more aggressively censorial responses—they no longer could take for granted the primacy of their position in a way that might have been feasible in years past.

This connection of censorship with *transitions* in discursive power arrangements also seems to characterize the hyperaggressive response to pro-Palestine encampments and other forms of pro-Palestine speech at campuses across the nation in the midst of Israel's post–October 7 war in Gaza.[109] What had been

[105] Eric Reitan, "Rape as an Essentially Contested Concept," *Hypatia* 16, no. 2 (2001): 49 ("[I]f any one party has the power to unilaterally determine the conceptual framework that will be used in assessing a normative problem, that party will be able to preemptively silence certain dissenting voices.").

[106] Alison Jaggar, "Feminist Politics and Epistemology: The Standpoint of Women," in *The Feminist Standpoint Theory Reader: Intellectual and Political Controversies*, ed. Sandra Hardin (Routledge, 2003), 56.

[107] Alison Bailey, "The Unlevel Knowing Field: An Engagement with Dotson's Third-Order Epistemic Oppression," *Social Epistemology Review Reply & Collective* 3, no. 10 (2014): 62.

[108] Schraub, "Academic Freedom," 72.

[109] See Jonathan Allen and Caitlin Ochs, "Police Arrest Dozens of Pro-Palestinian Protesters at Columbia University," Reuters, May 1, 2024, https://www.reuters.com/world/us/pro-palestinian-protesters-occupy-building-columbia-university-cnn-2024-04-30/.

for many years a relatively uniform (at least among mainstream political actors) sense of sympathy for Israel suddenly was confronted with an emboldened pro-Palestine faction that, while certainly not a dominant force in American politics, was now flexing unprecedented levels of social influence.[110] The censorial instinct here—manifesting in canceled speakers,[111] ad hoc restrictions on campus gatherings,[112] and attempts to prescribe limits to acceptable speech on Israel/Palestine[113]—is less a function of drunken power and more one of acutely felt vulnerability (which, as the slavery gag-order example makes clear, is not the same thing as saying such vulnerability should always be accommodated). After all, while it takes some (certainly significant) amount of public influence to ban speech, that pales in comparison to the power reflected in being able to have your ideologies or preferences accepted as default presuppositions that need no defense.

Indeed, if you possess the right type of power, you can unilaterally recode certain types of arguments as nullities that are per se excluded from conversation—and you can do so (here's the real kicker) while holding yourself out as *defending* open inquiry. This is most common in attempts to characterize antidiscrimination appeals (e.g., claims of racism, sexism, antisemitism, or other like forms of discrimination) as a form of "silencing." To be sure, such appeals may be right or they may be wrong in any given case, but as a class they certainly touch on exceptionally important questions of justice that deserve serious consideration. Yet frequently they are not treated that way. They are instead viewed as barriers to open inquiry, an obstacle that must be surmounted before the real work of deliberation can begin.[114]

[110] See Kenichi Serini, "Tens of Thousands Have Joined Pro-Palestinian Protests across the United States. Experts Say They Are Growing," PBS, December 15, 2023, https://www.pbs.org/newshour/politics/tens-of-thousands-have-joined-pro-palestinian-protests-across-the-united-states-experts-say-they-are-growing.

[111] See "USC Cancels Speech by Pro-Palestinian Valedictorian, Citing Safety Concerns," *NBC Los Angeles*, April 15, 2024, https://www.nbclosangeles.com/news/local/usc-cancels-valedictorian-speech-over-safety-reasons/3388883/; Zachary Small, "Indiana University Cancels Major Exhibition of Palestinian Artist," *New York Times*, January 11, 2024, https://www.nytimes.com/2024/01/11/arts/design/indiana-university-samia-halaby-exhibition-canceled.html.

[112] See Aubrey White, "IU Changes Policy Day before Encampment Arrests," Indiana Public Media, April 26, 2024, https://indianapublicmedia.org/news/legal-action-may-be-necessary-after-students-faculty-banned-from-iu-campus.php.

[113] See Ellie Silverman, "Judge Sides with U-Md. Pro-Palestinian Group, Clears Way for Oct. 7 Vigil," *Washington Post*, October 1, 2024, https://www.washingtonpost.com/education/2024/10/01/university-maryland-vigil-ruling/; Univ. of Md. Students for Justice in Palestine v. Bd. of Regents of the Univ. Sys. Md., 2024 WL 4361863 (D. Md. Oct. 1, 2024).

[114] Objecting to preemptive dismissal of discrimination claims as being made in "bad faith," I argued that "the bad faith response is dominating speech in a very literal sense—it takes an important claim, one that should occupy our attention as citizens concerned about fair and egalitarian treatment, and removes it from the domain of acceptable public discourse. It dominates speech about discrimination." David Schraub, "Playing with Cards: Discrimination Claims and the Charge of Bad Faith," *Social Theory & Practice* 42, no. 2 (2016): 286.

For example, one law professor, Adam MacLeod, published the introductory speech he gives to his first-year law students wherein he announces his ban on using "-ism" terms in class discussion. Here is how he begins that lecture:

> Before I can teach you how to reason, I must first teach you how to rid yourself of unreason. For many of you have not yet been educated. You have been dis-educated. To put it bluntly, you have been indoctrinated. Before you learn how to think you must first learn how to stop unthinking.
>
> Reasoning requires you to understand truth claims, even truth claims that you think are false or bad or just icky. Most of you have been taught to label things with various "isms" which prevent you from understanding claims you find uncomfortable or difficult.
>
> Reasoning requires correct judgment. Judgment involves making distinctions, discriminating. Most of you have been taught how to avoid critical, evaluative judgments by appealing to simplistic terms such as "diversity" and "equality." ...
>
> [Hence] except when describing an ideology, you are not to use a word that ends in "ism." Communism, socialism, Nazism, and capitalism are established concepts in history and the social sciences, and those terms can often be used fruitfully to gain knowledge and promote understanding. "Classism," "sexism," "materialism," "cisgenderism," and (yes) even racism are generally not used as meaningful or productive terms, at least as you have been taught to use them. Most of the time, they do not promote understanding.
>
> In fact, "isms" prevent you from learning. You have been taught to slap an "ism" on things that you do not understand, or that make you feel uncomfortable, or that make you uncomfortable because you do not understand them. But slapping a label on the box without first opening the box and examining its contents is a form of cheating.[115]

In its rhetoric, at least, this lecture appears to appeal to many of the same values I have defended throughout this book—things like grappling with uncomfortable ideas or not preemptively dismissing arguments simply because they're challenging. But in reality, MacLeod's defense of these values is quite asymmetrical. Most obviously, by simply banning the discussion of "-ism" claims in his class, the professor is effectuating a silencing in a far more explicit and draconian way than anything his students are likely able to muster. (It is not wrong to say that professors must have the authority to impose some sorts of silencing inside their

[115] Adam J. MacLeod, "Undoing the Dis-Education of Millennials," *New Boston Post*, November 9, 2017, http://newbostonpost.com/2017/11/09/undoing-the-dis-education-of-millennials/.

classrooms simply by virtue of their position, but that shouldn't stop us from calling it what it is.)[116] A whole range of "truth claims"—ones that perhaps MacLeod himself may find "false or bad or just icky"—are now excluded from the range of issues the class will consider. Importantly, MacLeod is *not* making the reasonable demand that, if his students wish to condemn something as "racist" (or what have you), they must justify their conclusion rather than simply rest on the label. It would, of course, be perfectly fair for any professor to insist that his or her students demonstrate they understand the argument they are critiquing and publicly reason through *why* and *how* it is racist. (Indeed, this would be fair of a professor to demand of any normative conclusion—of praise or condemnation—that a student might proffer on any subject.) But while MacLeod could have said "You cannot use an '-ism' unless you explain first what you mean by it," he did not in fact make this anodyne demand. He is quite explicit in writing out the entire field of inquiry from permissible discussion whatsoever (or at best, demanding that it be bowdlerized)—whether it be well-warranted and fully explained or not.[117]

More troubling is the sense that this exclusion was pronounced without much regard for the potential validity of the claims so silenced, or indeed any significant attempt to even understand their potential validity. MacLeod extols the value of learning from Aristotle and Hammurabi and thinks such elder statesmen are unjustly dismissed by students on account of "chronological snobbery." By contrast, he derides his students' youthful obsession with valuing "equality" and "diversity"—two terms, he posits, which are incoherent in conjunction with one another, for "equal simply means the same. . . . And diversity simply means difference. So when you say that we should have diversity and equality you are

[116] For a systematic exploration of the issues raised by teachers necessarily having the authority to "silence" students in their classroom, see Eamonn Callan, "When to Shut Students Up: Civility, Silencing, and Free Speech," *Theory and Research in Education* 9, no. 1 (2011): 3–22.

[117] In Chapter 2, we discussed (citing Lawrence Blum) the possibility that certain replies that I label "dismissal" are really efforts to demand a more complex vocabulary around matters of racism and discrimination; the sin objected to is the allegedly sweeping usage of "racism" to cover a wide range of behaviors and practices which should not be roped together under the same term. Perhaps the most charitable reading one can give to MacLeod is that his ban on "-ism" suffixes is an attempt to facilitate development of this more nuanced vocabulary so that students must be precise in what they mean when making an allegation of racial justice. In that previous discussion, I posited that one test of whether this explanation is accurate would be to see how the purveyor reacts to the use of certain neologisms, such as "microaggressions," which do fill out our vocabulary in a more nuanced fashion but which are typically not greeted warmly by persons, like MacLeod, who claim that contemporary education on matters of "equality" and "diversity" have functioned as forms of "indoctrination." While MacLeod does not appear to directly register an opinion on this matter, he has favorably quoted a critic who contended that "slogans of diversity, equity, safe spaces, trigger warnings, microaggressions, and preferred pronouns" have made "American schools increasingly resemble the authoritarian Chinese schools that aim at transforming human beings into an instrument that serves the state." Adam J. MacLeod, Facebook post, November 25, 2020, https://www.facebook.com/permalink.php?id=107919034096361&story_fbid=225368359018094.

saying we should have difference and sameness."[118] Of course, equality need *not* "simply mean the same"—Aristotle taught us that[119]—and it is extraordinarily uncharitable to think that, however unformed their minds might be, the young students who prize both "equality" and "diversity" are lumbering into a paradox *that* obvious. Perhaps there's more to their ideological commitments than first meets the eye. Certainly one suspects that the books and articles which fed the "dis-education" of the students have at least considered the cutting objection "equal means the same and diversity means different." But we'll never know because the thoughts that might be shared around this topic have been preemptively judged as unmeritorious and thus have been taken off the table tout court. In effect, the professor is closing off a whole range of topics by unilaterally reframing the entire field of inquiry as transparently ludicrous (and therefore unworthy of consideration).

The final way MacLeod is able to recast his suppression of (certain avenues of) inquiry as a defense of reasonable inquiry is by arbitrarily dividing the discursive terrain so as to remove the undesirable concepts from the broader goal of pursuing truth. "-ism" claims, MacLeod suggests, are a way we *avoid* thinking—or thinking critically—about political, legal, or philosophical arguments. They are reflexive labels slapped on to an argument whenever "you" ("you" here being young, presumably progressive millennials and Gen Z-ers) stumble across "things that you do not understand, or that make you feel uncomfortable, or that make you uncomfortable because you do not understand them." We call an argument racist when we don't want to think about it; thinking about a concept commences only once we agree not to dismiss it as racist. In this way, Macleod makes an attempted turnabout—to declare something "racist" is itself an act of dismissal; his restriction on using the term is a countermeasure to ensure that the ideas under review actually receive due consideration.

The problem, of course, is that exploring whether or not an argument is racist is something that is *part of*, not outside of, the broader act of consideration. The attempted bifurcation doesn't promote open inquiry; it contorts it so that facets that may well be critical are gerrymandered out of the bounds of legitimate debate.

To take one last example: after arguing in the *New York Times* for why the concept of a "Jewish state" is unjustifiable as inherently undemocratic, Joseph Levine concluded, "[I]t's time the question was discussed openly on its merits, without the charge of anti-Semitism hovering in the background."[120] Certainly one should be able to discuss the moral validity or democratic compatibility

[118] MacLeod, "Dis-Education."
[119] Aristotle, *Nicomachean Ethics* (Oxford University Press, 2009), 1131a–1132b.
[120] Joseph Levine, "On Questioning the Jewish State," *New York Times*, March 9, 2013, https://opinionator.blogs.nytimes.com/2013/03/09/on-questioning-the-jewish-state/?_r=0.

of Zionism or a Jewish state "openly on its merits."[121] But what's baffling about Levine's formulation is his implication that the question of antisemitism is not itself *part* of the "merits." One might think that the issue of antisemitism—its definition, contours, effects, and remediation—would play a very important part in an "on the merits" discussion of Zionism. One might even think that a putatively "on the merits" discussion of Zionism that *does not* include (arguably, does not *foreground*) antisemitism would be transparently stilted, biased, and incomplete. Talking about antisemitism by no means compels a particular answer to questions about Zionism, Israel, or any other Jewish-related topic, but refusing to talk about antisemitism inevitably will yield distorted conclusions—which (the cynic might suggest) is perhaps the point. When "-ism" claims are given unique treatment as conversation stoppers, things which cannot be allowed into the discursive arena lest the entire space be obliterated,[122] what is left is frequently "a coerced agreement . . . that concedes the key intellectual contest."[123]

What we see in these examples are circumstances where certain people can elect not to listen to whole classes of discomforting claims—sometimes (ironically enough) on the rationale that in doing so they actually are *promoting* the full and fair consideration of the hard thoughts. This sometimes can be expressed through formal or quasi-formal power (as in the professor leading a class discussion), but in many cases it need not leverage any sort of juridical authority. Empowered persons can sequester themselves in deliberative locales where they need not consider thoughts that upset them; if they do deign to engage, it is at their discretion and always with the possibility of beating a hasty retreat. This

[121] One could try to circumvent the issue by arguing that Levine's question is a narrow one—Is a Jewish state inherently *undemocratic*?—that is studiously unconcerned with any broader assessment of whether it can be justified, and that while considering the issue of antisemitism may be relevant to the latter, it is not germane to the former. The problem is that Levine clearly does mean for his inquiry to take on the broader moral register—through most of his essay he phrases his critique as being whether Jews have a "right to a state of their own"—and when playing in that register one cannot easily wall off the moral imperatives that historical and ongoing antisemitism generate. Even when he does, toward the end of his essay, pivot more explicitly toward speaking of the tension between a "Jewish" state and a "democratic" state, he does so by reference to a relatively broad understanding of democracy that—while by no means outlandish—does itself tacitly incorporate far more into its ambit beyond simple "majority rule" or even "majority rule with respect for basic political and social rights." Levine's view of democracy is that a democracy must, in order to show requisite respect for all its citizens, not just secure the rights of all citizens regardless of ethnicity but present itself in all respects as equally the state of all ethnic groups contained in the polity equally. This is hardly implausible, but again, once democracy is defined more expansively to include these sorts of broadly *liberal* values, it becomes harder to assert that other potential and seemingly germane political values, such as the need to be responsive to or counteract ongoing or historical antisemitic marginalization, are extra-topical.

[122] David Hirsh, "Struggles over the Boundaries of Legitimate Discourse: Antizionism, Bad-Faith Allegations and the Livingstone Formulation," in *Global Antisemitism: A Crisis of Modernity*, vol. 5: *Reflections*, ed. Charles Asher Small (ISGAP, 2013), 89.

[123] Jerome McCristal Culp Jr., "To the Bone: Race and White Privilege," *Minnesota Law Review* 83, no. 6 (1999): 1641.

isn't recognized as a form of censorship, and perhaps fairly so—as will be argued in the next chapter, the ability to withdraw from deliberation is itself an essential component of liberal freedom. But if our focus is less on what rights people have in discourse and more on what problems emerge from the full exercise of these rights, then it is entirely reasonable to show concern over how this evinces a form of worrisome dismissal.

6
Not Listening, to Nietzsche

Thus far, "consideration"—listening, argument, and analysis—has mostly been the hero of our deliberative story. Our lodestar quote has been Gilligan's remark regarding how those with power can opt not to listen with impunity;[1] our imagined reader has been one holding power and our implied tone has been one of reproach when they do elect not to listen.[2] But this is not the complete story.

In the previous chapter, we gestured at some at least facially reasonable rationales for declining to listen and spoke of the important emphasis free speech gives to (at least the possibility of) "averting one's eyes." This chapter delves into this topic more deeply. Typically, the case for not listening is premised on time or resource constraints. Drawing on Nietzsche, I suggest that additionally, at least some of the time, not listening may be an important component of political empowerment. What does it mean for an oppressed person—the downtrodden, the slave, the member of the out-group—to be empowered? Often, to be empowered is to be able to *opt not to listen*—the flip side of the Gilligan quote we have relied upon so regularly. To not have to take orders from a master, to not have to ask "How high?" when commanded to jump—these are markers of empowerment. Under this view, liberation comes not when the powerful start listening to the powerless (thereby ceding their power) but when the powerless no longer feel compelled to listen to the powerful (therefore becoming empowered themselves).

Understanding how, in the right circumstances, *not* listening can be an important component of political freedom does not obviate the dangers of dismissal articulated in the previous chapters. Rather, it identifies a tension and destabilizes a too-simple solution to the above problems—adopting complete and uncomplicated postures of open-minded receptivity to any and all claims and attacking or dismantling whatever structures, conditions, or entitlements enable people to successfully decline to address claims. Certain articulations of

[1] "The 1984 James McCormick Memorial Lecture: Feminist Discourse, Moral Values, and the Law—A Conversation," *Buffalo Law Review* 34, no. 1 (1985): 62. The other participants in the discussion were Ellen G. DuBois, Mary C. Dunlap, Catherine A. MacKinnon, and Carrie J. Menkel-Meadow, with Isabel Marcus and Paul J. Spiegelman moderating.

[2] See Emily Beausoleil, "Listening to Claims of Structural Injustice," *Angelaki: Journal of the Theoretical Humanities* 24, no. 4 (August 2019): 120–35.

Deliberation, Dismissal, and Democracy. David Schraub, Oxford University Press. © Oxford University Press (2025). DOI: 10.1093/9780197816424.003.0007

self-described "free speech culture" sometimes verge on taking such a position—treating virtually *any* circumstance where a deliberator retains or exercises a capacity not to listen (e.g., blocking someone on social media or canceling a subscription to a newsletter with a malign editorial line) as a betrayal of free speech. The claim that such moves are per se breaches of a commitment to free speech is conceptually incoherent and undesirable in practice. But this does not resolve the aforementioned tension—if anything, it deepens it. Shorn of the ability to treat refraining from dismissal as a sort of blanket moral rule, we instead are better off framing our approach as one of cultivating a particular sort of deliberative disposition—an inclination against dismissal, an exercise of the virtue of consideration even when it isn't mandatory and even when it isn't comfortable. It is precisely because there are *not* any hard-and-fast rules that can compel this sort of consideration that it is most important to foster it as a virtue.

What's the Problem with Listening?

Instinctually, we are not often accustomed to viewing free speech or open listening as villains of the deliberative story. More often, we are concerned with encouraging these practices as virtues, as against the vices of dismissiveness or ideological self-sequestering.[3] Yet on further reflection, we all know how the language of free speech and open inquiry is quite often appropriated by individuals or groups seeking to (re)open debate on settled political or moral questions in ways that seem problematic, if not outright toxic. If we hear someone say "I just want to have a free discussion on the Holocaust, where everyone comes in with an open mind and without any presuppositions," our gut reaction is generally not to laud the speaker for their humility and epistemic virtue. Yet it is no accident that the Holocaust denier frequently speaks in precisely these terms: "I just want to ask the question. Why won't you have the debate? What are you afraid of hearing?"[4] When we can think of listening only as an unadulterated good, it is difficult to convey a response to this challenge that does not suggest that we should be less dismissive toward the "hard thought" (the challenger might say) that the Holocaust really was a hoax.

[3] See John D. Inazu, *Confident Pluralism: Surviving and Thriving through Deep Difference* (University of Chicago Press, 2016), 84.

[4] As Robert Wistrich observes, Holocaust deniers often cast their practice in terms of free speech and open inquiry—as in the Committee for Open Debate on the Holocaust, an organization dedicated to placing Holocaust denial tracts at American universities. Robert Wistrich, "Introduction: Lying about the Holocaust," in *Holocaust Denial: The Politics of Perfidy*, ed. Robert Wistrich (de Gruyter, 2012), 18–19. Indeed, the house publisher for David Duke's antisemitic invective is actually named Free Speech Press or Free Speech Books. *See, e.g.*, David Duke, *Jewish Supremacism* (Free Speech Press, 2003); David Duke, *My Awakening* (Free Speech Books, 1998).

So, does the Holocaust denier have a point here? Are those persons who reject his invitation objecting to open-mindedness and free inquiry? To answer that, imagine that someone relates a similar "open inquiry" message about the Holocaust as that given above, but retrospectively: "I came from a community where the Holocaust wasn't really part of our educational system or public discourse, so growing up I didn't know anything about the Holocaust. A few years ago, however, I decided to research it myself—with an open mind and no presuppositions—and I came to the conclusion that the Holocaust did occur, resulting in the death of millions of Jews, in a manner that tracks the general historical consensus and narrative on the subject." In contrast to the person who contemporaneously demands an "open inquiry" about the Holocaust, the reaction to this story would likely be quite positive. Clearly, they were quite earnest in approaching the question with an open mind and no presuppositions—hence why they ultimately came to the conclusion supported by the best available evidence.[5]

The reason we find the call for an open inquiry on the Holocaust suspicious isn't because we are afraid of what the results of such an investigation would be. There is no worry directed toward persons who *actually* engage in unbiased and diligent research about the Holocaust. The reason we are suspicious of the sorts of persons who loudly call for "open inquiry" on the Holocaust is that we strongly suspect the persons calling for such a debate are coming in with an agenda: they have an answer they *hope* to be true (or even—contra their assertion of open-mindedness—already and irrebuttably *believe* to be true), and it is the one that fits with a wider range of unsavory, biased, or otherwise bigoted views about Jews, Jewish history, and Jewish political practice. Put another way, under conditions of deliberative scarcity, the desire (often fervently expressed desire) to place *this particular issue* back onto the deliberative agenda is a motivated one—the idea that the prevailing consensus on the Holocaust is wrong is plausible primarily if not solely because of prejudiced attitudes toward Jews and other victims of Nazi predation.

This might suffice as a reason for why we need not indulge the neo-Nazi in his "just asking the question" parlor game.[6] But I want to suggest that there is a more fundamental connection between *not listening* and human freedom. Return, once again, to Gilligan: those who "have power can opt not to listen.

[5] Of course, given the overwhelming character of the evidence, if someone retrospectively claimed to have engaged in this "investigation without presuppositions" and determined that the Holocaust was a myth, our suspicion would be that they were lying about the lack of presuppositions—or at best, that they were led astray by culpably negligent research practices.

[6] Note that we are still speaking of one's ethical obligation to engage—what in Chapter 5 I described as the "deliberative" register of free speech. It does not necessarily suggest that there should be a juridical carve-out prohibiting the neo-Nazi from speaking. Put another way, this logic justifies closing one's ears, not closing a public forum.

And they do so with impunity." We took that to be an implicit rebuke of the powerful—they need not behave as good deliberative citizens; they can ignore or dismiss their less-advantaged fellows with impunity. And to be sure, that is almost certainly the register that Gilligan meant to evoke.

Yet one can also read that quote in a very different light. If one of the attributes of having power is that one can "opt not to listen" without consequence, it follows that possessing this capacity is an important marker of being *empowered.* Rachel McKinney offers an important countertheme to the idea of freedom of speech—typically presented as giving persons the freedom, means, and opportunity *to* speak—in her discussion of the ability of powerful actors to "extract" speech from the marginalized as a means of facilitating their continued marginalization.[7] A confession elicited under torture would be a prime, albeit extreme, example. More mundane forms might be compelled forms of deference, submissiveness, or obsequiousness, where refusal to engage in this form of "expression" marks one as "angry," uppity, or a troublemaker. We might say, then, that for marginalized individuals freedom of speech is often the freedom *not to speak*—or at least, not to do so on demand or under compulsion.

Similarly, it is a characteristic of being a marginalized group that one is obliged to listen to the demands or the discourse of the powerful. They tune this "expression" out—treating it simply as ambient or background noise, jabbering conspiracy theorizing, or mere ridiculous whining—at their own peril. Under conditions of oppression, even ridiculous or nonsensical (to say nothing of the "merely" unreasonable or unjustifiable) demands of dominant actors nonetheless often require some form of response and so must be listened to attentively. This, too, serves as a counterweight to the more positive and optimistic modes of thinking or listening as a purely salutary and virtuous activity. Given this backdrop, the ability to simply *ignore* more privileged peers can hold significant liberatory potential. Indeed, Jürgen Habermas suggests that this capacity lies at the heart of what it means to be an autonomous subject: "Private autonomy extends as far as the legal subject does *not* have to give others an account or give publicly acceptable reasons for her action plans. Legally granted liberties entitle one to *drop out* of communicative action, to refuse illocutionary obligations; they ground a privacy freed from the burden of reciprocally acknowledged and mutually expected communicative freedoms."[8]

The prior chapters have envisioned a positive discursive climate where participants equally speak and listen to others speak. Here, by contrast, we imagine the capacity to stay silent and ignore the speech of others in turn. Far from

[7] Rachel Ann McKinney, "Extracted Speech," *Social Theory & Practice* 42, no. 2 (2016): 258–84.
[8] Jürgen Habermas, *Between Facts and Norms: Contributions to a Discourse Theory of Law and Democracy* (MIT Press, 1998), 120.

envisioning a polity of mutually engaged, perpetual listeners, here freedom looks to be something quite different (at least some of the time): the ability simply to tune out hostile, disparaging, or even merely discomforting messages. This matters. If we return to the example of the Holocaust denier who "just wants to have a discussion," we can see how important it is as a matter of political freedom that Jewish interlocutors be empowered to *not* engage in the conversation. Insofar as Jewish individuals are effectively compelled, over and over, to listen and respond to the Holocaust denier's assertions, that is highly suggestive of a world where Jewish persons are significantly disempowered such that they felt *forced* to repeatedly defend the bare facts of their own collective genocide.

From here we can gain new perspective on the pained—and in some ways, self-refuting—statement from members of oppressed groups that they should not have to argue for their equal human worth, that there are not "two sides" to oppression, racism, transphobia, and so on. On the one hand, were they in a position not to have to make such an argument, they would likely not be in a condition of oppression to begin with. To speak of an oppressed group is to speak precisely of a group which *does* have to take overt and conscious action to assert and secure its equal social standing. But the reason the plea has resonance is because of how it identifies its end goal. While there may be a great many subjects of political controversy where all one can ask for is the right to participant in collective deliberations as an equal, when it comes to matters of basic human worth this will not suffice. In these contexts, equality doesn't mean the right to participate in arguments *about* equality—even "as an equal." It does not even suffice to prevail on the issue after the argument has concluded. "Equality comes when equality is normal—so normal that you don't have to be perpetually on your guard to defend it. So normal that it wouldn't occur to anyone to try and take it away."[9] And if that may often be utopian in nature, the next best alternative is for equality to be so normal that those who wish to take it away *can* be overlooked and ignored—not listened to—with impunity.

"Not Listening" as Collective Liberation

> ***Europeans, open this book, look inside. After taking a short walk in the night you will see strangers gathered around a fire, get closer and listen. They are discussing the fate reserved for your trading posts and for the mercenaries defending them. They might see you, but they will go on talking among themselves without***

[9] David Schraub, "Post-Racialism and the End of Strict Scrutiny," *Indiana Law Journal* 92, no. 2 (2017): 602.

> *even lowering their voices. Their indifference strikes home: their fathers, creatures living in the shadows, your creatures, were dead souls; you afforded them light, you were their sole interlocutor, you did not take the trouble to answer the zombies. The sons ignore you. The fire that warms and enlightens them is not yours. You, standing at a respectful distance, you now feel eclipsed, nocturnal, and numbed. It's your turn now. In the darkness that will dawn into another day, you have turned into the zombie.*[10]

This is how Jean-Paul Sartre introduces his reader, imagined to be European, to Frantz Fanon's *The Wretched of the Earth*. It unsettles—why? Not for what is said—few details are given. Not because of what is unsaid—the subject is clear enough. What unsettles is the indifference: the natives pay you no heed. Their conversation, like that book, is neither written for European ears nor modulated in the knowledge that European ears are listening. They do not bother to even lower their voices. Those accustomed to being able to ignore the natives now are placed in the uncanny position of being the one who is ignored. The European interlocutor can imagine the natives plotting against him but cannot imagine them being unaffected by his presence. They are supposed to listen to him, listen *for* him, alter their voice and pitch and tenor knowing that he is around.[11] What must have changed to make it possible for them to stop listening for his footsteps?

As mentioned above, a characteristic aspect of oppression is that those in a more marginalized position must take heed of the demands of dominant actors—even if only to better resist them. That the natives aren't doing even this in Sartre's introduction is part of the reason why the image is meant to be so unnerving to the European reader—it speaks to a far more total loss of domination and control than even overt opposition would be. And so at the group level, the desire to (have the capacity to) not listen can be thought of as an important motivator of decolonization movements (particularly when they manifest as a desire for *self*-determination, as opposed to gaining formal equal citizenship within the structure of the colonial power). The resistance by recently decolonized nations in the Global South to the imposition of Western human rights norms can be seen in this light: independence and self-determination exist only if one can simply *ignore* what your former masters demand of you—even if it is expressed as a demand, even if they really insist that you listen to their mandate.[12] Where the "formerly" colonized nations cannot, in practice, ignore these

[10] Jean-Paul Sartre, "Preface," in Frantz Fanon, *The Wretched of the Earth* (Grove, 2004), xlviii.

[11] Consider the act of "code-switching"—speaking in different vernacular in front of in- versus out-group members—in this light. See Vershawn Ashanti Young, "'Nah, We Straight': An Argument against Code Switching," *JAC* 29, nos. 1–2 (2009): 49–76.

[12] Marie-Luisa Frick locates the "unease" in the Global South over Western human rights standards in their still precarious ability to assert autonomy: "In [the] course of decolonization countries

demands, decolonization is not yet complete. Kwame Nkrumah hence defines neocolonialism as a situation where a state is, "in theory, independent and has all the outward trappings of international sovereignty [but] [i]n reality its economic system and thus its political policy is directed from outside."[13]

Strength and empowerment here take on a Nietzschean tenor. Freedom means the freedom to cavalierly ignore those who are accustomed to being listened to. Much as the "private" space is one in which "publicly acceptable reasons do not have to be given,"[14] so too can political autonomy at the group level be conceptualized as the freedom to not have to justify oneself to an external authority. It is a freedom of indifference. And this Nietzschean understanding seems significantly reflected in the praxis of 20th-century national liberation movements. These movements can be understood as, at least in part, seeking the ability to have the option to not listen to the hitherto dominant groups.[15]

Returning to Gilligan's line, it seems clear that—stripped of its egalitarian gloss—Nietzsche would endorse wholeheartedly the descriptive thrust of the passage. Hawks do not need to listen to the bleating of little lambs. (Lambs, by contrast, must pay keen attention to the cries of the hawks.)[16] What is mistaken, for Nietzsche, is the thought that this creates a moral claim on behalf of the lambs against the hawks—that the bird of prey is "*accountable* for being a bird of prey."[17] The slave revolt in morality begins by taking an attribute of the lambs—the fact that they have to listen—and demanding it of the hawks: they, we are told, "have" to listen as well, because that's what justice demands.

The concept of accountability seems closely related to the genesis of the "bad conscience" Nietzsche develops in the second essay of *The Genealogy of Morals*—namely, its growth out of the creditor-debtor relationship. As he puts it, "[T]he feeling of guilt, of personal obligation, had its origin . . . in the oldest and most primitive personal relationship, that between buyer and seller, creditor and debtor: it was here that one person first encountered another person,

of the global South may have (re-)gained political autonomy, but hardly any economic independence, and—according to many—still less independence from Western epistemic hegemony." Marie-Luisa Frick, "Universal Claim and Postcolonial Realities: The Deep Unease over Western Centered Human Rights Standards in the Global South," in *Human Rights and the Third World: Issues and Discourses*, ed. Subrata Sankar Bagchi and Arnab Das (Lexington, 2013), 16.

[13] Kwame Nkrumah, *Neo-Colonialism: The Last Stage of Imperialism* (International, 1965), ix.

[14] Shane O'Neill, "The Politics of Inclusive Agreements: Towards a Critical Discourse Theory of Democracy," *Political Studies* 48, no. 3 (2000): 507.

[15] To be clear, my goal is not to defend nationalism, or even these particular forms of nationalism, as being wholly amenable to Nietzsche's outlook. Contrary to some later exploitations, Nietzsche was very much not a nationalist. See Walter Kaufmann, ed., *The Portable Nietzsche* (Penguin, 1982), 442 ("Being nationalistic, in the sense in which it is now demanded by public opinion would, it seems to me, be for us who are more spiritual not mere insipidity but dishonesty, a deliberate deadening of our better will and conscience."). But I do want to say that this particular characteristic at least echoes some of Nietzsche's important themes in interesting ways.

[16] See Friedrich Nietzsche, *On the Genealogy of Morals* (Vintage, 1989), 44–45 (I §13).

[17] *Id.* at 45 (I §13).

that one person first *measured himself* against another."[18] *Ressentiment* is about calling in an imagined debt—the little lamb demanding the hawk account for its misdeeds.

At first blush, one could associate the creditor stance with being master—being able to compel others to pay for their wrongs. Certainly the slaves conceive of it this way: Nietzsche states that when a person low in the social order is allowed to take on the role of the creditor and *punish* those who have wronged him (even if that punishment is simply the ceded authority to hate the wrong-doer), it will appear to him as "a foretaste of higher rank. In 'punishing' the debtor, the creditor participates in a *right of the masters*."[19]

Yet elsewhere Nietzsche is clear that the creditor is by no means a true master. Hawks, after all, do not devour lambs as *payment for misdeeds*. Believing mastery to lie in an entitlement owed by another is to substitute slave morality for master morality. The concept of not needing to listen is closer to the mark and emerges in a telling passage about Mirabeau:

> To be incapable of taking one's enemies, one's accidents, even one's misdeeds seriously for very long—that is the sign of strong natures in whom there is an excess of the power to form, to mold, to recuperate and to forget (a good example of this in modern times is Mirabeau, who had no memory for insults and vile actions done him and was unable to forgive simply because he—forgot). Such a man shakes off with a *single* shrug many vermin that eat deep into others; here alone genuine "love of one's enemies" is possible—supposing it to be possible at all on earth.[20]

Nietzsche continues with this theme when discussing mercy. "As the power and self-confidence of a community increase, the penal law always becomes more moderate"—why? Because an individual's transgressions "can no longer be considered as dangerous and destructive to the whole as they were formerly."[21] Whereas a weak community cannot afford to let its debts go unredeemed, the strong man can forgive the debts and—eventually—ignore them altogether. The apex of this development comes when society gains such a "*consciousness of power* that it could allow itself the noblest luxury possible to it—letting those who harm it go *unpunished*. 'What are my parasites to me?' it might say. 'May they live and prosper: I am strong enough for that!'"[22]

[18] *Id.* at 70 (II §8).
[19] *Id.* at 65 (II §5).
[20] *Id.* at 39 (I §10).
[21] *Id.* at 72 (II §10).
[22] *Id.* On this passage, consider Michael Ure, "The Politics of Mercy, Forgiveness, and Love: A Nietzschean Appraisal," *South African Journal of Philosophy* 26, no. 1 (2007): 63, who argues instead

To stay in the role of the creditor is ultimately to still feel compelled to listen to another—first, to see if they are paying their debt and, later, to bask in their gratitude as one magnanimously discharges it. The one who is strong has overcome this need—they do not avenge slights but forget them, they do not collect debts (or even forgive debts) because they feel no need to issue them in the first place. If they are "wronged" by parasites, they pay no mind because they are strong enough to shrug off such nips and bites without a thought.

Consider in this light the 20th-century American civil rights movement. The celebrated liberal iteration, promoted by Martin Luther King Jr., was focused on calling White people to account. They had engaged in injustice, and they owed Black people recompense (even if that recompense was simply reforming their behavior to end racist mistreatment). Dr. King explicitly used the language of credit and debt in his "I have a dream speech": "When the architects of our republic wrote the magnificent words of the Constitution and the Declaration of Independence, they were signing a promissory note to which every American was to fall heir. . . . It is obvious today that America has defaulted on this promissory note insofar as her citizens of color are concerned."[23]

The civil rights movement, in its establishment liberal manifestation, primarily focused on changing White people—getting Whites to stop being racist. King's invocation of a creditor-debtor relationship is, under the Nietzschean view, precisely the wrong framework for securing true Black empowerment. And so when the Black Power movement challenged the liberal orthodoxy, this was its key point of departure.[24] As Kwame Ture and Charles Hamilton put it, "The civil rights leaders were saying to the country: 'Look, you guys are supposed to be nice guys, and we are only going to do what we are supposed to do. Why do you beat us up? Why don't you give us what we ask? Why don't you straighten yourselves out?' For the masses of black people, this language resulted in virtually

that the lesson to be drawn is that unconditional forgiveness can be extended only to those one views as vermin, parasites, or otherwise subhuman. See also Jean-Jacques Rousseau's advice to the Poles regarding how they should view the Russians: "I should not wish, however, that any invectives against the Russians, or even any mention of them, be permitted at these solemnities; it would be doing them too much honor. This silence . . . will say all that needs to be said about them: you ought to despise them too much to hate them." Jean-Jacques Rousseau, "Considerations on the Government of Poland," in *Jean-Jacques Rousseau: Political Writings*, ed. and trans. Frederick Watkins (University of Wisconsin Press, 1986), 170.

[23] Martin Luther King Jr., "I Have a Dream," August 28, 1963, http://www.ushistory.org/documents/i-have-a-dream.htm.

[24] King also drew the connection between Nietzsche and the Black Power movement, contending that both placed "love" and "power" in a false binary with one another. Martin Luther King Jr., *A Testament of Hope: The Essential Writings and Speeches of Martin Luther King, Jr.*, ed. James Melvin (Harper & Row, 1991), 247. *See* James M. Patterson, "A Covenant of the Heart: Martin Luther King Jr., Civil Disobedience, and the Beloved Community," *American Political Thought* 7, no. 1 (2018): 145n23, for discussion.

nothing."[25] The alternative proffered by the Black Power and Black Nationalist movements was to cease appealing to White people and instead place Black people in a position to control their own destiny, regardless of whether Whites were racist or not. The Black Nationalist mantra, "Do for self," is a testament to this ambition.[26] It is not a call for selfishness. It is a reminder to the Black community that they should take action not to please White people or look good in front of White people or be respectable before White people. One may well end up taking actions that are generous and amenable to White interests, but the reason one does them should be inwardly motivated.

One can tell a similar story about Jewish liberation in an overlapping period.[27] A prominent manifestation of the non-Zionist Jewish political efforts aimed at securing Jewish equality in the United States, Europe, and the Middle East was classically liberal in character. Jews sought to convince non-Jewish-dominated polities to include Jews as equals. Separate church and state, eliminate religious tests for offices, stop beating us up, form a neutral state and polity that includes Jews as equals. These were, in Ture and Hamilton's terms, calls for non-Jews to "straighten yourselves out." And between the Holocaust in Europe and the mass expulsions of Jews from the Middle East, it is fair to say that (at least outside America) "this language resulted in virtually nothing."

The Zionist movement, by contrast, was not primarily focused on getting non-Jews to straighten themselves out. It was designed to create a new type of Jew, a strong Jew. Sometimes this conception of "strength" was decidedly nonphilosophical—a buff, muscular, well-armed sabra Jew in contrast to the weak, nebbish, effeminate shtetl Jew who cowers in his Yeshiva as the Cossacks approach. But Zionism also conceptualized a more political form of Jewish strength in the formation of a sovereign state which was entitled to the immunity and autonomy that had long been denied to Jews. The establishment of the state of Israel represented the first time in over a millennium that Jews possessed a space where, in any realistic sense, they could opt not to listen to non-Jewish overlords. Zionism and Black Power thus both represent a type of Nietzschean nationalism[28]—a nationalism based on enabling groups to exercise this power not to listen.

[25] Kwame Ture and Charles V. Hamilton, *Black Power: The Politics of Liberation* (Vintage, 1992), 50–51.

[26] See, e.g., Clarence Thomas, *My Grandfather's Son: A Memoir* (HarperCollins, 2007), 62 ("I never went along with the militant separatism of the Black Muslims, but I admired their determination to 'do for self, brother,' as well as their discipline and dignity. . . . [T]o be truly free and participate fully in American life, poor blacks had to have the tools to do for themselves.").

[27] On the connection between Black Power and Zionism, *see* Marc Dollinger, *Black Power, Jewish Politics: Reinventing the Alliance in the 1960s* (Brandeis University Press, 2018), ch. 6.

[28] Again, I want to stress that I am not arguing that Nietzsche would endorse even this form of nationalism. I mean once again to spotlight the thematic overlap between Nietzsche's understanding of power (and empowerment) and this particular impetus for a form of nationalism. Others have identified this overlap as well, while not necessarily claiming a direct affinity between these

To be sure, Nietzschean nationalism need not be separatist—it can be in a step toward integration. The original Black Panthers were a political party, after all. Ture and Hamilton's core ideology was that "*Before a group can enter the open society, it must first close ranks.* . . . [G]roup solidarity is necessary before a group can operate effectively from a bargaining position of strength in a pluralistic society."[29] The difference between integration and supplication is whether one is wholly at the mercy of what others put on offer. One *can* enter open society as an equal only if one does not *have* to, if others must bargain with one as much as one must appeal to them. Actual integration occurs when there is equipoise between all parties' capacity to enter into and withdraw from deliberative engagements with the other, the freedom to do the latter underpinning the genuinely voluntary decision to do the former. Nietzsche does not view his higher man as being ignorant or unhearing; to the contrary, in *The Gay Science* he tells us, "Higher human beings distinguish themselves from the lower by seeing and hearing, and *thoughtfully* seeing and hearing, immeasurably more."[30] But, as Brian Leiter argues, what this reflects is a *capacity* to hear more that can and should be used thoughtfully and judiciously.[31]

What a Nietzschean nationalist cannot do is shun power—at least, not without returning to a state of disempowerment and dependence. It is worth teasing out exactly what this means, however. Gilligan's formulation is that power allows one to *opt* not to listen—it does not *demand* that the powerful not listen to others or *require* that they plunder the interests and desires and bodies of their fellows. Does Nietzsche agree? He attacks the idea of separating "strength from expressions of strength, as if there were a neutral substratum behind the strong man, which was free to express strength or not to do so."[32] Even more harshly: "To demand of strength that it should *not* express itself as strength, that it should *not* be a desire to overcome, a desire to throw down, a desire to become master, a thirst for enemies and resistances and triumphs, is just as absurd as to demand of weakness that it should express itself as strength."[33] Power is as it does, so it seems at first glance that Nietzsche condemns the putatively powerful who refuse to act upon the power—who keep their gun holstered.

But consider the illustration Nietzsche uses to emphasize the point. Nietzsche claims it is impossible "that the strong man is free to be weak and the bird of prey

nationalist impulses and Nietzsche's own beliefs. *See, e.g.*, Eddie Glaude, *Is It Nation Time? Contemporary Essays on Black Power and Black Nationalism* (University of Chicago Press, 2002), 5, n8; Jacob Golomb, *Nietzsche and Zion* (Cornell University Press, 2004).

29 Ture and Hamilton, *Black Power*, 44.

30 Friedrich Nietzsche, *The Gay Science*, ed. Bernard Williams (Cambridge University Press, 2001), 170 (§301).

31 Brian Leiter, "Nietzsche and the Morality Critics," *Ethics* 107, no. 2 (January 1997): 282.

32 Nietzsche, *Genealogy*, 45 (I §13).

33 *Id.*

to be a lamb."[34] What makes the lamb a lamb? It is not that the lamb listens to the hawk; it's that the lamb *has no choice* but to listen to the hawk. It would be strange for Nietzsche to define power in such a way as to radically restrict the choices available to the strong man. But it makes perfect sense to say that one cannot lose the *choice* not to listen while still pretending to possess power. Power means one can opt not to listen—with the potential for all the terrible implications that flow from Gilligan's initial, more egalitarian read of the phrase. If one loses that capacity—the ability to choose to ignore others—one no longer has power.

There is no such thing as a weapon that can be used only for defense. The same tools that empower us to not listen and to determine the contours of our own lives also allow us to attempt unjust dominion over others. Ture and Hamilton were perfectly cognizant of the risk and accepted it: they were quite forthright that while the purpose of Black Power was not to dominate White people, it is impossible to give Blacks power without also creating, at least in some spaces, the potential for such domination.[35] Consider how Melanie Kaye/Kantrowitz discusses nonviolence in response to abuse: if you can't even conceptualize committing violence (let alone if you lack the physical tools to do so), you're not a pacifist, you're just weak. Pacifism is a choice only if you can imagine and are capable of plunging the knife in first.[36]

It is also interesting to consider how groups with power have responded to these very different (liberal vs. nationalist) challenges. When the challenge takes on the standard liberal tones, the retort is simple enough: either deny the debt or assert it has already been discharged. (Witness Justice Antonin Scalia's implied rebuke to Dr. King: "[U]nder our Constitution there can be no such thing as either a creditor or a debtor race.")[37] But the Nietzschean argument does not rest on any sort of unpaid debt. It is not directed at the putative masters at all. It seeks nothing more than for those who were previously compelled to listen to the masters to instead possess the power to opt not to. It skirts the creditor-debtor framework entirely.

Yet this creates *ressentiment* of its own, and of a very particular sort. The hawk that imperiously proclaimed his mastery over the sheep will find he has lost something very precious indeed if lambs really become able to opt not to listen to the hawks. For centuries, knowing that the other *had to listen* was part of the cultural patrimony that Whites possessed over Blacks and that Christians and Muslims possessed over Jews. When that perceived entitlement to compel consideration—in effect, to dominate—is undermined, of course it will be felt as

[34] *Id.*

[35] Ture and Hamilton, *Black Power*, 47–49.

[36] Melanie Kaye/Kantrowitz, "Women, Violence, and Resistance," in *The Issue Is Power: Essays on Women, Jews, Violence and Resistance* (Aunt Lute Books, 1992), 20.

[37] Adarand Constr., Inc. v. Pena, 515 U.S. 200, 239 (1995) (Scalia, J., concurring).

a loss. And this loss is in many ways far more biting than whatever behavioral changes the liberals might have requested. The liberals, after all, still come as supplicants, still accept the basic hierarchy that accepts who has authority to dictate terms (even if the terms do turn out to be perfectly benevolent or egalitarian).

And here, often, we do see the hawks start to act like lambs, and assume that the motivating instinct that inflicts this terrible loss upon them must be a desire to punish—an even more extreme and outrageous claim of debt to coincide with a greater and more painful loss of patrimony. Consider the argument, made most prominently by former Dutch prime minister Dries van Agt, that Israel should have been created in Germany because "the Middle East had nothing to do with World War II."[38] The wrong people are being punished! I have never once heard any Jew—Zionist or anti-Zionist—suggest that Israel should have been created in Germany, because Jews never thought of Israel as punishment for goyish misdeeds. Israel wasn't established as a form of reparation; Israel was established in order to create a space where—for the first time in modern history—Jewish day-to-day politics were not an exercise in compulsory listening to non-Jews. It is a product of gentile *ressentiment* to be unable to conceptualize Zionism as anything but an effort to extract a pound of flesh. The Black Power movement endured a similar framing in the White imagination—they presented it as an even more radical claim against White people rather than a transcending of the creditor-debtor frame altogether.

While I attempt here to give a corrective to the presumption that more consideration is always better, and give a valid positive account of the virtues of not listening, we should not swing too far in the opposite direction. Explaining why not listening holds liberatory potential does not erase the dangers and vices that accompany the practice. Many have criticized the Black Power movement for stifling internal diversity under the guise of solidarity.[39] Such risks are not obviated by the fact that African Americans were and are responding to an ongoing system of oppression. For one, the censorial burden at issue may be especially acute for internal minorities who face structures of oppression from within the minority group as well as from the outside—this alone complicates any attempt to claim that an uncritical solidaritistic impulse is necessary for collective liberation. But beyond that, history is replete with examples of hitherto oppressed groups engaged in a genuine anticolonial or liberationist struggle using that status in ways which re-create different patterns of domination, censorship, or authoritarianism.

[38] "Former Dutch PM: Jews Should Have Had a State in Germany," *Times of Israel*, November 11, 2012, https://www.timesofisrael.com/former-dutch-pm-jews-shouldve-had-a-state-in-germany/.

[39] See Michael C. Dawson, "A Black Counterpublic? Economic Earthquakes, Racial Agenda(s), and Black Politics," in *The Black Public Sphere*, ed. Black Public Sphere Collective (University of Chicago Press, 1995), 206.

The example of Zionism perhaps illustrates this in stark fashion. Albert Memmi, the great Tunisian Jewish scholar of colonialism and decolonization, was emphatic in identifying Zionism as a remedy for Jewish colonization, with Israel representing "*the still-precarious result of the liberation of the Jew, just as decolonization represents the liberation of the Arab or black peoples of Asia and Africa.*"[40] But Zionism's empowerment of Jews "not to listen with impunity" includes a capacity to not listen to Palestinians, whom it has placed under a decades-long occupation, as well as to critical international legal and political institutions which are increasingly vocal in insisting that Israel's conduct toward the Palestinian people is incompatible with basic universal human rights commitments. This impulse towards refusing to listen manifests, among other ways, in the contention that Jews should be able to unilaterally impose a "solution" onto the Israeli-Palestinian conflict, without much if any in the way of consideration of Palestinian positions, claims, or interests.[41] It can be more radical and vicious still: writing in *Tablet Magazine*, Jeremy England endorses carte blanche authority for Israel to kill Palestinian civilians and permanently conquer Palestinian territories, by labeling the entirety of the international human rights legal corpus as part of a "lingering ideological subjugation to the Western tradition": "Israel must stop pretending it is a nation like any other, begging to be judged fairly by whatever standards the current hegemon has decreed we all agree upon. We need to look [instead] for standards from within our tradition to set a moral example for the whole world."[42] In turn, the status of Israeli Jews claiming a right to "not listen with impunity" generates counterentitlement among some Palestinian liberationists, who likewise contend that respecting Palestinian

[40] Albert Memmi, *Jews and Arabs*, trans. Eleanor Levieux (J. Philip O'Hara, 1975), 96 (emphasis original). Memmi thus defined a Zionist as "anyone, Jew or non-Jew, who, having found that the Jewish situation is a situation of oppression, looks upon the reconstruction of a Jewish state as legitimate: so as to put an end to that oppression and so that Jews, like other peoples, may retrieve their dimensions as free men." Even more bluntly: a Zionist is "anyone who considers the liberation of the Jews as a Jew desirable." *Id.* at 97.

[41] See, e.g., Seth J. Frantzman, "How Can Israel Win the Palestinian Conflict? Historian Explains," *Jerusalem Post*, January 7, 2023, https://www.jpost.com/arab-israeli-conflict/article-726743 (quoting Daniel Pipes arguing that "a just resolution of the conflict requires the Palestinians to lose hope. Only when they give up their war goal of eliminating Israel will the conflict come to an end. Israel must win and the Palestinians must lose."); Martin Indyk, "Biden Can Clean Up Trump's Israeli-Palestinian Policy Mess, but Can He Broker Peace?," *NBC News*, November 17, 2020, https://www.nbcnews.com/think/opinion/biden-can-clean-trump-s-israeli-palestinian-policy-mess-not-ncna1247996 (describing Donald Trump's proposed "Deal of the Century" as an "attempt to impose a solution on the Palestinians. It was conceived without consulting them and came down on Israel's side on all the final-status issues.").

[42] Jeremy England, "Live by the Law or Die on the Cross," *Tablet Magazine*, May 28, 2024, https://www.tabletmag.com/sections/news/articles/live-law-die-cross-israel. I do not think it is a coincidence that England begins his column with a description of his parents as former Marxist revolutionaries, and his own upbringing "marinating in progressive ideas." *Id.*

empowerment means an affirmative refusal by putative "allies" to critique or otherwise police Palestinian choices regarding what liberation looks like or how it might be achieved.[43]

Recognizing these cross-cutting pressures may still help to illuminate the ferocity which greets international legal and political pressure targeting Israel's military campaign in Gaza, and the occupation and treatment of Palestinians more broadly. From one vantage point, this campaign is simply an enforcement of universal legal and moral principles to which all members of the international community should be forced to adhere. Israel's refusal to heed the overwhelming consensus of the international community is a threat to the entire notion of a "rules-based" international order.[44] From another vantage, the obsession outside actors have with bringing Israel to heel is simply a desire to restore a lost patrimony where Jew was forced to listen to gentile. The frustration felt by Israel's "flouting" the international community is a frustration that Jews, in a collective capacity, no longer sit in their historically subjugated position of needing to listen—in other words, it is antisemitic resentment at losing a form of dominance.[45] And from yet a third perspective, that the campaign for Palestinian rights is not modulating its rhetoric or demands in order to accommodate the tender feelings of Israeli and diaspora Jews, is reflective of Palestinians coming into their own power—after however many years of being forced to publicly aver condemnations of "terrorism" or recognize "Israel's right to exist" before (maybe) being permitted to stake claims,[46] now they can, at least to some extent, "opt not listen" and press their arguments via whatever means or mechanisms they feel are most appropriate or most effective.

[43] See, e.g., Charlotte Silver, "Corrie Lawyers Expose Army Smear Campaign against ISM," *Electronic Intifada*, May 26, 2011, https://electronicintifada.net/content/corrie-lawyers-expose-army-smear-campaign-against-ism/10014 ("We [the International Solidarity Movement] are very careful not to be colonial activists, not telling Palestinians how to resist, or what they need to do.").

[44] See H. A. Hellyer, "How Joe Biden Sabotaged the 'Rules-Based Order,'" *Foreign Policy*, May 10, 2024, https://foreignpolicy.com/2024/05/10/biden-israel-gaza-arms-rules-based-order/.

[45] This, of course, echoes critiques of human rights enforcement leveled by many Third World/Global South nations that have likewise presented these demands as efforts to reinscribe colonial domination. Appropriating from Nkrumah, the widespread international pressure and compulsion on Israel (as the Jewish state) to alter its policies toward the Palestinians would be read instead as a means of leveraging economic and political power to restore a prior state of affairs where Jewish life was being "directed from outside" and Jewish sovereignty reduced to a mere "trapping." *See* Nkrumah, *Neocolonialism*, ix.

[46] Consider, in this vein, how Rep. Charlie Rangel (D-NY) responded to demands on Black Americans to condemn Louis Farrakhan. Confronted with an antisemitic statement by Farrakhan (that Judaism is a "dirty religion"), Rangel agreed that the statement was "garbage" but also expressed concern that condemnation of Farrakhan was being treated as a "passbook" Black Americans needed to carry in order to discuss any issue of concern to the Black community. Discussed in Derrick Bell, *Faces at the Bottom of the Well: The Permanence of Racism* (Basic Books, 1992), 120.

The problem is that all three positions have some validity to them. The notion that Palestinians must wait for Israelis (or anyone else) to write them a permission slip before they may advocate for their own liberation is untenable. The probability that the historic entitlement non-Jews have had to dictate Jewish practice would manifest as fury and frustration at Jewish self-determination is undeniable. And the position that any nation—of whatever background or genealogy—can claim exemption from the basic rules of international governance is unacceptable. So we're left with the problem of how to accommodate a series of dueling intuitions. One possibility is to retreat into a naïve cosmopolitanism which rejects any claimed entitlement "not to listen" wholesale as incompatible with one's civic obligations; the account above was an effort to explain why that approach is unlikely to be successful or viewed as acceptable by its putative targets. Another flawed attempt to traverse the problem is to try to organize by fiat who is and is not entitled to "not listen" based on some notion of ideological or tribal congeniality, so we can say that, for example, only Israel is entitled to "not listen" to Palestinians specifically or global critics generally (or vice versa).[47] This simply tries to wave away someone's valid deliberative entitlements and right to autonomous self-determination; it is essentially a mechanism of avoiding a hard thought (typically, either that antisemitism is an inextricable factor in global perceptions of Israel and Zionism or that making Palestinian equality and self-determination contingent on Israeli approval is incontestably a form of unjust political domination). In this context or any other, we cannot either uncritically accept a "right not to listen" (for anyone), nor can we gainsay the important political values such a right seeks to instantiate. Instead, we need to cultivate a set of proper deliberative virtues fully cognizant of the competing pressures that rest on both sides of the ledger.

This call for complexity may seem intolerably wooly given the rapidly accelerating humanitarian crisis in the Gaza Strip, which as of this writing includes the Trump administration's openly promoting, to a receptive audience in the Israeli government, ethnic cleansing as its preferred conclusion to the

[47] The argument that some on the left try to divide the world into "oppressor" versus "oppressed," giving the latter unlimited deference and the former unbridled condemnation, is in essence a claim that just this mistake is being made. It is common in some Jewish circles to allege that such a taxonomy is responsible for an allegedly disproportionate focus on Israeli misdeeds. See, e.g., David L. Bernstein, *Woke Antisemitism: How a Progressive Ideology Harms Jews* (Wicked Son, 2022). For the most part, I think this critique is too simplistic (particularly once it extends itself outside of cloistered radical activists and presents itself as a mainstream moral zeitgeist). But a more fundamental problem is that, overwhelmingly, critics who make these claims pair them with a demand for heightened deference to Israeli and Jewish concerns as necessary accommodations for historical and ongoing antisemitism. In other words, their complaint is not with an "oppressor"/"oppressed" binary; it is that they think Jews and Israelis should properly be sorted into the latter category and are not receiving the bounty they're owed.

war in Gaza.[48] In such a circumstance, it is quite appropriate to impose limits on sovereign autonomy—whether objected to as "colonial" or not. But the point is that it is far too convenient to pretend that the dangers (and atrocities) we are trying to avert bear no connection to the promotion of "not listening" as a political virtue, including "not listening" by a group whose oppression historically very much took the form of being compelled to listen. Just as an uncritical insistence on always "having to listen" overlooks how such insistences can re-create patterns of domination, it also must be admitted that uncritical valorization of autonomously ignoring the demands of others—including in circumstances where that autonomy stands in contrast to a historical practice of subjugation—can license human rights atrocities of the most vicious sort.

[48] See Matthew Lee and Natalie Melzer, "Israel's Netanyahu Signals He's Moving Ahead with Trump's Idea to Transfer Palestinians from Gaza," AP, February 16, 2025, https://apnews.com/article/israel-palestinians-hamas-war-news-ceasefire-hostages-02-15-2025-1cf8b3cb7622489c368c610f85e51e35.

7

Cultivating (and Preserving) the Virtues of Deliberation

In conjunction with the preceding chapters, we now have both horns of the dilemma firmly in hand. On the one hand, good democratic citizenship requires that people listen and consider arguments and claims that are hard and which they'd rather avoid. On the other hand, political freedom insists that persons must be empowered to opt not to listen. These two demands cannot be reconciled into any sort of formalized rule (whether legal or ethical) regarding political consideration. Rather, they suggest the need for political and social arrangements that foster deliberative *virtues* (and diminish vices). What sort of arrangements might these be?

In this chapter, I concentrate on three important virtue categories relevant to a proper orientation toward dismissal. The first is the importance of feeling free to speak one's mind—but also of being taught when it is best to remain silent. "Self-censorship" can speak to an overly restrictive speech culture, but it also can reflect the mature recognition that not every thought one has must immediately and without reflection be aired. The second is the importance of epistemic friction. An unanticipated consequence of the leveling of access to deliberative spaces brought on by social media and the rise of the "citizen journalist" has been the removal of markers of authority that distinguish credible from uncredible sources. Where every speaker is equal and the same, there is little reason to prefer one speaker over another save how they cohere to one's preexisting political biases. One benefit of social diversity is that it provides a sort of epistemic "bumpiness" that can resist this otherwise stultifying homogeny paradoxically exacerbated by (a form of) deliberative equality. The third is the judicious usage of mechanisms through which one can temporarily and provisionally withdraw from debate. While often criticized (particularly when such mechanisms are given the name "safe spaces"), the existence of such opportunities is in fact essential to a healthy deliberative life—*so long as* they are appropriately limited in scope. What we should concentrate on is not whether "safe spaces" exist but rather on which sorts of deliberator are most liable to overuse them—that is, who is most likely to be able to permanently cocoon themselves off from grappling with hard thoughts. From this vantage point, it is dominant majorities who

Deliberation, Dismissal, and Democracy. David Schraub, Oxford University Press. © Oxford University Press (2025). DOI: 10.1093/9780197816424.003.0008

seem clearly most able to abuse the privilege—but this outlook does flag the risk that the salutary desire to expand marginalized communities' access to safe spaces could convert into an envy for the iniquitous capacity majorities have to insulate themselves from the proper (but not always pleasant) virtues of public deliberation.

The Virtues of Speaking Freely and of Staying Silent

It is sometimes asserted that the necessary virtues to be taught in order to create a healthy deliberative climate are straightforward. Teach learners (particularly young students) to welcome vigorous debate and avoid denigrating or disparaging dissident ideas—simple. Bonnie Snyder, director of high school programs at what was then known as the Foundation for Individual Rights in Education,[1] promotes this approach while railing against a "restrictive culture" of self-censorship surrounding speech in schools, one where "students are clearly on notice that certain opinions are best not expressed, unless you're willing to risk consequences ranging from mild social disapproval to abject humiliation or even outright ejection."[2] Students are acculturated into the latter set of habits at an early age, so that by the time they are in a position to direct their own learning, they are suspicious of open discourse and inquiry and lack the ability or the temperament to handle divergent views.

I do not want to wholly dismiss Snyder's concerns here. Speaking freely—even, or especially, when one does not believe one's view already commands the majority—is a skill, and it is one that requires cultivation. As already discussed, Mill was acutely aware of how the pressures of custom can exert a censorial effect as strong as, if not stronger than, even the formal hand of the magistrate. And Elisabeth Noelle-Neumann's "spiral of silence" cogently demonstrates how unwillingness to air a view that is (or is thought to be) unpopular can have cascading effects that narrow the bounds of important conversations.[3] Kristie Dotson's influential account of "testimonial smothering," the "truncating of one's own testimony in order to insure that the testimony contains only content for which one's audience demonstrates testimonial competence," is also germane to problematic self-censorship, though, perhaps unsurprisingly, it is not typically categorized under that rubric by those who profess most concern about the latter

[1] Bonnie Snyder is also the author of *Undoctrinate: How Politicized Classrooms Harm Kids and Ruin Our Schools—And What We Can Do about It* (Bombardier, 2021).

[2] Bonnie Snyder, "Taking the Battle for Free Speech to K–12," *Volokh Conspiracy*, September 20, 2021, https://reason.com/volokh/2021/09/20/taking-the-battle-for-free-speech-to-k-12/.

[3] Elisabeth Noelle-Neumann, *The Spiral of Silence: A Theory of Public Opinion—Our Social Skin* (University of Chicago Press, 1984).

topic.[4] Where speakers know both that the relevant listeners lack the competency to accurately take up the speaker's intended meaning, and that the listeners generally will not recognize their own ignorance and so will barrel ahead with an incorrect and typically pernicious ascribed meaning (this tracks the problem of "replacement epistemology" I discuss in Chapter 3), the speaker may well self-censor to avoid that problematic outcome. This practice (which is most likely to be endured by socially marginalized speakers) ends up diminishing our collective ability to hear and consider important testimony over hard thoughts and certainly is something a healthy deliberative system should try to ameliorate.[5]

The previous chapter, however, should already have demonstrated why an account that solely views "self-censorship" as a problem to be overcome is far too simplistic. The wide range in the putative "consequences" dissident speakers face—mild disapproval is one thing, outright ejection is very much another—is a powerful hint that more nuance may be required. It is likely impossible to prevent "certain opinions" from evincing at least "mild social disapproval." More than that: it is almost certainly *undesirable* to obstruct that reaction; in a different mood, defenders of free speech might well suggest *precisely* acts of social disapproval as a means of countering hostile or repugnant speech, as a replacement for more obviously censorial acts (such as "outright ejection"). Snyder's worries about self-censorship rapidly collapse in on themselves—what happens when the student suppresses their instinctive feelings of disapproval toward speech for fear of appearing, as per a given zeitgeist, intolerant or censorial? Condemnation, censuring (note the spelling), disappointment, disgust—these too are all dimensions of speech. If Snyder promotes a sort of brute free speech liberalism in the classroom, she also threatens to create the sort of student who is "liberal" in the classic aphorism of one "afraid to take his own side in an argument."

The fact is that certain opinions *are* best not expressed, and part—only part, but an important part—of cultivating a healthy relationship with speech is teaching students to self-regulate and learn what not to say.[6] Likewise, students must also learn how to effectively serve as evaluators and appraisers of the speech of others—a role which sometimes does entail signaling dissatisfaction and disapproval. A student who, as a speaker, emerges from the educational system with the belief that they should spit out any thought that enters their mind, with no

[4] Kristie Dotson, "Tracking Epistemic Violence, Tracking Practices of Silence," *Hypatia* 26, no. 2 (2011): 244.

[5] Though less prominent in the public zeitgeist, there is research that suggests liberal and minority individuals also must self-censor or quiet their own speech due to social pressure stemming from conservative or majority actors. *See* Finlay Malcolm, "Silencing and Freedom of Speech in UK Higher Education." *British Educational Research Journal* 47, no. 3 (June 2021): 520–38.

[6] John Horton, "Self-Censorship," *Res Publica* 17, no. 1 (2011): 101.

regard for its propriety, how it will be received, or how it might affect others, should not be our model of a free speech success story. Neither is the student who, as a listener, is capable of offering only a bland affective neutrality toward all the speech they encounter.

The model that most closely suggests the sorts of skills young people need to develop regarding speech is the case of the editor. Recall the dilemma, discussed in previous chapters, that editors face on a daily basis in their job—needing to present arguments and positions that do not simply mimic the views they or their readers already hold, while also needing to be critical evaluators capable of adjudging certain (perhaps many) potential contributions as unworthy of debate. No editor adopts a "take all comers" orientation toward prospective submissions, but good editors can differentiate between an idea they disagree with substantively but that merits discussion and one that deserves to be tossed in the trash outright. The problem is that one can easily use the importance of identifying the former to elide the obligation to dispense with the latter—*and vice versa*. Editors can just as easily hide behind the skirt of "open-mindedness" to justify publishing utter dreck as they can launder their raw personal preferences through a façade of critical judgment. Handling these twin obligations adroitly is a skill, and one best inculcated young—but it does no favors to view either side of the ledger as the sole capacity that needs development.

For this reason, Shannon Rea suggests that the term "self-censorship" be supplanted by the more value-neutral "refrainment from speech."[7] Certainly refrainment from speech can be bad if done for the wrong reasons—such as unjustified social stigma, fear of unwarranted retaliation, or even concern of immediate and degrading dismissal. But we should not presuppose that the reasons someone refrains from speaking are necessarily bad. Sometimes they are reflective of important deliberative virtues—self-control, humility, and a willingness to learn more before stepping onto controversial terrain. Indeed, some of these practices of "self-censorship" actually can net out to increasing the ability of all participants to speak freely. As Dotson notes, a listener who is appropriately aware of their lack of knowledge and is "wary of their comprehension" when faced with testimony from domains they are unfamiliar with is more likely to speak in ways that elicit engaged explanation from their partners.[8] And the speaker who gains confidence that their audience will relate to them with that sort of humility is less likely to testimonially smother herself. Instead of a spiral of silence, such behaviors can prompt a virtuous cycle of mutual engagement.

[7] Shannon Rea, "On Silence: Student Refrainment from Speech," in *Dilemmas of Free Expression*, ed. Emmett MacFarlane (University of Toronto Press, 2021), 252–68.
[8] Dotson, "Tracking Epistemic Violence," 246.

Rather than simplistic and one-sided attacks on self-censorship or disapproving responses to deleterious speech—positions that, paradoxically, degrade healthy speech culture because they do not treat *not listening* with appropriate seriousness—what is necessary is the cultivation of *dispositions* and *temperaments* toward listening and consideration. Unlike a moral rule, a disposition toward consideration is not absolute—it describes an orientation and a preference, not an ethical command. We want to tamp down on the instinct to move *too quickly* to dismissive condemnation and censuring, but we do not want to delegitimize them all together. Likewise, framing the virtues this way, as ones of *listening* and *consideration*, appropriately avoids an undue valorization of any and all speech. A climate where some participants feel entirely unable to participate or make deliberative offerings of their own would not be conducive to consideration, but this does not mean that any impulse toward holding back and refraining from speech is a destructive one. And from this more layered understanding, I suggest, some of the common targets of scorn in contemporary debates about free speech culture—concepts like "safe spaces" and "trigger warnings"—actually strike this balance far better than many critics credit.

In the remainder of this of chapter, I draw on Alexis de Tocqueville to illuminate a particular danger that paradoxically arrives from some forms of equalization in access to deliberative resources. Without markers of differentiation, listeners have little reason to distinguish one speaker from another save how a speaker coheres to their preexisting viewpoints or passions. Diversity (of viewpoint and of perspective) is essential to cultivating proper deliberative virtues because it provides the right sort of inequality—not one predicated on domination and subordination but one that generates exposure to alternative points of view and which generates sufficient epistemic friction such that critical analysis remains possible. I then combine this argument with the prior discussion of the empowering dimension of "not listening" to shed light on debates over voguish campus practices (like trigger warnings) that often are highly controversial in discussions about free speech culture. Trigger warnings, safe spaces, and the like are frequently presented as attempts to subvert the very values of scholarly inquiry, which center precisely on the need for open engagement even with hard thoughts. There is, I agree, a connection between such campus innovations and not listening, but it is more subtle than many critics let on. Ultimately, such practices are unlikely to present significant threats to anyone's reckoning with the hard thoughts. To the extent they may encourage some debilitation in the deliberative virtues of the marginalized persons they supposedly aim to protect, they likely do no more than afflict them with the same sorts of epistemic infirmities often possessed (though rarely acknowledged) by their more privileged peers.

The Virtue of Cultivating Epistemic Friction

In *Democracy in America*, Tocqueville observed that "[t]here is no philosopher in the world so great that he does not believe a million things on faith in others or does not suppose many more truths than he establishes."[9] This is due not to philosophical laziness but to practical constraints: it would be impossible for anyone to actually hold every single hypothesis up to critical scrutiny and establish it from foundational principles or first-person evaluation. For Tocqueville, this basic fact of limited investigative capacity has serious impacts when conjoined with growing social equality. Equality disinclines people to listen to their fellows—why should another person, equal to me, be more authoritative than I am?—and instead channels them to listen to the majority (the consensus of equals).[10] Equality thus yields the risk of democratic despotism: people see less and less need to exercise their free will as against the guiding hand of the benevolent "schoolmaster" centralized state, which, after all, represents the consensus of equals.[11]

The dangers Tocqueville warned about carry to the present day. One arena where equality's dark underbelly has revealed itself with alarming speed is in the proliferation of social media channels as a primary mechanism for many to receive the news, alongside a concurrent diminution of trust in "established" media organizations. Initially, the ability of "anyone" to bypass the media gatekeepers and become a citizen-journalist was hailed as democratizing: everyone, regardless of social position or rank, was equally capable of contributing to and influencing the trajectory of the public dialogue.[12] Today, however, that vision of equality has turned nightmarish—where all voices are "equal," it is impossible to distinguish the credible from the outlandish, the informed from the ignorant, the earnest from the hacks. The result of this trend has been simultaneously greater ideological siloing—people retreating into congenial political bubbles where they hear only news that pleases them (or, more frequently, enrages them in the right way)—but also paradoxically a disconnect and disenchantment with the entire project of informed deliberation. At one level, it seems, people do grasp that they're not getting a complete or accurate picture from the media sources

[9] Alexis de Tocqueville, *Democracy in America* (1835), ed. and trans. Harvey C. Mansfield and Delba Winthrop (University of Chicago Press, 2002), 408.

[10] *Id.* at 407–10.

[11] *Id.* at 663.

[12] See, e.g., Ivan B. Dylko, Michael A. Beam, Kristen D. Landreville, and Nicholas Geidner, "Filtering 2008 US Presidential Election News on YouTube by Elites and Nonelites: An Examination of the Democratizing Potential of the Internet," *New Media & Society* 14, no. 5 (2011): 832–49; Joshua A. Tucker, Yannis Theocharis, Margaret E. Roberts, and Pablo Barberá, "From Liberation to Turmoil: Social Media and Democracy," *Journal of Democracy* 28, no. 4 (October 2017): 48–49; Rubén Sánchez Medero, "Democratization in Political Communication," *Political Studies Review* 19, no. 4 (2021): 607–23.

they consume. But this recognition leads to a sort of cynical apathy toward the entire endeavor: a shrugging acceptance that any news source, any testifier, and any politician is (*equally*) slanted, untrustworthy, and probably manipulative—so what's the point of even trying to distinguish between them? As Arendt tells us, this outlook, above all others, is ripe for the emergence of totalitarianism: "The ideal subject of totalitarian rule is not the convinced Nazi or the convinced Communist, but people for whom the distinction between fact and faction (*i.e.*, the reality of experience) and the distinction between true and false (*i.e.*, the standards of thought) no longer exist."[13]

The rise of generative artificial intelligence and other "deepfake" technologies, accessible to all, is only going to exacerbate this problem. After Kanye West took out an ad during the Super Bowl to hawk a T-shirt bearing a swastika, a viral video of "Jews Against Kanye" purported to show a range of Jewish celebrities giving West the middle finger—fooling many before it was reported that the video was fake.[14] Even viewers pleased by the particular message of that video quickly recognized the underlying danger—if one could realistically mock up celebrities condemning antisemitism, one could realistically mock up celebrities endorsing antisemitism, or enacting it themselves.[15] More established media outlets were able to reveal the sham in relatively quick order—but notice that this capacity exists only insofar as there is an essential *inequality* between media institutions over the internet masses—the former enjoying heightened credibility and authoritativeness compared to the latter.

Institutional media gatekeepers have many faults, but they do provide this helpful "bumpiness" in epistemic terrain, enabling observers to make critical distinctions among sources. In a passage about art critics that could easily apply to social and political critics more generally, Jarrett Earnest addresses the question "How do we make sense of this world in which everything seems to be collapsed and equally viable?" "That idea," he continues, "is challenging because it means that there isn't any hierarchy of importance, and thus the critic isn't needed to

[13] Hannah Arendt, *The Origins of Totalitarianism* (Harvest, 1968), 474. *See also* Hannah Arendt, "Truth and Politics," in *Between Past and Future: Eight Exercises in Political Thought* (Penguin, 1993), 257 ("[T]he surest long-term result of brainwashing is a peculiar kind of cynicism—an absolute refusal to believe in the truth of anything, no matter how well this truth may be established. In other words, the result of a consistent and total substitution of lies for factual truth is not that the lies will now be accepted as truth, and the truth be defamed as lies, but that the sense by which we take our bearings in the real world—and the category of truth vs. falsehood is among the mental means to this end—is being destroyed.").

[14] Philissa Cramer, "In AI Video, Jewish Celebrities from Scarlett Johansson to Adam Sandler Give Kanye the Middle Finger," *JTA*, February 11, 2025, https://www.jta.org/2025/02/11/culture/in-ai-video-jewish-celebrities-from-scarlett-johansson-to-adam-sandler-give-kanye-the-middle-finger.

[15] Jeffrey Salkin, "I Liked the AI Jews-against-Kanye Video—and We Should All Be Terrified of It," *JTA*, February 12, 2025, https://www.jta.org/2025/02/12/culture/i-liked-the-ai-jews-against-kanye-video-and-we-should-all-be-terrified-of-it.

make those kinds of distinctions, which was traditionally their domain."[16] The role of a critic who is worthy of distinctive attention depends on there being some sort of hierarchy of authority—*this* voice distinctively matters, and it matters for reasons aside from it being an especially clear echo of what everyone else is saying. It's not the case that this hierarchy needs to be of a traditional dominative type, but there needs to be some sort of friction—an acknowledgment of differences that continue to matter—in order to pull ourselves out of this Tocquevillian trap.

Tocqueville offered one hypothesis for how a particular epistemic vice might develop—he was concerned that social equality (viewed as homogeneous sameness) would lead people to adopt a blind follow-the-masses approach as a substitute for developing their own critical cognitive faculties. The corollary is that certain forms of diversity or heterogeneity can provide the requisite epistemic friction necessary to continually provoke new and novel insights, or at least keep actors on their (epistemic) toes.[17] The enemy is the indistinguishable sea of "equal" content; the cure is markers of distinction and differentiation. Epistemic friction is necessary for deliberators to, literally, get a grip—to be able to make critical distinctions and assess arguments on terrain other than ideological congeniality or conformity to popular dogmas.

More contemporary explorations of how democracy can embody deliberative virtues, such as those forwarded by Hélène Landemore and Elizabeth Anderson, likewise focus on diversity as a crucial factor. Sometimes diversity assists at the input stage, ensuring that the pool of deliberators possesses knowledge or analytical insight from a wide range of different sources (Landemore).[18] Others suggest diversity is also important post-decision, ensuring that arrived-upon decisions can still be challenged, revisited, or revised (Anderson).[19] In either case, the necessary diversity is not just viewpoint diversity—though that often is important. It is also diversity of what Iris Marion Young calls "perspective," the fact that "differently positioned people have different experience, history, and social knowledge derived from that positioning."[20] The importance of perspective isn't that it dictates specific argumentative content—persons with similar perspectives can

[16] Quoted in Matthew Israel, *A Year in the Art World: An Insider's View* (Thames & Hudson, 2023), 84.

[17] On the concept of "epistemic friction," *see* José Medina, *The Epistemology of Resistance: Gender and Racial Oppression, Epistemic Injustice, and Resistant Imaginations* (Oxford University Press, 2012), 78.

[18] Hélène Landemore, *Democratic Reason: Politics, Collective Intelligence, and the Rule of the Many* (Princeton University Press, 2013).

[19] Elizabeth Anderson, "The Epistemology of Democracy," *Episteme* 3, nos. 1–2 (2006): 8–22.

[20] Iris Marion Young, *Inclusion and Democracy* (Oxford University Press, 2002), 136.

nonetheless have radically different opinions and political views. Rather, perspective helps create the set of questions and assumptions from which we begin to reason.[21]

José Medina pushes this argument further by defending not just the deliberative utility of "diversity" in the abstract, but specifically elevating the particular deliberative virtues of persons laboring under conditions of oppression. The debates over safe spaces tend to presuppose that their beneficiaries—imagined to be historically marginalized groups (since the "safe spaces" enjoyed by the majority are unmarked and so are not registered at all)—are being "insulated" from the challenging ideas which (paradoxically enough) are said to be quite common out in the "real world." Medina suggests this assumption is misplaced, if not backward: oppressive conditions can yield a sort of "meta-lucidity" whereby oppressed persons gain knowledge not just of their own subjective vantage (forged through personal experience) but also the hegemonic societal vantage (learned via its ubiquitous omnipresence).[22] This translates into a set of epistemic virtues Medina identifies—characteristics like humility, curiosity, and open-mindedness—which are contrasted against a set of epistemic vices (arrogance, laziness, and close-mindedness) which may characterize persons who do not experience epistemic friction or resistance and so are unaccustomed to having their views challenged. Put another way, persons who are at the bottom of a social hierarchy frequently have no choice but to become conversant in views "not their own"—they are curious not (necessarily) because it is virtuous but because it is a survival skill.

Consider the archetypical target of the attack: the undergraduate at a left-leaning college or university. It may well be true that, among the student body at a progressive liberal arts college, it is rare to hear aired the view that most or all undocumented immigrants ought to be deported immediately. But it is fanciful to suggest that students—particularly those who would be directly impacted by such policies (e.g., because they themselves or their family members are undocumented)—are consequently *unaware* of these arguments or have managed to "insulate" themselves from them in any meaningful respect. Such views are ubiquitous in our political discourse; it is virtually impossible to avoid encountering them regardless of what is or isn't taught inside any particular classroom. To be sure, it is easy to push this fact too far as well: one can be aware—quite concretely aware—of the existence of such positions in American political discourse without having encountered their articulation in a philosophically robust way. But just as we should retain some skepticism that one truly

[21] *Id.* at 137–40.

[22] Medina, *Epistemology of Resistance*, 187ff. Consider here Du Bois's famous concept of "double-consciousness" as well. W. E. B. Du Bois, *The Souls of Black Folk* (1903; Penguin, 1996), 5.

"knows" an argument one has not heard, we can also be cautious in assuming that any and all desire for epistemic insulation comes with the hope of avoiding hearing any argument outright.

By contrast, persons at the top of the social pecking order can (to return to Gilligan) opt not to listen. This, of course, implies that they also can choose *to* listen, and some do. But the point is that such persons (unlike their more marginal fellows) can, if they wish, luxuriate in the sensation of general agreement—the way they think is harmonious with the way the world acts upon them—and so lose the ability to engage in genuine critical conversation even as they become convinced of their own epistemological superiority.[23] There consequently are few guardrails preventing them from becoming epistemically complacent—secure in the knowledge that they already know any and all relevant information. When that sensibility is disturbed—when they are (for whatever reason) forced to account for challenges to their worldview—they may lack the tools to process that challenge in a healthy way, and so may become defensive, distraught, or even violent.

Medina's argument suggests that the focus on threats to open inquiry emerging from social outgroups—things like safe spaces and trigger warnings—is likely misplaced. There is, however, another element latent in Medina's language of epistemic virtues and vices that is less discussed. One need not be versed in the life of St. Augustine ("Lord, give me chastity and continence—but not yet!") to know that virtues are frequently a drag and vices are often a blast. Being forced to navigate an epistemic world which was not built for you and is often jarringly inconsistent with your own lived experience can enhance critical reasoning skills, intellectual adroitness, and facility with diverse views. It also can be exhausting, degrading, and humiliating. That it produces epistemic virtues does not in any way mean that these virtues are fun to live out. Hence it is entirely plausible and understandable that one thing marginalized persons might desire and associate with liberation is to access the epistemic life spaces occupied by their more privileged peers—to be able to bask in certainty, to be able to take certain things for granted, to not have to constantly and perpetually defend core personal or political commitments. So while we might think that the critics of contemporary collegiate culture are wrong to locate threats to open inquiry primarily inside of these subaltern movements, to the extent that they are identifying a real threat that threat could be the possibility that some outgroup members desire to trade a virtue for a vice.

[23] Medina refers to this as "meta-blindness." Medina, *Epistemology of Resistance*, 75. Mill's disdain, discussed above, for the "princes . . . who are accustomed to unlimited deference" and therefore are not habituated to considering challenging perspectives, is an obvious philosophical antecedent. Mill, *On Liberty*, 17.

Even this critique should not be jumped to too quickly. The desire for *some* epistemic "insulation" is not always unvirtuous. If persons of color succeed in getting us to stop debating whether White supremacy is a legitimate political outlook and instead simply agree to agree on the matter, they would be gaining "nothing more than what Whites long enjoyed effortlessly."[24] But that does not mean they'd be joining White people in a state of vice. There are good reasons why we should not have to reinvent every philosophical wheel; we would likely be better off residing in a society where racial equality (or the historical veracity of the Holocaust, for that matter) is taken for granted and not even thought of as debate-worthy compared to one where it remains an "open question."

Nonetheless, as Albert Memmi observed at the conclusion of his magisterial *The Colonizer and the Colonized* (and in a passage he returned to at the outset of the retrospective *Decolonization and the Decolonized* 50 years later), the liberation of the colonized entails the colonized becoming "a man like any other," with all "the ups and downs" that entails.[25] Neither the colonized nor the decolonized are saints, nor should they be expected to be,[26] and Medina's argument does not depend on any assertion of intrinsic and intractable virtue. But for this exact reason, it is possible—arguably even expected—that some of the virtues Medina identifies as necessities for persons living under conditions of oppression may fade as those oppressive circumstances begin to lift, and some contrasting vices may be indulged in now that they're available.

Yet even in those cases where the degree of insulation demanded is of a sort that ends up being incompatible with the virtues of open consideration, this wouldn't falsify Medina's larger point. In such a case, what marginalized persons are seeking is not some unique deviation from broader norms of open inquiry and freewheeling intellectual discourse. The deliberative lives of persons in positions of privilege are already shot through with safe spaces and the like; they are more often than not capable *by default* of avoiding the thoughts they would rather not think. Outgroups, by contrast, have to put in work to attain the same status—and the visibility of that work makes it (inaccurately) appear as if it is different in kind from the sorts of epistemic insulation privileged persons already enjoy. Hence, even if in some cases critics are accurate that the deliberative equilibrium desired by these outgroups does cross over from virtue to vice, all that we would be witnessing is outgroups leveling down to a denominator already set by persons in privileged positions. This would not support the rhetoric suggesting

[24] Schraub, "Academic Freedom," 72.

[25] Albert Memmi, *The Colonizer and the Colonized* (1957; Beacon, 1991), 153; Albert Memmi, *Decolonization and the Decolonized*, trans. Robert Bononno (University of Minnesota Press 2006), x.

[26] Memmi, *Decolonization*, xii ("Like the colonized, the decolonized is not a saint; how could he be and continue to live through such an agitated period of his history?").

that marginalized persons are receiving some sort of unique insulation from the hard knocks of a free society.

The Virtue of Having, and Transcending, Safe Spaces?

A common complaint leveled by guardians of free speech culture is that we have created too many opportunities to cloister ourselves from discomforting or problematic views. Debates over content moderation on social media sites have seen this debate play out in particularly aggressive fashion. But the complaint can also be witnessed in attacks on pedagogical innovations like trigger warnings or the existence of so-called safe spaces on campus. All of these, the accusation goes, are simply means of creating an epistemic bubble. Consistent with my arguments above, I will contend here that these criticisms, while not wholly meritless, miss the mark because they overlook the importance of being able to elect not to listen and thus try to impose a fundamentally unsustainable rule where persons are at all times and in all spaces constantly exposed to an unregulated firehose of content, without any means of channeling it or separating the wheat from the chaff. Once we accept that the admitted risks of epistemic bubbles can be adequately dealt with only by cultivating *dispositions* (rather than mandates) toward listening, we can better balance the important virtue of willingness to grapple with hard thoughts alongside the necessary benefits of being empowered to withdraw (at least some of the time) from certain undesirable conversations.

Start with the question of content moderation and "blocking" norms on social media. The democratic and libertarian ethos that drove much early internet innovation often manifested in platform owners extolling, at least initially, a strong commitment to free speech, by which they meant that the platform would generally not police or moderate the content of user contributions. Technology companies often express great hesitance at taking on the role of content filters—in part because the most shocking and offensive conduct often drives traffic (and therefore profit) but, in fairness, also because they can honestly claim to lack either democratic legitimation or topical competence to be deciding what sorts of statements are in versus out of bounds. Declaring a free speech open forum seems, at first blush, a way of washing their hands of the problem. And it is moreover presented as a healthy choice from a deliberative perspective—by ensuring all views can be aired, it ensures that all users are exposed to a diverse range of competing perspectives.

Unfortunately, as often as this commitment is put forth, it always proves itself to be unsustainable. As S Peter Davis observes, the platforms which have "attempted the free speech absolutist project" have universally "gone one of two ways eventually: They have ultimately embraced content moderation, or they have become homogeneously radical right-wing websites."[27] Customers—posters, observers, advertisers, and other users—fundamentally do not want a free speech free-for-all. If participation in a platform means they realistically cannot "stop listening" to certain unwelcome speech intrusions, they will leave. The most recent iteration of this cycle manifested after Elon Musk's purchase of Twitter (which he renamed X). Musk presented himself as a "free speech absolutist" and quickly began eliminating or scaling back practices and features which aided users in avoiding undesired online interactions while simultaneously welcoming back onto the platform an array of extremist voices that had previously been banned for misinformation, harassment, or bigotry.[28] These reforms precipitated widespread advertiser and consumer departures from the platform to newly launched competitors like Bluesky.[29]

At one level, these debates mimic the ones grappled with throughout this book. Once social media sites elect to engage in content moderation, they encounter the evergreen (and, for ordinary people, unavoidable) problem of how to distinguish between an idea that is "merely" uncomfortable or controversial and one that should be outright suppressed. Facebook, for instance, had for many years a highly intricate and quasi-legal process for deciding how to apply its policies on misinformation[30]—ironic, given that under First Amendment rules actual legal actors do not and in fact cannot engage in similar decisions about what content to approve or disapprove. Merits or demerits of a quasi-legal approach aside (and in the next chapter I'll note some of the potential benefits of adopting at least some insights from legal practice into questions of nonlegal deliberative ethics), the difficulties they experience are not really legal in nature—they are rather similar in kind, though not in scale, to the general tension everyone experiences being an open-minded participant in wide-spanning debates while maintaining certain red lines which cannot be crossed. When,

[27] S Peter Davis, "The Hard Problem of Social Media: Why Free Speech Platforms Ultimately Fail," *Plato Was a Dick: The S Peter Davis Newsletter*, December 8, 2023, https://speterdavis.substack.com/p/the-hard-problem-of-social-media.

[28] See, e.g., Antonio Pequeño IV, "X Will Soon Let Users See Tweets from People Who Block Them—The Controversial Change, Explained," *Forbes*, October 17, 2024, https://www.forbes.com/sites/antoniopequenoiv/2024/10/17/x-will-soon-let-users-see-tweets-from-people-who-block-them-the-controversial-change-explained/; Kate Conger, "Elon Musk Brings Conspiracy Theorist Alex Jones Back to X," *New York Times*, December 9, 2023, https://www.nytimes.com/2023/12/09/technology/elon-musk-alex-jones-twitter-x.html; David Klepper, "Report: Tweets with Racial Slurs Soar since Musk Takeover," AP, November 10, 2022, https://apnews.com/article/elon-musk-technology-business-government-and-politics-2907d382db132cfd7446152b9309992c.

[29] Abid Rahman, "#Xodus: Bluesky Hits 20M Users as People Continue to Flee X," *Hollywood Reporter*, November 19, 2024, https://www.hollywoodreporter.com/business/digital/bluesky-20-million-users-twitter-exodus-elon-musk-1236065566/.

[30] See Peter Stern, Sarah Shirazyan, and Abby Fanlo, "How Can Platform Engagement with Academics and Civil Society Representatives Inform the Development of Content Policies? A Look at Meta's COVID-19 Misinformation Policies," *Journal of Online Trust & Safety* 1, no. 4 (2022), https://tsjournal.org/index.php/jots/article/view/90/32.

following the election of Donald Trump, Facebook announced a major retreat from its previous fact-checking and content-moderation standards, it presented its decision as an initiative to end "censorship" and embrace "free expression."[31] In reality, it was an abdication of its duties as a deliberative participant and was widely (and in my view fairly) seen as a partisan decision to promote a particular (right-wing and conspiratorial) deliberative vision. That Facebook has the First Amendment right to make this decision (just as you or I have the right to read and extol the virtues of the *Protocols of the Elders of Zion*) does not mean its decision cannot be subject to withering criticism on an ethical level.

But what we also see in controversies over content moderation on social media are claims that particular actors or perspectives are *entitled* to access a specified online audience and are being unjustly injured or censored if they are locked out. Texas and Florida, for instance, passed legislation attempting to sharply limit social media platforms' ability to engage in content moderation, allegedly because they were censoring "conservative" voices.[32] Though it surely overstates the case that "conservatives," writ large, were targeted by content-moderation efforts, there's little doubt that the social media platforms were responding in part to the desires of their customer base (both users and advertisers), who had no interest in participating in a "forum" that included harassers, bigots, conspiracy theorists, and other assorted cranks. One might think, then, that the free speech values at stake were straightforward: the moderated material was content that the platform didn't want to host and users didn't want to consume. But to that point, defenders of this legislation appealed directly to the notion that websites like Twitter were a modern-day public forum,[33] and, as discussed above, an important purpose of the public forum is to allow ideas to be transmitted to generally *unwilling* listeners. Under this view, social media platforms could and should be compelled to host speech that they find obnoxious and destructive, precisely so that their users' desire not to listen to that speech can be stymied. Indeed, in one of his most high-profile legal maneuvers since acquiring Twitter, Musk has sued advertisers who departed his platform (largely due to surging hate speech and misinformation on the platform), claiming that their refusal to patronize his forum was an antitrust violation.[34] The

[31] Clare Duffy, "Meta Is Getting Rid of Fact Checkers. Zuckerberg Acknowledged More Harmful Content Will Appear on the Platforms Now," CNN, January 7, 2025, https://www.cnn.com/2025/01/07/tech/meta-censorship-moderation/index.html.

[32] See Moody v. NETCHOICE, LLC, 144 S. Ct. 2383 (2024).

[33] See NETCHOICE, LLC v. Paxton, 49 F. 4th 439, 474–76 (5th Cir. 2022); Richard A. Epstein, "Keeping Free Speech Free on Social Media," Hoover Institution, January 31, 2024, https://www.hoover.org/research/keeping-free-speech-free-social-media.

[34] Kate Conger, "X, Owned by Elon Musk, Brings Antitrust Suit Accusing Advertisers of a Boycott," *New York Times*, August 6, 2024, https://www.nytimes.com/2024/08/06/technology/x-antitrust-suit-advertisers-elon-musk.html.

most basic decision to *not* wish to associate with certain views was presented as both unlawful and toxic to free speech itself; as his CEO Linda Yaccarino put it, "People are hurt when the marketplace of ideas is undermined and some viewpoints are not funded over others as part of an illegal boycott."[35] Under the Trump administration, the Federal Trade Commission likewise considered imposing (as a condition for approving a merger) a requirement on advertising companies that they not boycott platforms "because of their political content by refusing to place their clients' advertisements on them."[36] The government sword compelling unwilling participants to remain in conversation with Nazis, Holocaust deniers, and misinformation peddlers of all stripes—one struggles to imagine a clearer illustration of the importance of the right not to listen and to drop out of certain deliberative endeavors that we discussed in the last chapter.

These arguments also shed some insight on a parallel debate targeting competitors that have been more accommodating of content-moderation requests. Bluesky, for instance, has developed its own culture promoting relatively unrestrained "blocking" of undesired accounts and content (in contrast to an older internet ethos where to block often was presented as a tacit concession that one was too weak-kneed to handle a powerful argument). This has in turn launched a roaring discussion regarding whether the site is turning into an echo chamber.[37] X, for its part, pivoted sharply in the opposite direction by announcing it would functionally neuter the block function and allow users to continue to see content from those who had putatively blocked them.[38]

Defenders of social media blocking argue that there is a qualitative difference between not wishing to be constantly in a debater's posture with the internet's most toxic trolls and closing oneself off from any divergent or challenging view whatsoever. And the very willingness of large numbers of users to depart sites like X for greener pastures undermines the notion that these sites have effective monopolies over public discourse that renders them tantamount to the new

[35] *Id.*

[36] Lauren Hirsch, Benjamin Mullin, Kate Conger, and Tiffany Hsu, "F.T.C. May Put Unusual Condition on Ad Mega-Merger: No Boycotting," *New York Times*, June 12, 2025), https://www.nytimes.com/2025/06/12/business/ftc-omnicom-interpublic-merger.html.

[37] *See, e.g.*, Daniel W. Drezner, "Is Bluesky An Echo Chamber?," *Drezner's World*, September 25, 2024, https://danieldrezner.substack.com/p/is-bluesky-an-echo-chamber; Matthew Field, "'MAGA Cockroaches': The Left-Wing 'Echo Chamber' Rivalling Elon Musk's X," *Yahoo News*, November 21, 2024, https://www.yahoo.com/news/maga-cockroaches-left-wing-echo-110000482.html; Phoebe Maltz Bovy, "The Problem with Bluesky: It Won't Broaden Our Horizons," *Globe & Mail*, November 22, 2024, https://www.theglobeandmail.com/opinion/article-the-problem-with-bluesky-it-wont-broaden-our-horizons/.

[38] Antonio Pequeño IV, "X Will Soon Let Users See Tweets from People Who Block Them—The Controversial Change, Explained," *Forbes*, October 17, 2024, https://www.forbes.com/sites/antoniopequenoiv/2024/10/17/x-will-soon-let-users-see-tweets-from-people-who-block-them-the-controversial-change-explained/.

"public square."[39] That users are willing to depart X when it does not moderate speech is powerful evidence that when it does moderate speech it is less akin to a government regulator engaging in censorship and more like a private media company making curatorial decisions over what views to promote and what views to cast aside. In this light, coercive efforts like the Texas and Florida legislation or Musk's lawsuit against his reluctant advertisers speak to actors who feel entitled to an audience and for whom the decision to "avert one's eyes" is tantamount to censorship.

This isn't to say that there are not or will not be problematic deliberative norms that develop on Bluesky or any other platform—including norms that swing too far toward dismissiveness. Increasing the power of individual users to block others is a transfer of regulatory power to the user—now they, more than the platform or the government, control who and what crosses their feed. This power should come with responsibility, a responsibility that is accentuated precisely because the power is largely unregulated. There is a difference between embracing the mantra "Block early, block often" in response to internet trolls and adopting the belief that one should not have to think at all about one's decision to block. But those problems, if and when they emerge, cannot be adequately addressed without a basic recognition that *not listening* is itself a valuable component of deliberative freedom that in some circumstances needs protection. Bluesky's problem is not that people are empowered to block. It might be, depending on how that power is being exercised, that they are blocking too cavalierly.

Students on campus directly engage in content moderation or "blocking". But there are substantial debates over other mechanisms through which students can regulate or control what sorts of ideas they are exposed to (or at least, in what context they will encounter them). Depending on one's vantage, the use of "trigger warnings" and "safe spaces" are presented either a part of or a threat to healthy pedagogical development. Here too we find allegations that individuals exploit these practices in order to evade hard thoughts. And here too a deeper dive into the practices suggests that this criticism is far too simplistic, adopting a fundamentalist antagonism to not listening rather than a more layered understanding of how listening and not listening can coexist in equipoise in a healthy deliberative ecosystem.

A trigger, or content, warning is "a statement about the content of material that one is teaching, issued in advance, so that students may prepare themselves for it. Those who issue these warnings typically do so for things like graphic

[39] See *Paxton*, 49 F. 4th at 476 (arguing for why modern social media platforms are tantamount to monopolies over a "particular niche of online discourse").

depictions of sexual violence."[40] Trigger warnings are often alleged to be tactics by which certain students, typically those from underrepresented or minority backgrounds, can evade having to reckon with difficult or challenging ideas in the classroom. Terri R. Day and Danielle Weatherby, for example, describe trigger warnings as an effort to avoid material that might prompt trauma in students. Yet, they argue, these efforts are counterproductive because encountering this "triggering" material is critical in order for persons to eventually overcome trauma. They draw an analogy to physical therapy used to recover from an injury: it's hard, and it directs pain exactly at the point of trauma, but doing just that and doing it repeatedly is precisely what helps one eventually heal.[41]

The analogy to exposure therapy has some resonance, particularly given the accustomed claim that higher education is valuable in part because it provides exposure to alternative or discomforting views. But there is something odd about why the critique is applied against trigger warnings specifically. After all, as Jennifer Saul observes, a trigger warning is definitively *not* a warning against using such content in class. (If they were meant to serve that role, they'd be redundant: a professor who does not want to teach certain material can simply omit it from the syllabus.)[42] Rather, they provide advance notice to students regarding certain content which they will encounter in the class, in circumstances where they might not otherwise be anticipating it. In this way, trigger warnings may actually facilitate encountering challenging material by giving persons the notice necessary to craft a properly structured environment so they can truly engage with the traumatic stimuli.[43] The comparison to therapy is perhaps more revealing than Day and Weatherby acknowledge. Physical therapy is highly structured, disciplined, and foreshadowed—one doesn't rehabilitate an injured knee by having people bash it with a hammer at random and unpredictable intervals. By contrast, Kate Manne compares the "exposure therapy" argument for forgoing trigger warnings as "akin to occasionally throwing a spider at an arachnophobe."[44] That trigger warnings are seen as serving this "insulating" function, when they are more accurately viewed as a means of facilitating communicating hard thoughts to an otherwise unreceptive or hostile audience, is

[40] Jennifer Saul, "Beyond Just Silencing: A Call for Complexity in Discussions of Academic Free Speech," in *Academic Freedom*, ed. Jennifer Lackey (Oxford University Press, 2018), 125.

[41] Terri R. Day and Danielle Weatherby, "Speech Narcissism," *Florida Law Review* 70, no. 4 (2018): 839–82.

[42] Saul, "Beyond Just Silencing," 126.

[43] See Kendall Gerdes, "Trauma, Trigger Warnings, and the Rhetoric of Sensitivity," *Rhetorical Society Quarterly* 49, no. 1 (2019): 3–24 (categorizing trigger warnings as an accessibility practice that enables students of all backgrounds to participate in the curriculum effectively).

[44] Kate Manne, "Why I Use Trigger Warnings," *New York Times*, September 20, 2015, https://www.nytimes.com/2015/09/20/opinion/sunday/why-i-use-trigger-warnings.html.

demonstrative of how powerful—but misleading—the stereotype of the coddled minority student is.

It is an oddity about trigger warnings that their critics would seem to fully endorse their use were it not for the name, which drives them to paroxysms of anxiety about the imminent demise of open academic inquiry. University of Chicago professor Jerry Coyne, for example, devoted an entire essay to the efforts by some students to put a trigger warning in front of Ovid's classic work *Metamorphoses*. A sexual assault survivor, not realizing that the myths included vivid accounts of rape, described herself as "triggered" upon reading it and was further upset when the professor dismissed her concerns. Coyne is appalled by what he takes to be the students' censorial instincts, the possibility of a slippery slope (what *won't* be "triggering" to *someone*?), the failure to understand that "life is triggering," and so on.[45]

So, does Coyne think there should be any accommodation made for the "triggered student"? Well, yes, Coyne concedes: "[P]erhaps [the professor] might have mentioned beforehand that there is violence and sexual assault in Ovid, but that's as far as I'd go."[46] In other words, he suggests that there should have been a trigger warning.

There seems to be very little dispute about the appropriateness of using trigger warnings in at least some academic contexts, save for the name itself. George Mason University law professor Ilya Somin describes his "warning against trigger warnings" that he delivers to his students at the beginning of his course on constitutional law: "I don't believe in trigger warnings. But if I did, I would have to include one for virtually every day of this course. We are going to cover subjects like slavery, segregation, sexism, suicide, the death penalty, and abortion. There is no way to teach this course without discussing these issues. And there is no good way to cover them without also considering a wide range of views about these subjects and their relationship to the Constitution."[47]

Despite the moniker, I pointed out to Somin that this paragraph functions basically like a trigger warning: "It tells students, accurately, about some of the content they'll be reading, and notes that much of it deals with issues of deep injustice and controversy."[48] Somin, however, resisted incorporating his warning under the ambit of "trigger warnings." He argued that only an "absurdly broad definition" of the term would include his generic statement advising students of

[45] Jerry A. Coyne, "Life Is 'Triggering.' The Best Literature Should Be Too," *New Republic*, May 14, 2015, https://newrepublic.com/article/121790/life-triggering-best-literature-should-be-too.

[46] *Id.*

[47] Ilya Somin, "A Warning against Trigger Warnings," *Washington Post*, August 25, 2016, https://www.washingtonpost.com/news/volokh-conspiracy/wp/2016/08/25/a-warning-against-trigger-warnings/.

[48] David Schraub, "Warning against Warning against Trigger Warnings," *Debate Link*, August 25, 2016, http://dsadevil.blogspot.com/2016/08/warning-against-warning-against-trigger.html.

some of the potentially triggering content they might experience in the course. Somin suggested that a trigger warning must be exceedingly specific in precisely what content will be triggering, and its language should, at least by implication, suggest that such material will be addressed in a "hypersensitive" fashion.[49]

Somin has a particular vision of what a trigger warning is, where the "warning" is delivered in the most portentous form possible and the allegedly triggering content is described in the most minute detail so as to tick off every conceivable politically correct box. Certainly if one roots around one no doubt can find examples of trigger warnings which have these characteristics. Pretentious performances are a professional hazard of the professoriate, and trigger warnings perhaps offer a particularly alluring opportunity to indulge. But labeling trigger warnings as *by definition* encompassing only such extreme measures is an attempt to box them off from more ordinary statements that are a regular part of the toolkit of any responsible academic.[50]

It is true that, under the more expansive understanding of "trigger warning" that I advocate here, in many cases a "normal" syllabus may qualify as providing a trigger warning insofar as it makes it abundantly obvious that potentially sensitive material will be on the docket. But this strikes me as precisely the point: the goal of trigger warnings is not to perform some tribute to sensitivity and wokeness; it is to place students on notice of triggering material. Where the presence of such material is facially evident, there likely will not need to be any self-conscious declaration of a trigger warning to accomplish this notification. (If the criminal law class will be discussing murder tomorrow, there is no need to warn people that violence is on the agenda.) The more explicitly labeled trigger warnings are for those cases where the student would not reasonably anticipate the coming content—as in, for example, the case of *Metamorphoses*, where many students not steeped in the classics would not necessarily be aware of the plot. It is a feature of trigger warnings that they need to be explicit only when the presence of potentially triggering content is not evident in advance.

To give one last example: A colleague who teaches First Amendment law at one point covers the "antipornography" ordinances proposed by feminist activists led by Catherine MacKinnon and Andrea Dworkin.[51] As part of this section,

[49] Somin, "A Warning against Trigger Warnings." See also Jack Halberstam, "Trigger Happy: From Content Warning to Censorship," *Signs* 42, no. 2 (Winter 2017): 537 ("The trigger warning . . . believes in a student or viewer who is unstable and damaged and could at any moment collapse into crisis.").

[50] It also arguably is an example of "desiring disagreement," discussed in Chapter 3: preferring to associate "trigger warnings" with extreme or outlandish practices so as to *avoid* the possibility that their advocates are, in important respects, making arguments that Somin in fact endorses as good pedagogical practice.

[51] See "The MacKinnon/Dworkin Pornography Ordinance," reprinted in *William Mitchell Law Review* 11, no. 1 (1985): 119–25.

she shows the students a clip from a graphic rape pornography film of the sort targeted by the ordinances. She never uses the term "trigger warning"; however, at the end of the immediately prior class, she notifies her students that she'll be showing such a clip and asks them to be prepared to react and discuss it.

We can debate whether or not it is sound pedagogy to show excerpts of rape pornography in the classroom, even for illustrative purposes. What cannot be debated is that if one *is* going to show such a clip, then it is absolutely proper—if not imperative—to notify the students that one is doing so in advance. The alternative—"Surprise! Rape porn!"—would be a wildly inappropriate pedagogic approach; it is difficult to imagine any reasonably competent professor disagreeing on that score.[52] That my colleague was right to give advance notice of the content did not oblige her to deliver any pretentious sermons or even to use the term "trigger warning" (which she does not). And once that fraught label is taken away, the substantive content of the trigger warning stops being a debilitating threat to open inquiry or the soft-hearted coddling of weak-minded students and turns into a valued part of the toolkit of responsible, reasonable academics.

Safe spaces raise similar concerns and merit a similar response. As Jacob Levy's compelling, if slightly qualified, defense of safe spaces makes clear, much of academia is a safe space in the sense that nobody is expected to perpetually be in an accept-all-challengers intellectual posture at all times.[53] Physicists need not spend *all* (or even much) of their time responding to a philosopher's quibbles about the metaphysical nature of reality; political scientists need not spend all (or even much) of their time debating chemists about whether social scientific experiments are real experiments. That may seem like a trivial point, but as Levy observes (echoing Tocqueville), intellectual advancement requires "building blocks," which means at some point taking for granted certain presumptions or presuppositions without constantly holding them up for challenge (which is not the same as *never* taking the time to reassess them, which in turn is not the same as *primarily* re- and re-reassessing the foundational basics).[54]

[52] Jack Halberstam posits that in certain cases, some shocking material *must* be presented as a surprise in order to properly impact the student observers. He gives the example, in the context of a course on the Holocaust, of showing the graphic depictions of genocide and its aftermath in the movie *Night and Fog*: "One could argue here that the clips from *Night and Fog* need to be seen without warnings ahead of time in order to allow the students to grapple with their own shocked reactions before delving into the history of the representation of genocide." Halberstam, "Trigger Happy," 540. I am unconvinced. Putting aside whether the students in a class on the Holocaust are already on notice that they will be encountering violent and disturbing material, I find it unlikely that such images would fail to adequately shock unless students were taken entirely by surprise when the images were presented.

[53] Jacob T. Levy, "Safe Spaces, Academic Freedom, and the University as a Complex Association," lecture, Georgia State University, February 15, 2016, transcript available at op://bleedingheartlibertarians.com/2016/03/safe-spaces-academic-freedom-and-the-university-as-a-complex-association/.

[54] *Id.*

More immediately germane is the universal need we all have to sometimes step back, rest, and recharge away from the maelstrom of political controversy. Members of dominant groups have long enjoyed the equivalent of safe spaces in the form of country clubs, fraternities, dinner societies, and the like—even the old saw that "a man's home is his castle" evokes in many ways this entitlement to a place of retreat and repose.[55] Members of such groups are well aware of their benefits, and they presumably do not think of their resort to such venues as tantamount to a tout court refusal to ever engage in the rough and tumble of difficult deliberation. They might therefore be expected to have sympathy for the student who is shadowed by the constant threat of deportation wanting *some* spaces and times where the question "Should you be physically dragged off and expelled from the country?" is not up for debate.[56] It is fair to say that if this student is taking a course on immigration policy, they may have to engage in that question regardless of how close to the bone it cuts—in this way, it is fair to assert that the university as a whole cannot be a "safe space" everywhere and at all times. But that one *must* engage the question in the immigration seminar falsifies the notion that, in *not* wanting to have to engage the question in the chemistry lab, what the student desires is full-fledged insulation from an opposing view. What the putatively safe space would provide is a *partial* insulation in particular social locations—coupled with an acknowledged reality that in other contexts the student can and will have to encounter the idea in an open intellectual setting. Like with trigger warnings, the purpose of safe spaces is less to block uncomfortable or challenging hard thoughts outright, and more to provide a mechanism for regulating the context in which they are encountered. Framed this way, both trigger warnings and safe spaces likely do more to facilitate conversations over the hard thoughts than they do to thwart them.

So why, then, do innovations like social media block lists, trigger warnings, and safe spaces provoke so much visceral anger in many circles? One possibility is that the furor is not really about speech at all—it is actually resentment toward hitherto disempowered people claiming some right and capacity to *elect* when and in what contexts to listen. Trigger warnings, block lists, and safe spaces do not and are not intended to fully insulate their beneficiaries from

[55] Indeed, as will be discussed in the final chapter, the strong instinct that it is inappropriate to protest even an otherwise deserving target outside their household is based on this recognition that it is important to preserve and protect at least some spaces where people do *not* have to listen, even when the claim being forwarded is an important one.

[56] Importantly, that is the state of being that *most* students enjoy far more than "some" times. In general, the average student *never* has to consider the argument "Should you, personally, be physically dragged off and expelled from the country?" At most, they might encounter in a very abstract way a fringe article or essay suggesting such a thing as recompense for America's settler-colonial status. But even if the student finds the idea disconcerting, it rarely will occupy their mind for longer than a seminar session or two.

hard thoughts. What they do offer is the promise that these thoughts will not be foisted upon them at any moment. To persons accustomed to being listened to or listened for—whether it is Nietzsche's hawks or Sartre's colonizers—losing this prerogative can be quite jarring.

Yet we should not confuse the loss of this entitlement with a broader corrosion in social consideration of the hard thoughts. There is little risk that members of marginalized groups will (absent a broader upheaval in their social status) ever become *uniquely* empowered such that they can "opt not to listen." The risk that is genuinely present is Tocquevillian—the prospect that social equality will lead to a society-wide deterioration where all persons, in their equality, regress to the stilted epistemic position previously available only to arrogant princes. But this risk cannot, even in concept, be ameliorated via the imposition of a hard and fast rule demanding consideration of all thoughts at all times. Held in balance, the Nietzschean form of empowerment facilitates the *capacity* not to listen, which must be tempered by the self-motivated desire to nonetheless *choose* to listen. Here, finally, the Millian values which demand open listening can be synthesized with the equally important liberty interest in not listening—or, perhaps more accurately, being able to choose, at least some of the time, not to listen. The importance of cultivating deliberative virtues—training citizens to lean into difficult questions and to be judicious in the exercise of their inevitable discretion to dismiss—is accentuated precisely because they must, at the end of the day, be matters of virtue rather than rule.

8
Bypassing Dismissal
Law as a Cognitive Expressway

Law is but one of many channels through which a given social controversy might be argued.[1] While the preceding chapters have certainly engaged in specifically legal questions, they have also cast their net more widely to consider other vectors of social discourse where dismissal circumvents or obstructs important public debates. But law is not just another forum for civil discourse. It has certain specific characteristics which suggest it occupies a crucial niche in the deliberative ecosystem. This chapter accordingly offers a comparative institutionalist account of the judiciary's unique posture vis-à-vis dismissal.[2] It is comparative institutionalist because it seeks to measure the *relative* strength of the judiciary at handling a particular problem (here, that of dismissal) as compared to other political or social forums which could be assigned the same task. That we are in the realm of *relative* strengths and weaknesses matters a great deal: my argument is certainly not that the judiciary perfectly resolves the concerns over dismissal that have been flagged in the preceding chapters. Nonetheless, I will argue that certain features of the legal system make it uniquely well-positioned to overcome the problem of dismissal—at least some of the time—and push important public conversations forward.

This chapter proceeds in three parts. I begin by analyzing the problem of inequalities in the social distribution of knowledge, which acts to make certain groups more vulnerable to inadvertent injuries imposed by majoritarian actors. Theories of moral negligence suggest that whether victims have even a moral claim that the harms they endure are wrongful may depend upon whether the alleged wrongdoer could reasonably be expected to be aware of the injury, making it especially important that vectors exist for this knowledge to be transmitted

[1] See generally Catherine R. Albiston, Lauren B. Edelman, and Joy Milligan, "The Dispute Tree and the Legal Forest," *Annual Review of Law and Social Science* 10 (2014): 106–9 (noting that dispute resolution is not a pyramid where initial claims are progressively winnowed down until a rump remainder receive legal adjudication, but rather a tree whereby different disputes take different paths toward resolution).

[2] On comparative institutionalism, see Neil K. Komesar, "Taking Institutions Seriously: Introduction to a Strategy for Constitutional Analysis," *University of Chicago Law Review* 51, no. 2 (1984): 366 (urging that law pay attention to "the *relative* strengths and weaknesses" of the different branches of government in determining how to allocate decision-making authority) (emphasis added).

Deliberation, Dismissal, and Democracy. David Schraub, Oxford University Press. © Oxford University Press (2025). DOI: 10.1093/9780197816424.003.0009

from politically marginalized groups to political decision-makers. I then identify several unique properties of the judiciary which help overcome this form of inequality. The Rules of Civil Procedure—indeed, the fact that courts are bound by rules of procedure at all—place courts in a distinctive deliberative niche where they have to listen to at least certain types of claims (including quintessential "hard thought" claims). These rules, which (literally) regulate the practice of dismissal, mean that courts are often compelled to give reasons for their decisions, thus taking questions that might in other venues be shunted aside and transforming them into live subjects of debate. This can sometimes result in direct victories for the claimant, where courts—forced to reason over a given claim—find that there really isn't any compelling argument against it. But even where claimants lose, they still can reap significant benefits simply by placing an issue on the public agenda as a live controversy. Sometimes the only way to force the court of public opinion to open its doors is to first walk into the court of law.

Moral Negligence and the Social Distribution of Knowledge

Moral behavior is often said to depend on what we know, or should know, about our fellows. In articulating the concept of moral negligence, Seana Shiffrin suggests that negligence as a moral wrong entails not properly considering the moral worth of other persons impacted by one's behavior.[3] For example, if there is an easily avoidable risk that endangers another person, and we take that risk anyway, we are not acting in a manner which adequately respects their worth as a person. The same is true if we fail to do due diligence in exploring how our behavior has predictable hostile impacts on others.

"Negligence" implies (un)reasonableness. The wrong is not the harm experienced by others per se, even a harm that in an ideal state of affairs could have been avoided. The wrong is that one acted *unreasonably* in imposing that harm, that given the available resources (material and deliberative) a reasonable person who possesses the proper moral attitudes toward his or her fellows could and would have acted differently. The most straightforward negligent failures are those of knowledge: one is consciously aware of the relevant risks but proceeds anyway. But knowledge is not strictly necessarily; we are not generally willing to let people off the hook that easily. There are certain generalities about people that we can all be assumed to know—people don't like being abused, for example—such that a person who abuses another can fairly be said to have failed in their moral duties regardless of whether they possess actual intimate knowledge of the

[3] Seana Valentine Shiffrin, "The Moral Neglect of Negligence" in *Oxford Studies in Political Philosophy*, ed. David Sobel, Peter Vallentyne, and Steven Wall (Oxford University Press, 2017), 197–228.

other's preferences. (Absent exceptional circumstances, the naked forwarding of the possibility "How was I to know he wasn't a masochist?" will not be accepted as a defense.) Moreover, we often develop specific knowledge regarding the preferences and commitments of others that create more fine-grained moral duties. If I know that a friend has a deathly fear of dogs, most would expect me to lock my pet Labrador in another room if that friend comes to visit. That specific knowledge can't be generalized: if a stranger with a similar phobia comes to my home, sees the dog, and is terrified, we might consider it unfortunate but not a moral failing on my part.

In short, the "knows or should have known" language, common in negligence-speak, suggests a more robust obligation centered not on what happens to be in any one person's subjective state of mind, nor on what entitlements the putative victim can justly claim abstractly, but rather on the surrounding milieu of social knowledge—the sort of knowledge and information that we generally expect typical society members to have access to such that it is reasonable to assume (indeed, demand) that they possess and consider. James Baldwin alluded to this point when, speaking of White persons whose racial practices "are destroying hundreds of thousands of lives" yet who claim innocence regarding any knowledge of these effects, he declared that it "is the innocence which constitutes the crime."[4] White people *should* know and can *reasonably be expected* to know of how certain practices or policies perpetuate racial injustice; when they maintain ignorance on these topics they are nonetheless committing a moral crime. Negligence is thus based not solely on the primary issue of what it means to treat someone else equally—what claims they have upon others in an ideal world—but also on the secondary issue of what knowledge of others we can assume is generally possessed. This latter concern—the social distribution of knowledge—affects what is and is not considered to be a reasonable behavior and thereby governs when we can say someone has been derelict in their duties toward others.

The negligence perspective frontloads the moral salience of the social distribution of knowledge. It suggests that a significant amount of moral reasoning can be thought of as a species of information processing.[5] How people are treated depends significantly on how vast quantities of information that might reveal morally salient facts are channeled to or shunted away from relevant decision-makers. The problem runs deeper than simple factual disagreement. (I think a minimum wage will increase working-class incomes; you think it will eliminate their jobs altogether.) In many cases, we will not know what it is we do not know

[4] James Baldwin, *The Fire Next Time* (Vintage, 1993), 5–6.

[5] For a review that applies this concept to administrative bodies, see Jennifer Nou, "Intra-Agency Coordination," *Harvard Law Review* 129, no. 2 (2015): 421–90.

(the "unknown unknowns," in Donald Rumsfeld's memorable typography), and in many others the causeways that render certain information available will not be neutral but will in fact (deliberately or unintentionally) be slanted to favor certain informational sources favoring certain moral judgments.

Focusing on the distribution of epistemic resources asks not just who knows what, but what and whose knowledge is readily accessible to and usable by other social actors when they engage in the project of moral reasoning. That there will be a distribution of knowledge is inevitable—there is no circumstance where every social actor can possess perfect information about all of his or her fellows. The problem exists not in the distribution but in the *mal*distribution. When we dismiss the testimonial offerings of certain perspectives because we deem them generally incredible, or when we lack the epistemic tools to render intelligible the claims of particular out-groups, we alter the social distribution of knowledge in ways likely to diminish the prospect that their just moral claims will resonate or be taken seriously.

In this vein, José Medina discusses several connected vices and virtues related to conditions of epistemic inequality.[6] For example, privileged persons may exhibit a sort of epistemic laziness wherein they exhibit no curiosity toward those areas of life which they do not (by virtue of social position) have to encounter. For example, for much of history, men could be epistemically lazy toward the field of housework. While nothing was stopping them from learning how their home was kept, because such work was often relegated to women they were not compelled to do so, and many chose to look no further. Medina's contention is not that all men are epistemically lazy in this respect—perhaps some were, for self-motivated reasons, interested in the day-to-day upkeep of the hearth—only that conditions of inequality can smooth the path toward this sort of behavior. A similar vice is that of arrogance—overconfidence in one's epistemic capacities that makes one disinclined to explore new perspectives and resistant to contrary evidence. In many circumstances patterns of segregation, media dominance, and other like social structures can deprive persons of natural sources of resistance to their package of epistemic assumptions. The epistemically arrogant subject may infer from this gap that there is nothing to challenge, that they know all that they need to know, and this too can lead to a lack of curiosity toward other potential outlooks on the world.

These vices come with corresponding virtues. A person possessing epistemic humility, for example, is not too wedded to his or her assumptions about the world; she concedes there are things she does not know and is open to the possibility of revising her beliefs or encountering alternative perspectives. This can

[6] José Medina, *The Epistemology of Resistance: Gender and Racial Oppression, Epistemic Injustice, and Resistant Imaginations* (Oxford University Press, 2013), 30–40 (vices); 40–48 (virtues).

lead to a second virtue of epistemic diligence or curiosity. These persons are motivated to explore the epistemic world around them (they are very interested in how the house is run) and perform accordingly—seeking out new sources of knowledge and alternate avenues to enrich their own perspectives.

While Medina tends to explicate his concepts in terms of individual behavior (albeit mediated by surrounding social structures), it is possible to translate his arguments onto institutions. Certain types of deliberative structures may embody various epistemic virtues and vices better than others, either in general or for certain types of disputes. For example, one defect (among others) of making decisions in the proverbial smoke-filled back room is that such an arrangement seems unlikely to elicit much curiosity about the views of persons not present. A well-publicized meeting in an accessible space, by contrast, could reduce the barriers inhibiting persons whose views differ from the dominant voices from effectively airing their concerns.

What is clear is that what we know, or can be reasonably expected to know, significantly mediates our moral obligations toward others, and also can structure our attitudes toward particular out-groups in important ways. Sometimes ignorance can assist in the maintenance of demeaning or disparaging attitudes toward a given group, enabling settled presumptions about their behavior to remain undisturbed. In this way, ignorance—a lack of knowledge—can be a motivated phenomenon: we prefer to remain in the dark about certain features of social life so that we can preserve comforting beliefs about ourselves, about others, or about the justice of entrenched social systems.[7] And even outside conscious or unconscious motivation, structural factors—for example, patterns of residential segregation—can deprive persons of opportunities for regular interaction across differences that would facilitate correcting mistaken views.[8]

For example, lack of knowledge regarding particularities of a given group's experience or behavior can cause people to believe that members of the group aren't satisfying certain duties that the group does, in fact, take seriously. Consider a prominent conservative objection to the Black Lives Matter movement: that the movement doesn't pay sufficient attention to so-called Black-on-Black crime.[9] The complaint underlying the objection is that, supposedly, there are

[7] Consider, for example, the works collected in Shannon Sullivan and Nancy Tuana, *Race and Epistemologies of Ignorance* (SUNY Press, 2007).

[8] David Schraub, "Sticky Slopes," *California Law Review* 101, no. 5 (2013): 1304 (observing that "social stratification . . . can act to insulate [its] beneficiaries from [its] effects; they experience all of the pleasure and see none of the pain").

[9] "So-called" because there are some who object to this term outright. The objection does not deny that sometimes there are crimes committed by a Black perpetrator against a Black victim. Indeed, given patterns of residential segregation, it is unsurprising that most crimes involve members of the same race occupying the perpetrator and victim positions. Rather, the argument is that such crimes are not typically *racialized* in the same way that transracial crimes are—for example, they do

significant efforts to protect Black lives only in situations where White people can be blamed; this alleged absence undermines the activist's contention that they truly care about Black lives at all and suggests that the "problem" is a concocted one. "Where," they ask, "are the movements and protests in cases where White people are not the perpetrators?"

One trouble with this objection is that it makes an important leap: from "I have not observed these movements" to "These movements do not exist"—a classic manifestation of Medina's vice of epistemic arrogance. In reality, of course, Black Americans (particularly in cities) are quite aware of the extent of violence suffered by their community and are emphatic in their efforts to change it—regardless of who is perpetrating it.[10] That these efforts gain little traction in the broader political climate *except* in certain cases where White people are involved does not mean that they do not exist. The ignorance displayed by the conservative objector to Black Lives Matter straddles the line of moral negligence, because it is fair to demand that the virtuous hearer should assume in these circumstances lacking awareness of the political practices of an out-group does not signal that the group is engaging in malign or negligent actions.[11] Yet—unless we are to assume that anything short of perfect virtue is a case of negligence—there will undoubtedly be situations where persons will be reasonably in the dark about the views of others and make inaccurate inferences from ignorance.

The preceding example offers a case where lack of knowledge can build or sustain malign attitudes toward a particular group. But maldistributions of social knowledge can cause harms in other ways. Consider two examples involving a camper in a forest. She intends to start a fire for the night and is looking for kindling. Fortunately, there are many potential sources of firewood nearby, such that while one source might be most convenient, selecting another comes with only trivial cost. In the first example, the most readily apparent source of kindling is a neatly arranged stack of logs about 20 feet from a cabin. There are no signs or fencing explicitly demonstrating that the logs are the property of the cabin owner (though it turns out they are), nor is the camper subjectively aware that they are the personal property of another. In the second example, there is no cabin or other property in the vicinity; however, it turns out that (unbeknownst

not implicate concerns about implicit shooter bias or racialized assumptions of self-defense. "Black-on-Black" is not purely descriptive—we do not, for example, typically refer to "White-on-White" crime—but rather attempts to present the *criminal* pattern as something specific to Blackness.

[10] *See* Jamelle Bouie, "Know Who Cares about Black-on-Black Crime? Black People," *Patriot-News*, December 2, 2014, https://www.pennlive.com/opinion/2014/12/know_who_cares_about_black-on-_1.html.

[11] Cf. Miranda Fricker, *Epistemic Injustice: Power and the Ethics of Knowing* (Oxford University Press, 2007), 172 (noting that in "contexts where there is not sufficient time" to attend to a given claim, the virtuous response would be "*reserving* judgment" on the claim's merits).

to the camper) these logs are in fact property of a local Druids' group and are an essential part of a ritual to be performed later that evening.

It seems that, if the camper takes the firewood, she is properly labeled negligent in the first example but not the second. The reason why lies not in the cost of avoidance (stipulated to be trivial in both cases) nor in the degree of harm suffered by the victim (however much harm we think results from taking another's property, presumably taking *sacred* property is more serious still). We could locate the difference in the failure of the Druid group to take adequate steps to warn potential encroaching campers that this is their log pile—but then the cabin owner likewise did not take any significant steps to publicize the ownership of their logs either.

The difference, rather, lies in what relevant knowledge we think can be socially assumed. We think that most people either know, or should know, that a neatly stacked pile of logs next to a cabin provides sufficient indicia of ownership such that one is rightfully on notice that they may be the property of another and should not be taken (especially where other easily available substitutes exist). By contrast, we do not expect that the average person is aware of the schedule or practices of small Druid groups such that any similar red flags would be raised by this particular log pile. Of course, we can play with the facts and the relevant social norms to change this outcome. Maybe this Druid group's practices are in fact widely known in the community such that most campers would know full well not to take from lumber piles of this sort. On the other hand, maybe there is a communal norm that says unfenced log piles are free for the taking, such that it would not be unreasonable for the camper to assume the pile near the cabin was available for use. The point is that negligence depends on what people are assumed to know—the social distribution of knowledge. The contours of this distribution thus become very important.

Indeed, as the above discussion illuminates, the social distribution of knowledge can also cause problems in assessing standards of due care. What one can reasonably be expected to know will typically be socially understood by reference to the standard package of knowledge available to members of the dominant social groups—the "reasonable person" implicitly becoming "the reasonable White upper-middle-class straight Christian man." Note that it is not necessary to impute any bad faith or ill will to such a "reasonable" person to identify a problem. To the contrary, one significant result of maldistributed social knowledge is that it can prevent even persons who recognize gaps in their knowledge and who are committed to filling them from successfully doing so.[12]

Consequently, while adding a negligence component to moral inquiry is certainly a significant expansion—for example, it is how we can deem the camper in

[12] Medina, *Epistemology of Resistance*, 43.

the first example to have engaged in at least some moral wrong—it does not mean that every loss suffered by a particular person comes with a specific morally blameworthy perpetrator. The Druids seem to have experienced a tangible and unfortunate loss, one that as a respectful and tolerant society we would prefer them not to have suffered, but there is no readily available person we can easily label as a wrongdoer. For some, the inquiry stops here: if no person can fairly be said to have wronged (negligently or deliberately) the person suffering the loss, then that is that. Yet this is a very cramped read on the project of moral analysis. It seems we should be at least interested in minimizing feelings of hurt or suffering where feasible, regardless of whether they are at any given point attributable to a malicious or even negligent actor.

Alan David Freeman's influential distinction between "perpetrator" and "victim" perspectives on discrimination illuminates why identifying a specific agent acting wrongly is insufficient.[13] Put roughly, the "perpetrator" outlook seeks to identify specific wrongful actors and punish them for their malfeasance. This can occur through formal levers of the state (tort law, criminal sanctions, etc.), but it also can apply to our appraisals of how to think about antidiscrimination norms as a social practice; there is no discrimination "problem" unless there is a specific malign perpetrator causing it. The "victim" perspective, by contrast, looks to see how marginalized communities experience losses or harms and seeks to rectify such problems as best as possible. The requirement that the wrongs be "caused" by a morally culpable perpetrator is unnecessary.

The focus on moral negligence is an attempt to expand the perpetrator perspective—perhaps a laudatory one, but also a limiting one. While it raises the behavioral bar, once it has been established that no identifiable party has been negligent (or intentionally malign), the analysis stops. The baseline of "reasonable knowledge" is left untouched, and there is little room for any more wide-spanning remedies and recompense for the out-group.[14] Indeed, sometimes too much of a focus on questions of perpetration—negligent or otherwise—can lead to the undesirable conflation of systematic reform efforts with aspersions of blame. If the project of addressing moral wrongs simply

[13] Alan David Freeman, "Legitimizing Racial Discrimination through Antidiscrimination Law: A Critical Review of Supreme Court Doctrine," *Minnesota Law Review* 62, no. 6 (1978): 1049–119.

[14] Shiffrin approaches the problem in the opposite direction: she wishes to minimize the focus on remedies because she worries that concentration on what sort of negligence can be remedied may have a distorting impact on our conception of negligence itself: "On the one hand, where remedies are limited, their contours may exert a distorting influence on what can be recognized as negligence. On the other, where remedies are overwhelmingly large or harsh, concerns about disproportionality and unfair burdens may infect and depress one's assessment of the moral significance of negligence." Shiffrin, "Moral Neglect," 206. I view this as the flip side of the same coin: if remedies are limited by what is negligent, then we may be too stingy in imagining remedies; if negligence is limited by what can be effectively and proportionately remedied, then we may be too cramped in conceptualizing negligence.

is the project of ascribing blame, then persons will assume that institutional reform endeavors are—implicitly or explicitly—labeling them as wrongdoers; the reforms themselves will be conceptualized as a form of punishment.

To be sure, Freeman's victim perspective does not itself give us a means to determine which deprivations are *wrongful* deprivations and which ones are merely unfortunate tough breaks to be endured. If the deprivation occurs in a truly idiosyncratic or random fashion, for example, there might be no reason to rejigger social structures to avoid it (nor, for that matter, are there usually easily ascertainable mechanisms for avoiding truly idiosyncratic or random harms). But very often that is not the case. The social distribution of knowledge provides unequal protection to different groups within a society, and does so predictably. Just as we might expect social out-groups to more commonly be the victims of moral negligence (because dominant actors are less likely to respect them as moral equals), it seems clear that social out-groups are more likely to be "victims" of nonnegligent deprivations as well, where the harms they suffer are not attributable to an unreasonable failure of deliberation by the "perpetrator."

One implication of this analysis is that it can alter how we assess claims for restitution, accommodation, or legislative alteration *ex post*—once the hitherto socially unknown harms come to light. As our unfortunate Druids can attest, everyday persons (including legislators and other policymakers) are often unaware of the tenets and practices of minority religions. Among other things, this makes it more likely that they will pass laws which substantially burden said minority's religious faith. In some circumstances, of course, this might be a product of malice: the minority sect is actively disliked, and majoritarian actors seek to suppress it. But in other cases in seems fair to suspect that there is no malevolence in play: it just did not occur to the legislators that there was a conflict.[15] It is perfectly reasonable to suspect that, in at least some cases, the legislators would be willing to alter the law or admit to an accommodation had they been fully aware of its consequences on the out-group.

Majority (or at least socially prominent) religious groups are less likely to face this particular problem. An American legislative body is unlikely to be simply unaware of how a given proposal might be in tension with Christian beliefs. Indeed, it is, if anything, easier to imagine a case of outright prejudice (particularly against Christian subgroups—Catholics or evangelicals) motivating a given law, especially in a community where that group is a (localized) minority. Cases of explicit prejudice are of course wrongful, but the wrong is not the failure to understand how the proposed policy would negatively impact the group. (In the

[15] See Michael W. McConnell, "Free Exercise Revisionism and the *Smith* Decision," *University of Chicago Law Review* 57, no. 4 (1990): 1136n117 ("Most legislators are unaware of the problems of minority religions, and many (though not all) minority religions are poorly positioned to defend their own interests.").

case of animus, such impacts are a feature rather than a bug.) More frequently, of course, there is no prejudice, and the competing interests—the objectives of the law versus the religious hardships it imposes on the majority—are explicitly considered and incorporated into the debate.

This observation indicates that deliberators assessing the need for an accommodation *post hoc* should be more attentive to religious accommodation requests by minority faiths and more deferential to the enacted judgment of the legislature when the challengers are members of the majority creed. The reason here is not that minority faiths are more deserving of protection or should enjoy special dispensation from majoritarian legal judgments. Rather, the reason relates to the differing pathways through which we can reasonably expect the relevant moral knowledge to enter into the deliberative processes. In most cases, laws which substantially burden majority religious practices will never even be proposed; legislators are perfectly aware of the majoritarian creed and have no interest in gratuitously attacking it.[16] It can therefore be reasonably assumed that, where such a conflict does manifest, the legislature carefully and deliberately weighed the relevant moral interests and concluded that the objective being pursued was sufficiently weighty as to justify the religious burden.[17] The Supreme Court's *Hobby Lobby*[18] case provides a good example (albeit in a context where the Court, in my view, came to the wrong conclusion). There, a mandate requiring employers to cover contraceptive healthcare was challenged by a company whose Christian owners had religious objections to contraception. Clearly, the decision to cover (and require that employers cover) contraceptive healthcare was not made in ignorance of the strong opposition to such policy by Catholic and conservative Christian sects. In enacting such a rule regardless, the political branches presumably concluded that the importance of securing affordable and comprehensive healthcare access for all persons, regardless of where they were employed, trumped the (acknowledged) religious objection. Consequently, the Supreme Court should have been less aggressive in second-guessing this legislative judgment in a context where there is little reason to think the religious freedom concerns were ignored, dismissed, or otherwise underappreciated.

By contrast, consider cases where smaller (often Indigenous) religious groups require access to hallucinogenic drugs as part of their sacramental practices.[19] It

[16] Frederick Mark Gedicks, *The Rhetoric of Church and State* (Duke University Press, 1995), 115 ("What the majority believes interferes with its religious practices . . . is unlikely to become law; what the majority considers necessary for its religious practices . . . is unlikely to be prohibited by law; and what the majority finds objectionable . . . is not likely to be made a legal obligation.").

[17] David Schraub, "When Separation Doesn't Work: The Religion Clause as an Anti-Subordination Principle," *Dartmouth Law Journal* 5 (2007): 162.

[18] Burwell v. Hobby Lobby Stores, Inc. 573 U.S. 682 (2014).

[19] See, e.g., Gonzales v. O Centro Espirita Beneficente Uniao do Vegetal, 546 U.S. 418 (2006); Employment Division of Oregon v. Smith, 494 U.S. 872 (1990).

is unlikely that the legislators who drafted the Controlled Substances Act were even cognizant of, let alone deeply deliberated over, the effect this law would have on these religious minorities. Unlike *Hobby Lobby*, it would be unrealistic to assert that Congress had explicitly or implicitly weighed the competing interests in passing the law; it is more reasonable to infer that they had not thought on the question at all because the relevant knowledge was not socially salient. In such circumstances, an individualized *ex post* challenge by members of the group provides a better mechanism for incorporating the previously unaccounted-for knowledge into the process of moral reasoning.

The upshot is not that majoritarian accommodation claims should be universally rejected or minority claims universally acceded to. It is possible that the legislature's deliberations—though perfectly cognizant of the harms imposed upon the majority faith vis-à-vis the relevant policy interests—were nonetheless lacking in weighing the balance; this would be a standard-issue instance of moral negligence. Likewise it is entirely possible that a judge, now entirely on notice regarding the minority claimant's objections and having given them full, fair, and charitable consideration, would nonetheless determine that an accommodation is unwarranted.[20] Rather, the point is to suggest that we are far more likely to make mistakes in our moral reasoning—and make those mistakes unevenly—when we fail to acknowledge what knowledge is socially available as a default and what requires additional steps to access. In different—but surprisingly resonant—ways, both legal processes and protests can offer a pathway for getting underserved currents of knowledge onto the deliberative radar screens of relevant decision-makers.

Law's (Literal) Rules for Dismissal

The Federal Rules of Civil Procedure (particularly Rule 12, which concerns motions to dismiss) formalize the circumstances wherein courts cannot hear or consider a claim that is presented before them. In doing so, the concept of dismissal also establishes that, if a claim does meet the criteria that make it into a justiciable case or controversy, then the parties are entitled to their day in court.[21] A claim which survives a motion to dismiss is a claim which, at some

[20] Consider Bowen v. Roy, 476 U.S. 693 (1986) (rejecting a Native American family's claim that assigning their daughter a social security number would violate their religious beliefs); Jeremy Waldron, "The Core of the Case against Judicial Review," *Yale Law Journal* 115, no. 6 (2006): 1398 ("People—including members of topical minorities—do not necessarily have the rights they think they have. They may be wrong about the rights they have; the majority may be right.").

[21] See, e.g., New Orleans Pub. Serv., Inc. v. Council of New Orleans, 491 U.S. 350, 358 (1989) ("Our cases have long supported the proposition that federal courts lack the authority to abstain from the exercise of jurisdiction that has been conferred."); Cohens v. Virginia, 19 U.S. 264, 404 (1821) ("We

level, must be heard. This quality of the courts—their status as a place where decision-makers *have to listen*—was recognized from America's earliest days. In *Democracy in America*, Alexis de Tocqueville observed, "It is the essence of judicial power . . . not to come of itself to the assistance of those who are oppressed, but to be constantly at the disposition of the most humble among them. *However weak one supposes him, he can always force the judge to listen to his complaint and to respond to it*: that is due to the very constitution of judicial power."[22] One hundred years later, Charles Hamilton Houston explained the NAACP's litigation-centric strategy in pursuit of African American civil rights in similar terms: "[W]e use the courts as a medium of public discussion, since it is the one place where we can force America to listen."[23]

Law offers a unique opportunity to confront the problem of dismissal because—for those claims which *do* fit inside the proper templates—courts must generally hear the cases presented to them. While pundits, politicians, and everyday people are free to consider any claims they like, they are rarely obligated to do so. The unabridged freedom of the private sphere which allows any claim to be heard also allows any claim to be ignored. If a person responds to an uncomfortable assertion by dismissing it out of hand, there is rarely anything their interlocutor can do to force the issue.

Writers who have considered the judiciary as a vector of public deliberation have often overlooked these advantages, evincing a marked skepticism toward the judiciary's ability to enhance public dialogue. There is ample reason to be skeptical of the ability of judges to provide any unique deliberative insight beyond what is already present in the broader population.[24] Judges, after all, "come from society and thus are likely to harbor prejudices similar to those held in society at large (or at least society's elite)."[25] Consequently, it is far from clear why they should be expected to possess any particular deliberative advantage unmatched by other, nonjudicial actors. For their part, judges insist on reminding the public that the role of the judiciary is not to "right every wrong, suture

have no more right to decline the exercise of jurisdiction which is given, than to usurp that which is not given.").

[22] Alexis de Tocqueville, *Democracy in America* (1840), ed. and trans. Harvey C. Mansfield and Delba Winthrop (University of Chicago Press 2000), 668 (emphasis added).

[23] Mark V. Tushnet, *The NAACP's Legal Strategy against Segregated Education, 1925–1950* (University of North Carolina Press 1987), 18.

[24] See Douglas NeJaime, "Winning through Losing," *Iowa Law Review* 96, no. 3 (2011): 949 (presenting these reasons, among others, for why many scholars believe that courts are "constrained" and litigation is an "empty promise" for social reform movements); Gerald N. Rosenberg, *The Hollow Hope: Can Courts Bring about Social Change?*, 2nd ed. (University of Chicago Press, 2008).

[25] David Schraub, "Unsuspecting," *Boston University Law Review* 96, no. 2 (2010): 410; see also David Schraub, Comment, "The Price of Victory: Political Triumphs and Judicial Protection in the Gay Rights Movement," *University of Chicago Law Review* 77, no. 3 (2010): 1463 ("Where there is no social support for protecting a given minority, it is unclear why judges, who are part of that same society, should be expected to consistently rise above the prejudices of their times.").

every societal wound, and correct every injustice."[26] And even where there is a valid role for the judiciary to play in addressing a given social problem, judges can nonetheless select only from a narrow range of possible interventions—large swaths of potentially productive or useful remedies remain outside of their purview.[27]

Whereas in private conversation we are free to explore any thoughts or claims which catch our fancy, legal concepts must be sufficiently clear such that citizens have considerable *advance* warning regarding what sorts of behaviors are permissible or not, and must have a broad enough base of popular support to be enacted into positive law. Consequently, law by necessity will often exclude many types of claims which do not fit inside preexisting doctrinal boxes. This is what Robert Cover famously referred to as law's "jurispathic" quality.[28] Law can accommodate only a small sliver of the potential understandings which might animate a given conception of rights, justice, or the good. Bound by the need for order and predictability, it must "kill" other potential sources of legal understanding.[29] The (civil procedure) tool of dismissal in many ways operates to screen out those claims which—whatever their merits as an abstract notion of justice—do not fall inside the relatively narrow borders of accepted legal doctrine.

Compared to the legislative branch (to say nothing of informal efforts at popular persuasion), the judiciary is by design a narrow and constrained body—one that can redress claims only through the very narrow prism afforded by established legal precedent. Many claims—even very important, very justified claims—cannot be legitimately made in the argot of the law. For this reason, legal forums are often asserted to be "especially problematic" arenas for the deliberative project because of "the restrictions they impose upon admissible argument and so free dialogue."[30]

These arguments are not wrong. But they are incomplete. It is true that courts are in an important respect less "open" to claims than are, say, newspapers or legislators. Newspapers can publish whatever they want; there is no "jurisdictional" bar that they need to account for first. Likewise, legislators are largely free to focus their attention on any cause or interest group that strikes their fancy; they are not limited in their ability to conduct hearings in the same way that a

[26] Gerald E. Rosen, "The Hard Part of Judging," *Suffolk University Law Review* 34, no. 1 (2000): 9.
[27] See Freeman, "Legitimizing Racial Discrimination," 1052–57 (discussing the limited ways in which courts can truly address racial inequality in America given law's understanding of racial discrimination through the lens of discrete perpetrators).
[28] Robert M. Cover, "Foreword: Nomos and Narrative," *Harvard Law Review* 97, no. 1 (1983): 40.
[29] *Id.* at 53.
[30] John S. Dryzek, *Deliberative Democracy and Beyond: Liberals, Critics, Contestations* (Oxford University Press, 2000), 71.

court is.[31] And of course private conversation is open to any topic or debate that holds participants' interests. But in another respect, courts possess an important advantage over other deliberative institutions. Nobody can force the newspaper to publish your column, or a senator to meet with your interest group, or a congressional committee to hold a hearing on your bill. The same freedom that allows them to listen to everything equally grants them the right to ignore anything.

But judges are not free in this way. As Chief Justice John Marshall observed in *Cohens v. Virginia*:

> The judiciary cannot, as the legislature may, avoid a measure because it approaches the confines of the constitution. We cannot pass it by because it is doubtful. With whatever doubts, with whatever difficulties, a case may be attended, we must decide it, if it be brought before us. We have no more right to decline the exercise of jurisdiction which is given, than to usurp that which is not given. The one or the other would be treason to the constitution. Questions may occur which we would gladly avoid, but we cannot avoid them. All we can do is, to exercise our best judgment, and conscientiously to perform our duty.[32]

Just as judges are limited in what they can hear, so too are they limited in what they can decline to hear. The rules of judicial dismissal (indeed, the basic fact that, unlike its private or legislative counterparts, judicial dismissal is bounded by rules at all) can act to force consideration of certain claims that would otherwise go unheard. Law occupies a virtually unique deliberative niche in that certain claims *must be heard*—even if they are uncomfortable, even if the relevant decision-makers would rather ignore them.

What law provides against dismissal is a demarcated path through which certain claims, framed within preset and (relatively) stable borders, are entitled to be heard. When Robert Bolt described law as "a causeway upon which, so long as he keeps to it, a citizen may walk safely,"[33] this is not what he meant—but the metaphor resonates. Law may not recognize certain forms of discrimination, and people may find discrimination claims distasteful generally, but an employment discrimination claim that dutifully follows the borders of the *McDonnell Douglas* test will at the very least make it to summary judgment.[34] As a consequence,

[31] *Cf.* John Locke, *Second Treatise of Government* (1690), ed. C. B. Macpherson (Hackett, 1980), 83–88 (discussing the "prerogative" powers of government).

[32] Cohens v. Virginia, 19 U.S. 264, 404 (1821).

[33] Robert Bolt, *A Man for All Seasons* (Heinemann, 1996), 92.

[34] McDonnell Douglas Corp. v. Green, 411 U.S. 792, 802–4 (1973) (articulating the "prima facie case" that must be made demonstrating employment discrimination, with the employer then obliged "to articulate some legitimate, nondiscriminatory reason" for its decision and the plaintiff then required to point to evidence challenging that rationale as a pretext for discrimination). But see

law can offer an expressway past the first two cognitive checkpoints discussed in Chapter 2. Unlike everyday conversation, a legal claim that adheres to certain preset conventions generally *has to be heard*—a court cannot shunt it aside simply because it is inconvenient or uncomfortable.

From the Court of Law to the Court of Public Opinion

Courts can also, in the right circumstances,[35] help alleviate some of the problems identified above regarding how social deliberation accretes conclusions ignorant of the perspectives of marginalized stakeholders. Negligence relates to questions of personal responsibility through a standard of reasonableness; generally, such standards will be constructed against a backdrop of knowledge, practices, and understandings that are relatively common among society (or, perhaps more accurately, those social actors empowered to make decisions). Precisely because this backdrop is not neutral, it will still result in out-groups suffering a disproportionate share of *non*negligent wrongs. A just polity, therefore, should be highly attentive to the creation of additional pathways where uncommon knowledge can enter into public debate and deliberation.

As Iris Marion Young observes, "Normative judgment is best understood as the product of dialogue under conditions of equality and mutual respect. Ideally, the outcome of such dialogue and judgment is just and legitimate only if all the affected perspectives have a voice."[36] In broad democratic spaces legislating prospectively, it may be impossible or impracticable for "affected perspectives" to be incorporated simply because it is difficult to know in advance who they will be—especially among relatively unknown out-groups. Once a case hits the judiciary, by contrast, the problem has been narrowed down into a concrete "case or controversy" where affected parties are entitled to be heard and can correct misunderstandings. The judicial mode of deciding cases—focusing on the specificity of a *particular* controversy with *particular* facts implicating *particular* parties—differs importantly from more abstracted legislative reasoning

Elizabeth M. Schneider, "The Dangers of Summary Judgment: Gender and Federal Civil Litigation," *Rutgers Law Review* 59, no. 4 (2007): 709 (citation omitted) (suggesting that judicial "dislike of or discomfort with certain claims—whether employment discrimination, sexual harassment, or Family Medical Leave Act cases"—has prompted judges to be disproportionately willing to dispense of such cases at the summary judgment stage); David Schraub, "*Torgerson*'s Twilight: The Antidiscrimination Jurisprudence of Judge Diana E. Murphy," *Minnesota Law Review* 103, no. 1 (2018): 65–92 (suggesting that judges had placed distinct hurdles in front of discrimination cases which enabled them to more easily dispose of them at summary judgment).

[35] Of course, not every problem is amenable to judicial resolution. So judicial review can serve as at best only a partial corrective to social ignorance.

[36] Iris Marion Young, *Intersecting Voices: Dilemmas of Gender, Political Philosophy, and Policy* (Princeton University Press, 1997), 59.

and makes it easier for groups that might otherwise be drowned out in the din of public conversation to make themselves heard.[37] And because courts grapple with concrete "cases and controversies" rather than broad and abstracted legislative programs, they are able to zero in on the precise injuries and harms suffered by particular victims who might otherwise go unheard. Such persons are least likely to have their interests considered by democratic associations deliberating generally—sometimes due to bias, but often simply due to ignorance. The comparative advantage of the judiciary is not (necessarily) that they are comprised of better or wiser or more dispassionate deliberators but that they are an institution wherein—some of the time—affected parties must be given a hearing.

The ability to get to a hearing matters not just as a tool for overcoming ignorance but as a tool for overcoming dismissal. It matters—tangibly and as a matter of personal dignity—that "hard thought" issues of central importance to marginalized group members be seen and treated as worthy of debate.[38] Just as the inability to articulate a given claim in legal language can render it infirm even outside the courtroom, the fact that a claim has legal resonance comes with legitimizing force. When Catherine MacKinnon identified the importance of law recognizing the concept of sexual harassment, she did not focus on the tangible remedies that might result from a winning suit. What was more important was that women were "given a forum, legitimacy to speak, authority to make claims"—only after this litany did she conclude with "and an avenue for *possible* relief."[39] An important element of oppression is often its denial that the disenfranchised group even has the right to present claims.[40] A judicial forum can be

[37] As Oliver Wendell Holmes put it, "General propositions do not decide concrete cases." Lochner v. New York, 198 U.S. 45, 76 (1905) (Holmes, J., dissenting). David Strauss has argued that this "common law" method of adjudication—which is highly attentive to the specific context of particular controversies rather than being wedded too closely to abstract moral or even legal theorizing—represents the distinctive professional niche that judges and lawyers are trained to occupy. David A. Strauss, *The Living Constitution* (Oxford University Press, 2010).

[38] See Iris Marion Young, "Communication and the Other: Beyond Deliberative Democracy," in *Intersecting Voices: Dilemmas of Gender, Political Philosophy, and Policy* (Princeton University Press, 1997), 71 ("In a discussion situation in which different people with different aims, values, and interests seek to solve collective problems justly, it is not enough to make assertions and give reasons. One must also be heard."); Robert Dahl, *Democracy and Its Critics* (Yale University Press, 1989), 109 (arguing that the principle of effective democratic participation includes giving each citizen "adequate and equal opportunities for placing questions on the agenda and for expressing reasons for endorsing one outcome rather than another").

[39] Catherine MacKinnon, "Sexual Harassment: Its First Decade in Court," in *Feminism Unmodified: Discourses on Life and Law* (Harvard University Press, 1987), 104 (emphasis added).

[40] Cf. Dred Scott v. Sandford, 60 U.S. 393, 405 (1857) (concluding that descendants of enslaved Africans, even if they are acknowledged as citizens of a state, nonetheless would not be citizens of the United States and therefore would not be "entitled to sue as such in one of its courts"); Hannah Arendt, *The Origins of Totalitarianism* (Harvest, 1994), 296 ("The fundamental deprivation of human rights is manifested first and above all in the deprivation of a place in the world which makes opinions significant and actions effective.").

a rare arena where those claims must be given at least the trappings of reasoned analysis.

Arguments favoring an enhanced judicial role in the protection of minority groups typically focus on how judges are relatively insulated from popular pressure and prejudices which promote discriminatory legislation.[41] This position immediately runs into trouble, as it is by no means clear that courts are *systematically* more likely to be sympathetic to the interests of dispossessed groups than are the democratic branches.[42] There is, after all, something a bit odd about responding to the problem of minority dispossession by delegating the issue to a body that is whiter, maler, straighter, richer, and older than the American electorate writ large. Moreover, there is a more general paradox identified above: if judges are unlikely to differ significantly from popular conceptions of key political issues, how can they possess any significant advantage as reformers vis-à-vis democratic or social actors?

The focus on dismissal, however, illuminates an institutional advantage of judges that cuts through this Gordian knot. It is plausible—indeed it seems likely—that two otherwise similarly situated deliberators will reach differing conclusions over a contentious issue if one is forced to provide reasons for their position and the other is not. Judges do not necessarily reason *differently* than everyday people, but they are forced to reason *more often*, particularly in politically or emotionally fraught situations. Judges may be most likely to give due accord to marginalized voices, not because they are especially moral, wise, or insulated from democratic pressures but simply because the norms of their position often force them to engage in an argument where others do not have to.

Consider the rapid evolution of Americans' views on same-sex marriage.[43] For many years, the prospect of gay marriage could be dismissed as radical, extreme, a nonstarter, ludicrous—all responses that do not require any serious engagement of the issue on its merits. But courts are limited in their ability to resort

[41] See, e.g., United States v. Carolene Prods. Co., 304 U.S. 144, 152n4 (1938) (promoting heightened judicial scrutiny in circumstances where laws target "discrete and insular minorities" burdened by prejudice in the political system).

[42] See Waldron, "Core of the Case," 1404–5 (noting that the "argument for judicial review depends on a particular assumption about the distribution of support for the minority's rights. The sympathy is assumed to be strongest among political elites."); Christine Bateup, "The Dialogic Promise: Assessing the Normative Potential of Theories of Constitutional Dialogue," *Brooklyn Law Review* 71, no. 3 (2006): 1148–49 (criticizing as "empirically questionable" the notion that "judges remain better suited to decide matters of principle due to their comparative institutional competences" supposedly stemming from their "political insulation"); Chris Guthrie, Jeffrey J. Rachlinski, and Andrew J. Wistrich, "Inside the Judicial Mind," *Cornell Law Review* 86, no. 4 (2001): 783 (internal quotations and citations omitted) ("Inasmuch as judging is choice, the conclusions drawn from psychological research on human judgment and choice likely apply to judges as well.").

[43] See Pew Research Center, "Changing Attitudes on Gay Marriage," May 14, 2019, http://www.pewforum.org/fact-sheet/changing-attitudes-on-gay-marriage/ (documenting a 30-point swing in favor of gay marriage between 2004 and 2019).

to *those* sorts of response. Nominally, a court cannot dismiss a complaint on the grounds that it is "a nonstarter." They need to provide logically and legally cognizable reasons. Now to be sure, the evaluative aspect of motivated cognition gives judges plenty of opportunities to turn aside novel or unpopular claims even while purporting to deal with them on their merits.[44] And losing "on the merits" can come with significant dignitary harms too, particularly where the proffered reasons are themselves biased or demeaning toward the claimant.[45] Getting past the first two cognitive checkpoints clearly is not everything. But it is not nothing either. Being in the realm where one's opponents have to provide reasons against your claim is, for many groups, a significant and meaningful advance.

And just as a dismissed or avoided claim can lead to a "spiral of silence" further marginalizing its proponents, where law successfully places an issue on social radar screens it can have a cascading effect on public attitudes. Once gay marriage broke through with legal victories[46] it became correspondingly more difficult in public discussion to simply dismiss the concept outright. The early judicial decisions affirming gay marriage did not end the debate, but they did signal that a debate must be had.[47] And being in the realm of substantive debate is a much better place for gay marriage advocates to be than they were when the issue could be tossed aside as one of fringe radicals. Meanwhile, as people start to rethink the issue (or really, think critically about it for the first time), they can reason from and rely on the signals provided by the instigating legal decisions.[48]

Even claims which lose in the courts can have a salutary effect in promoting important social conversations.[49] Sometimes legal decisions spark public

[44] Not to mention the obvious point that, sometimes, marginalized groups nonetheless simply are wrong on the merits of their claims. *See* Waldron, "Core of the Case," 1398 ("People—including members of topical minorities—do not necessarily have the rights they think they have. They may be wrong about the rights they have; the majority may be right.").

[45] See Martha Minow, *Making All the Difference: Inclusion, Exclusion, and American Law* (Cornell University Press, 1990), 92–93 (citation omitted) (describing the negative effects of bringing a discrimination claim that "define some people as different, and inferior, in light of the norm").

[46] See, e.g., Baehr v. Lewin, 852 P.2d 44, 67 (Haw. 1993) (holding a law that prohibited same-sex marriage per se unconstitutional under the equal protection clause of the Hawaii Constitution); Goodridge v. Dep't of Pub. Health, 798 N.E. 2d 941, 969 (Mass. 2003) ("We declare that barring an individual from the protections, benefits, and obligations of civil marriage solely because that person would marry a person of the same sex violates the Massachusetts Constitution.").

[47] See, e.g., Jane S. Schacter, "Sexual Orientation, Social Change, and the Courts," *Drake Law Review* 54, no. 4 (2006): 871 ("[I]t may one day be said that Baehr and Goodridge started a process that culminated in same-sex couples securing widespread relationship protections, whether through marriage or civil union.").

[48] See David Schraub, "The Perils and Promise of the Holder Memo," *Cardozo Law Review* De Novo (2012): 201 ("[H]igh-profile legal discussions, particularly when instigated by known political actors who can serve as effective opinion leaders, become part of the larger cocktail of considerations voters use to assess a given social question.").

[49] See NeJaime, "Winning through Losing," 954 (citations omitted) (noting that, even among scholars who believe that *Brown* failed to directly make a significant dent in segregation, some nonetheless credit it for "fueling a powerful social movement by raising consciousness, driving

conversations leading to formal amendments to the relevant legal regimes. The Supreme Court's 2007 decision in *Ledbetter v. Goodyear Tire*, limiting the time-frame for workers to bring suit over discriminatory pay, was met with great public outrage and a swift statutory reversal.[50] But even where it results in no legal modifications, a losing claim can nonetheless have important social ramifications. When the Iowa Supreme Court held in 2013 that a male employer's decision to fire a female subordinate for being too sexually attractive was not illegal sex discrimination,[51] much of the public outrage did not take the form of technical quibbles with the court's legal analysis but rather with the harmful nature of such a rule as a broader moral principle.[52] The writers of these critiques seemed to view the decision of the court as the definitive, socially sanctioned answer to the question "Is firing a woman because she is supposedly too 'desirable' to her male supervisor justifiable as a matter of gender equality?" If they were right, then the decision is depressing indeed.[53] But the public reaction to the decision—largely critical and incredulous—is at least as important as the formal legal outcome. The legal proceedings placed this sort of behavior in public conversation, and the general consensus that emerged seemed to be that such an action is wrong. Identifying and articulating that consensus has value regardless of the formal legal disposition of the case. It is unlikely that 30, 40, or 50 years ago

fundraising, legitimizing a cause, and influencing other state actors"); Martha Minow, "Interpreting Rights: An Essay for Robert Cover," *Yale Law Journal* 96 (1987): 1867 (noting the importance of "even those claims that lose, or have lost in the past, if they continue to represent claims that muster people's hopes and articulate their continuing efforts to persuade").

[50] Ledbetter v. Goodyear Tire & Rubber Co., 550 U.S. 618, 628–29 (2007) (requiring that a plaintiff with a sex discrimination claim file an EEOC complaint within 180 days of the alleged violation because "current effects alone cannot breathe life into prior, uncharged discrimination"), abrogated by Lilly Ledbetter Fair Pay Act of 2009, Pub. L. No. 111-2, 123 Stat. 5, 6 (2009) (emphasis added) (recognizing that an "unlawful employment practice occurs . . . when an individual is affected by application of a discriminatory compensation decision or other practice").

[51] Nelson v. James H. Knight DDS, 834 N.W.2d 64 (Iowa 2013) (holding that terminating a female employee because of her appearance, while unfair, does not amount to illegal gender discrimination).

[52] See, e.g., Jessica Valenti, "Asking for It," *The Nation*, January 11, 2013, http://www.thenation.com/asking-it ("When this dentist in Iowa can fire his assistant for turning him on—even though she's done absolutely nothing wrong—the message again is that it's men's ability to work that's important."); Doug Barry, "Iowa Supreme Court Says It Was Totally Cool for a Dentist to Fire His 'Irresistibly Attractive' Female Employee," *Jezebel*, December 22, 2012), http://jezebel.com/iowa-supreme-court-says-it-was-totally-cool-for-a-denti-5970736 (criticizing the paradoxical nature of the *Knight* decision's failure to recognize gender discrimination in the face of purportedly straightforward evidence to the contrary). Of course, this is not to say that there is not space to argue that the decision was legally wrong, or that the decision was legally correct and that the law should be changed. But the point is that the decision was taken by many to entail not just the court's legal judgment on the meaning of the relevant antidiscrimination statutes but also a considered moral judgment on gender relations that was taken to be normatively dangerous. But see Nelson, 834 N.W.2d at 73 (stating that the relevant question was not whether "a jury could find that Dr. Knight treated Nelson badly," but rather whether the alleged facts constituted unlawful discrimination).

[53] See, e.g., Valenti, "Asking for It"; Joseph Diebold, "Iowa Supreme Court: It's Okay to Fire a Woman for Being Too Attractive," *ThinkProgress*, July 12, 2013, https://thinkprogress.org/iowa-supreme-court-its-ok-to-fire-a-woman-for-being-too-attractive-d022b15121e7/.

behavior like this would have even made it onto the social radar screen. Courts provided a vector for that social conversation to happen, and the results outside the courtroom were overwhelmingly positive.

The mere fact that—sometimes—judges have to listen is a critical and underappreciated institutional advantage of the judiciary, not just over the other political branches but over other modes of deliberation. An important part of political freedom is the ability to argue, before the relevant institutions, that one is being treated unfairly. Even in a just society "bad things happen: people get assaulted, mugged, sacked without due reason and so on. But what is crucial . . . is the victim's ability to *contest* the wrongful treatment."[54] If the "relevant institutional body" (the police, the courts, the grievance committee, etc.) does not hear—or does not fairly and impartially consider—the complaint, then this essential element of political freedom is lacking.[55]

When political or social deliberation functions properly, it offers a forum wherein people feel confident that the wrongs they experience will be carefully considered and reasonably redressed. This does not mean that claimants must always have their claims ultimately vindicated, but it does mean that they will be taken under consideration. To be sure, nobody can give full consideration to every potential claim or controversy. Deliberative resources are scarce; triaging is inevitable. But it is equally clear that these distributional decisions are fraught with danger. When given the opportunity to choose, deliberators will predictably focus their attention on those claims and claimants least likely to disturb or unsettle their deeply felt social or ideological priors.

Because courts offer a space where this discretion is constrained, they are uniquely advantaged vis-à-vis other deliberative institutions to offer a forum where even unpopular ideas or arguments can gain a hearing.[56] Put another way, what makes the judiciary different from other deliberative bodies—and potentially more open to claims of socially marginalized groups—is not that judges are especially educated, empathic, or even sensible people. Rather, it is that, unlike

[54] Miranda Fricker, "Silence and Institutional Prejudice," in *Out from the Shadows: Analytical Feminist Contributions to Traditional Philosophy*, ed. Sharon L. Crasnow and Anita M. Superson (Oxford University Press, 2012), 301; *see also* Philip Pettit, *Republicanism: A Theory of Freedom and Government* (Oxford University Press, 1997), 186–87 (articulating the basic features of "contestation" as an essential attribute of republican freedom); Alon Harel and Tsvi Kahana, "The Easy Core Case for Judicial Review," *Journal of Legal Analysis* 2, no. 1 (2010): 238–39 (articulating the contours of the "right to a hearing" consisting of "the opportunity to voice a grievance, the opportunity to be provided with a justification for a decision that impinges (or may impinge) on one's rights, and the duty to reconsider the initial decision giving rise to the grievance").

[55] Fricker, "Silence and Institutional Prejudice," 301.

[56] See Yuval Eylon and Alon Harel, "The Right to Judicial Review," *Virginia Law Review* 92, no. 5 (2006): 999 (identifying the "right to a hearing" as the core justification for judicial review).

the rest of us, judges by and large do not have boundless discretion to refuse to hear claims that are facially disconcerting.

To be clear, the deliberative advantage asserted here is comparative, not absolute. Courts retain the capacity to dodge hearing cases they would rather not address on their merits.[57] Yet it remains the case that courts possess an underappreciated, peculiarly democratic function in our governmental and social system. Limited though it may be, the legal system still "provides a uniquely democratic . . . mechanism for individual citizens to invoke public authority on their own and for their benefit."[58] The average citizen cannot get an audience with the president or a meeting with their senator; they are not guaranteed a voice in the pundit box or space in the editorial section. But every citizen has the right to walk into court and in some form receive an audience and response from an official representative of the U.S. government. In a world where certain types of claims and certain types of claimants are routinely and preemptively dismissed without serious engagement, that has equalizing power.

The prior chapters have emphasized that it is probably impossible to craft a general system of canons for confronting the problem of dismissal. Yet it is also true that there are benefits for carving out discrete deliberative forums where dismissal is limited by rule. And here law and the courts find themselves in an especially interesting position vis-à-vis dismissal. On the one hand, law is limited in its ability to address novel claims because law is by design a limited instrument. A significant purpose of law is precisely to winnow the theoretically infinite array of claims a litigant might make into a much narrower and more manageable set that is known in advance. Yet within those boundaries, law also offers significant opportunities. If a claim can be framed within the four corners of a recognized legal doctrine, courts are uniquely situated in public dialogue because they cannot simply refuse to listen. They cannot dismiss a claim simply because it is discomfiting or disconcerting, politically unpopular

[57] See, e.g., Alexander M. Bickel, "Foreword: The Passive Virtues," *Harvard Law Review* 75, no. 1 (1961): 42 (identifying judicial doctrines, such as standing, mootness, and jurisdiction, which assist in managing "the timing and limits of the judicial function"); Judith Resnik, "Managerial Judges," *Harvard Law Review* 96, no. 2 (1982): 424–31 (noting the risks of the increasing "managerial" role judges have taken over the cases they hear). A widely recognized recent case of this sort of behavior came in 2004, when the Supreme Court utilized the doctrine of "prudential standing" to overturn a Ninth Circuit opinion striking down the inclusion of "under God" in the Pledge of Allegiance without addressing the issue on its merits. Elk Grove Unified Sch. Dist. v. Newdow, 542 U.S. 1, 17–18 (2004). *See generally* Eileen Braman, "Reasoning on the Threshold: Testing the Separability of Preferences in Legal Decision Making," *Journal of Politics* 68, no. 2 (2006): 308–21.

[58] Frances Kahn Zemans, "Legal Mobilization: The Neglected Role of the Law in the Political System," *American Political Science Review* 77, no. 3 (1983): 692.

or a nonstarter. They have to give reasons.[59] And while that is not the end of the game, it is for many groups and many claims the beginning of broader public conversation that otherwise might have been avoided or dismissed outright.

[59] In recent years, the Supreme Court has made increasing use of the so-called "shadow docket" to make significant alterations to legal doctrine outside the normal process of briefing and argument, and often without much in the way of substantive reason-giving. See Stephen Vladeck, *The Shadow Docket: How the Supreme Court Uses Stealth Rulings To Amass Power and Undermine the Republic* (Basic Books, 2023). In *Trump v. CASA*, eliminating the practice of nationwide injunctions issued by lower courts, Justice Kavanaugh suggested that one way the judiciary could preserve legal uniformity is by accelerating the usage of the shadow docket to issue interim rulings addressing challenges to "major new statutes and executive actions." Slip op. at 10. Such an approach concentrates power in the Supreme Court in the precise context where the deliberative advantages of the judiciary outlined in this chapter are least prominent. It thus offer the worst of all worlds: all the dangers of a non-representative and insulated judicial branch, shorn of the norms compelling deliberation and reason-giving that have historically been part of the normal judicial process.

9
Deliberation under Protest

The previous chapter identified some of the ways civil litigation can serve to bypass practices of dismissal. In conversation with this discussion of law, however, I also want to suggest that a seemingly opposite form of contribution to public debate—protest—can serve a surprisingly similar function in how it interacts with the mechanics of dismissal.[1] At first blush, this connection might seem counterintuitive: legal proceedings are perhaps the quintessential example of working inside the confines of an extant system, while protests by their nature nearly always involve standing in defiance of prevailing rules and practices. For the most part, when law and protest are placed into conversation, it is asking how the former should regulate the latter. That is an important topic—and it is one that I will return to—but it often skips past important features of how protests fit inside a deliberative ecosystem.

Protests are both speech-facilitative and speech-suppressive. They are speech-facilitative in that protests are by their nature outbursts of passionate expression—claims that something is unjust, something must change, or someone is unheard. Yet many protests are speech-suppressive, undertaken to tamp down or silence other forms of speech. This is most obvious when the protest is directed at a speech, and particularly when the protest takes the form of a "shout-down" (seeking to drown out an undesired speaker with chants or heckles). Consequently, how we respond to protests inherently involves decisions about the *distribution* of deliberative resources; making choices about what sorts of speech get elevated and which are tabled.

This chapter thus begins not with how protests are regulated but rather by considering how protests can, in certain contexts, serve a deliberative role similar to how law was slotted as a deliberative practice in the previous chapter. In many circumstances, the function of protests is precisely to take certain topics or claims which have been systematically occluded from substantial consideration and force them into the public eye. This consideration-forcing attribute of protests—compelling people to at least think about issues they generally ignore—stands apart from whether the protest immediately increases or decreases attitudinal

[1] This chapter is adapted from portions of David Schraub, "They Managed a Protest: Prohibitory, Ethical, and Prudential Policing of Academic Speech," *Brigham Young University Law Review* 50, no. 3 (2025): 619–80.

Deliberation, Dismissal, and Democracy. David Schraub, Oxford University Press. © Oxford University Press (2025). DOI: 10.1093/9780197816424.003.0010

sympathy for the underlying cause, and indeed is potentially a virtue even if the protest does not directly result in any tangible alteration of its target policy commitments.

In this way, as a mechanism for bypassing dismissal, protests can be seen as the unruly cousin of law. In contrast to law, protests are not bound by much in the way of formal limitations on what issues can and cannot be raised. This gives them greater range of action but also places questions of deliberative scarcity into sharper relief—what justifies the protesters' preferred issue or hobbyhorse jumping the deliberative queue? Likewise, protests are not especially apt at facilitating a true give and take of reasoned arguments, an attribute that can amplify their relative power but also risks generating malformed deliberative practices where opposing (non-protesting) factions may see their interests or views systematically underaddressed.

Only after laying these foundations is it appropriate to consider how protests should be regulated—a question I examine with a particular eye toward the recent spate of campus protests. Much of the discourse on this question, I argue, has suffered by conflating a campus's prohibitory prerogatives (the rules it can set up to determine what sorts of protest can be prohibited, as well as which must be protected) from its attempts to cultivate a healthy deliberative ethos in the domain of protests (the endeavors, stopping short of censorship or coercive bans, to encourage sets of deliberative values conducive to healthy academic life). The values of these domains can often run orthogonal to one another. The prohibitory register of free speech is compatible with liberal neutrality as to substantive visions of the good, and that's a large part of its appeal. By contrast, ethical regulation by its very nature strains against liberal neutrality—it is all about taking a substantive position. Yet this does not mean the prohibitory register is superior to or can dispense with accompanying ethical regulation. Indeed, to a large extent the liberal neutrality stance in the prohibitory domain claims its power precisely because it *shifts* the substantive position-taking into the ethical/prudential domains.[2] It is one thing to say "It violates free speech to use formal administrative power to sanction speech on the basis of viewpoint." It is quite another to say "It violates free speech to assert that a given viewpoint is bad or wrongheaded"—nominally, making such assertions is exactly what we're supposed to do once we take administrative sanctions off the table. When Justice Louis Brandeis delivered his broadside against government censorship by calling for "more speech, not enforced silence," these ethical appeals were precisely the "more speech" he was referring to.[3]

[2] Franciska A. Coleman, "They Should Be Fired: The Social Regulation of Free Speech in the U.S.," *First Amendment Law Review* 16, no. 1 (2017): 3 ("[T]he First Amendment [reflects] a choice of social regulation over legal regulation.").

[3] Whitney v. California, 274 U.S. 357, 377 (1927) (Brandeis, J., concurring).

Given the different domains of speech regulation and the complex impact protests have on the critical question of how to *distribute* deliberative resources, I conclude by asking what we actually expect out of those tasked with enforcing academic speech rules and regulations. The conflicts between the demands of these different domains of free speech—unruly in the best of circumstances—are especially difficult to balance in the typically contentious, fast-moving, and confrontational environment of a protest, where efforts to advance or defend one of these registers of speech regulation may regularly undermine or squelch another. Failure to recognize these trade-offs means we will regularly give short shrift to the choices campus protest regulators are forced to make.

Protests as Law's Unruly Cousin

The previous chapter identified some of the ways civil litigation can serve to bypass practices of dismissal. At first blush, it is hard to envision a mechanism of social change more distant from legal proceedings than the protest. Lawsuits are formal, even ritualized, in their adherence to official procedural rules. Protests are informal, often rowdy or even chaotic, and in most cases self-consciously flout at least some governing rules or standards. Lawsuits are limited in scope to claims that are legally cognizable—a small subset of claims generally. Protests can be launched by anyone over any topic, without regard to how the claim fits inside some preexisting schema for ranking or categorizing political issues.

Yet there is one critical respect where protests have a lot in common with litigation: protests can be consideration-forcing. They can compel decision-makers, or the public writ large, to think about and grapple with arguments, contentions, or social realities that they have hitherto ignored or dismissed. As with litigation, this should not be confused with protests guaranteeing victory to their supported side. There are many protests that fail (and many protests that *should* fail), just as there are many lawsuits that lose and should lose. Rather, the deliberative virtue we are identifying is in the ability of protests to circumvent deliberative blockages and elevate to the top of the public agenda certain claims that are going un- or underaddressed.

To be sure, not every protest has this characteristic, nor is this the only characteristic that gives protests justification. The protests in Los Angeles against the Trump administration's draconian immigration crackdowns, for instance, surely were not motivated by a belief that Trumpist officials hadn't thought of or realized there was widespread opposition to their immigration policies.[4]

[4] See Marissa Wenzke, "Protests against Immigration Crackdown Continue in Los Angeles for a Fourth Day," *CBS News*, February 5, 2025, https://www.cbsnews.com/losangeles/news/protests-against-immigration-crackdown-continue-in-los-angeles-for-a-fourth-day/.

Sometimes the value of protests lies in assuring a community that they're not alone or isolated in their frustration, or simply in extracting costs that make implementing a given policy more onerous or pricey. But at least in some circumstances, protests can reshuffle the distribution of deliberative resources and take an issue area that decision-makers had been ignoring and force them to at least engage on the level of argument.

This understanding of the benefits of protests acts as a retort to the common complaint leveled against protesters that they're only hurting their cause. Even assuming that protests immediately reduce sympathy for persons targeted or inconvenienced, that trade-off might be worthwhile to get or keep an issue on the deliberative radar, and accordingly get one into the space of giving reasons. "Disruptive politics," Clarissa Hayward argues, "are not a matter of moral suasion. Their aim is less to convince those who are systematically advantaged by structural injustice that they ought to 'do the right thing' than to make it all but impossible for the privileged to not hear the voices of, to not know the political claims of, the oppressed."[5] The immediate goal of the protests is less about securing substantive policy changes (though those are of course typically desired) and more about ensuring that the protesters' agenda items take their place as deliberative issues that must be at least considered. For example, while few if any of the pro-Palestine encampments that swept the nation in 2024 succeeded in extracting a substantive promise from their university to commit to boycotting or divesting from Israel, a typical concession made to those encampments was that the protesters be allowed to at least pitch divestment to campus boards of trustees.[6] Even where the ultimate board vote is a failure, this still could be seen as an advancement compared to years past, when campus decision-makers might simply refuse to consider the proposals of the Boycott, Divestment and Sanctions movement at all.

What protests do, in this understanding, is circumvent the "normal" deliberative distributional channels that determine whose grievances gain meaningful consideration and whose are ignored. They change the distribution of deliberative resources. Whether that is a good or a bad thing depends on one's vantage point. The positive story sees protests as a mechanism for overcoming unjust blockages that prevent consideration of certain claims that are deserving of space. Claims and claimants that are putting forth arguments that demand

[5] Clarissa Hayward, "Responsibility and Ignorance: On Dismantling Structural Injustice," *Journal of Politics* 79, no. 2 (2017): 406.

[6] See, e.g., Michael Casey, "Brown Rejects Calls to Divest from Companies in Connection with Pro-Palestinian Protests on Campus," AP, October 9, 2024, https://apnews.com/article/campus-protest-brown-university-divestment-1bc45dfc0183ef008338678d09374529; Fiona Eilers, "LC Reaches Agreement with Student Protesters," *Mossy Log*, October 4, 2024, https://mossylog.org/2024/10/04/lc-reaches-agreement-with-student-protestors/.

consideration, but that are systematically ignored or suppressed, can claim access to the deliberative resources that are their due. Even if it is fair to say that under ideal circumstances deliberative agenda-setting should not be governed via the coercive mechanism of a protest, we do not live in ideal circumstances, and the more distance there is between the ideal state and gritty reality, the more those facing systemic deliberative disadvantages are justified in using confrontational or coercive tactics to level the playing field.[7]

The negative story sees protests as unjustly claiming disproportionate deliberative resources by resort to coercion and threat. They are not claiming something that is their due; they jump the queue at the expense of other deliberative stakeholders who are unable or unwilling to act in a similar coercive fashion. Recall that where deliberative resources are scarce (as they always are), the mere fact that a given claim is not receiving sustained consideration is not itself a wrong—it is impossible to deliberate over everything. The wrong, if there is one, lies in the maldistribution of deliberative attentions. But the appeal to latent inequalities in access to deliberative resources is unlikely to dissipate complaints over jumping the queue because many, if not most groups that are dissatisfied with the level of attention their claims are receiving from relevant decision-makers will also perceive themselves as the victims of a wrongful maldistribution of deliberative resources.[8] Meanwhile, where decisions on what to deliberate on are mediated primarily based on who is behaving most disruptively, the natural result is a race to be the most disruptive possible—a vicious cycle of protest and counterprotest where we end up considering an argument *only* if somebody is engaging in a sit-in on its behalf. Even as many campuses successfully de-escalated pro-Palestine encampments by promising them an audience with the board, this solution generated grievances among other campus stakeholders (e.g., Jewish or pro-Israel student organizations) who were *not* offered similar access and groused that the only way their voice would be heard is if they too

[7] See Archon Fung, "Deliberation before the Revolution," *Political Theory* 33, no. 2 (June 2005): 397–419; John D. Inazu, *Confident Pluralism: Surviving and Thriving through Deep Difference* (University of Chicago Press, 2016), 107 ("When a minority viewpoint lacks the political or social clout to be heard, some form of collective action might be the only practical recourse.").

[8] See Fung, "Deliberation," 410 (discussing student protesters who justified a sit-in at Harvard University in support of higher wages for university employees because "we have exhausted every avenue of dialogue with the administration that could lead to a living wage"). Fung presents this case as one where an argument that should have been considered by relevant Harvard decision-makers was not, a failure which justifies departing from ideal deliberative practices. He might be right in that particular case, but it should be clear that it will often be very difficult to distinguish two alternative possibilities: cases where the argument *was* fairly considered but ultimately rejected, and cases where the argument was *not* fairly considered but that failure is not attributable to any maldistribution of deliberative resources. At least in the first case, and arguably in the second, the disruption would not be justified—but in nearly every conceivable circumstance of passionate political disagreement there will be plausible arguments for any of the three possibilities.

occupied a campus building.[9] Some college administrators tried to traverse this problem by expressly stating that their willingness to meet with protesting students was *not* because they were protesting but because they were students, and that a similar offer was open to other students as well.[10] Even assuming this avowal was believed, such an approach, while rhetorically prudent, is not actually sustainable—it relies on denying the deliberative scarcity which in the real world means that a university president cannot always be open to every student complaint on an equal basis at all times.

Another important feature of protests is that they quite intentionally deprive targets of their "right not to listen." As Hayward says, their goal is "to make it all but impossible for the privileged to not hear the voices of, to not know the political claims of, the oppressed."[11] Of course, framed that way this sounds like an unadulterated good. But recall the importance, parsed in Chapter 6, of "not listening" as an important component of deliberative freedom. Just as the virtue of protest might not be directly a matter of moral suasion but rather might concentrate on ensuring underserved voices are heard, aversion to protest might not always be a desire to remain in a position of ignorance or dismissal but could stem from beliefs that certain discrete spaces or domains—not all, but some—ought to be ones where actors are entitled to withdraw from consideration.

Courts tasked with balancing protesters' rights against bystanders and bystanders' (and protest targets') interest in not being harangued have at least tacitly understood the distinction. We discussed in Chapter 5 the case of *Phelps-Roper v. City of Manchester*, allowing a city to limit the ability to protest and picket outside of a funeral.[12] The protests there were anti-gay and particularly provocative, but under well-settled First Amendment principles, courts have no role in deciding whether particular viewpoints—be they anti-gay, anti-militarism, anti-Israel, anti-abortion, or what have you—are or are not worthy of consideration. But the justification of the ordinance in *City of Manchester* had nothing at all to do with the merits or demerits of the protesters' views.

[9] See John Lauritsen, "Jewish Student Group Express Unease over U of M's Agreement with Pro-Palestinian Protesters," *CBS News*, May 3, 2024, https://www.cbsnews.com/minnesota/news/university-of-minnesota-jewish-students-concerned-pro-palestinian-encampmentIsrael/Palestine conflict:pro-Palestine encampments.

[10] See Alison R. Byerly, "Last Week's Sit-In at Laird," Carleton College Office of the President, May 23, 2024, https://www.carleton.edu/president/news/last-weeks-sit-in-at-laird/.

[11] Hayward, "Responsibility and Ignorance," 406; *see also* Clarissa Rile Hayward, "Disruption: What Is It Good For?," *Journal of Politics* 82, no. 2 (April 2020): 451–54 (suggesting that social disruption is a valuable tactic because it overcomes the motivated ignorance of its targets, ignorance which enables them to participate in social structures they would otherwise recognize as unjust without dissonance).

[12] 697 F.3d 678 (8th Cir. 2012) (en banc).

Rather, it is justified because a funeral is a space where we accept that people are entitled to not listen to *any* view if they don't want to. A funeral isn't the right domain where we justify compelling consideration. Similar dynamics might explain why protesting outside someone's home isn't justified[13]—again, not because homeowners should have a categorical right "not to listen" but because that *particular space* is one where we think there is an especially strong entitlement to be able to withdraw from participation in the project of reason-giving and -taking. By contrast, on the college quad we might think it is entirely reasonable that persons be confronted with potentially unwelcome or even hostile views.

Protests which targeted, for example, Dean Erwin Chemerinsky of UC-Berkeley Law at his home (where protesters interrupted a celebratory dinner he was hosting for graduating students) or University of Michigan regent Jordan Acker (whose home windows were smashed and car was spraypainted with pro-Palestinian messages in his driveway) are reasonably viewed differently and more critically compared to even rhetorically or tactically similar protests that occur in more public spaces.[14] The difference is not (just) one of substance—the unlawful vandalism, in the case of Acker. A similar act of vandalism on a campus sidewalk may still be punished, but it is, I think, viewed as different in kind from targeting an individual in his home—and that difference relates not to the act or the message but rather to the venue where the protest occurs. While many people might also express a preference to be able to walk around campus without being exposed to views they find obnoxious, a college quad is a quintessential example of a public forum designed to be a space where arguments and ideas can be presented without restriction, precisely *in order* that people who might otherwise prefer "not to listen" can be exposed to such perspectives.[15] The arguments which justify withdrawing from deliberative consideration at a funeral or in one's home do not extend to the campus sidewalk.

Finally, while protests may be well-suited as a means of overcoming ignorance and (potentially) dismissal, they are distinctively ill-suited to the reciprocal *exchange* of reasons. In Chapter 5, I noted (via Mill) the validity (in some cases) of "uncivil" actions like protests as a means of effectuating social change, while also highlighting the dangers of speech practices which do not treat one's interlocutors as having even potentially valid contributions in a dialogic

[13] See Frisby v. Schultz, 487 U.S. 474 (1988).

[14] See Vimal Patel, "At Berkeley, a Protest at a Dean's Home Tests the Limits of Free Speech," *New York Times*, April 12, 2024, https://www.nytimes.com/2024/04/12/us/uc-berkeley-palestinian-protest-free-speech.html; Jake Tapper and Chelsea Bailey, "University of Michigan Regent's Home Vandalized in Antisemitic Attack," CNN, December 9, 2024, https://www.cnn.com/2024/12/09/us/university-of-michigan-regents-vandalized-acker/index.html.

[15] See Sunstein, *#Republic*, 35.

exchange—both capable of being persuaded by reasons and capable of having arguments that might in turn be persuasive. In the context of a protest, this problem is at its most literal in cases where disrupters are about stopping certain views from being aired (as in the "shout-down" of an invited speaker). But even in other circumstances, the environment of a protest is not designed for encouraging or especially liable to encourage genuine deliberation over competing views. "Collective action," such as protests and boycotts, "that seeks to bend another's will is difficult to reconcile with tolerance, humility, and patience"—the virtues we hope to inculcate in a healthy deliberative community.[16] This is not to say that encouraging deliberation is or should always be the paramount value. But it is a value, and protests tend to sacrifice that value to advance others. That trade-off should be acknowledged, and further suggests that protests should not be *overly* valorized as the ideal way of (re)distributing our deliberative resources. As Martha Nussbaum observes, there are traits which "are virtues in the context of the struggle, advancing its goals, but not so good as elements in the overall life of an agent striving to live well"—for example, "uncritical loyalty and solidarity."[17]

For these reasons, protests represent an especially nettlesome arena for those seeking to instantiate free speech values. Protests offer certain deliberative benefits in terms of agenda-setting and promoting potentially marginalized views, benefits that are hard to replicate in other contexts. Yet protests also frequently press up against other important deliberative values—of fairness, of promoting reciprocal consideration, and (potentially) of just distribution of deliberative resources. The tensions between the cross-cutting benefits and burdens of protests are only amplified, moreover, when we consider the different domains through which protest is regulated. While First Amendment–inspired analysis typically concentrates primarily on when a protest can be prohibited (or when it must be permitted), protest regulators—particularly in the context of a university—also engage in important domains of regulation that are quite distinct from their prohibitory powers.

Regulating Protests Ethically

While campus protests are, almost by their nature, departures from and disruptions to the ordinary proceedings of the university, academic administrations still must come up with and enforce rules regulating them. All colleges and universities have some rules governing protests. These rules are frequently

[16] Inazu, *Confident Pluralism*, 106.
[17] Martha C. Nussbaum, *Citadels of Pride: Sexual Assault, Accountability, and Reconciliation* (W. W. Norton, 2021), 51 (citing Lisa Tessman, *Burdened Virtues: Virtue Ethics for Liberatory Struggle* (Oxford University Press, 2005)).

framed in terms of First Amendment values, and even private schools, which are not bound by the First Amendment, often voluntarily agree to hold themselves to principles protecting free expression meant to mimic the constraints placed upon government actors.[18] In framing, campus protest regulations typically recognize (albeit sometimes in a very vague and abstract fashion) the important free speech interests in protecting the right to protest, while also placing limits on when and how protests can occur. Unsurprisingly, questions of how to apply these rules are often subjects of controversy.

Many campus protest rules are inspired by First Amendment principles governing public forums (areas like parks and sidewalks), where the importance of protecting freewheeling and sometimes unruly speech is deemed to be at its apex. Even here, "time, place, and manner" restrictions are viewed as reasonable so long as they leave ample space for expression to be heard and do not discriminate on the basis of the content or viewpoint of the underlying speech.[19] Other protest rules are particular to the academic context—for example, prohibitions on "shouting down" an invited speaker. While disorderly or disruptive conduct can be prohibited consistent with the First Amendment, courts have not endorsed the idea that there can be a blanket prohibition on heckling, recognizing the free speech value of a "cogent remark, even though rudely timed and phrased."[20] Rather, courts have looked to the particular deliberative context to determine what does and does not constitute a true disruption—the sort of yelling and chanting that might be expected at a political rally would not be tolerated in a memorial service, for instance. In this context, it is reasonable enough to say that a classroom disruption or shouting down an invited lecturer falls far enough outside the norms of ordinary academic practice that it is reasonable to prohibit it outright (though we should still recognize that this choice represents in many ways a deviation from, rather than a straightforward application of, normal First Amendment principles).

[18] See, e.g., "3 Contentious Exchanges at the College Antisemitism Hearing," *New York Times*, December 6, 2023, https://www.nytimes.com/2023/12/06/us/harvard-mit-penn-presidents-antisemitism-hearing.html (quoting Elizabeth Magill, then-president of the University of Pennsylvania, as stating that her campus's "free speech policies are guided by the United States Constitution"); Letter from Adam Goldstein, Program Officer, Individual Rights Defense Program, Foundation for Individual Rights in Education (now Foundation For Individual Rights and Expression), to Nathan O. Hatch, President, Wake Forest University, March 28, 2019, https://www.thefire.org/sites/default/files/2019/03/28165326/FIRE-Letter-to-Wake-Forest-March-20191.pdf ("While [Wake Forest University] is not bound by the First Amendment, it has bound itself to freedom of speech, freedom of inquiry, and freedom of expression," and citing a range of First Amendment cases and doctrines to establish that Wake Forest violated the free speech rights of community members by investigating an allegedly offensive Instagram post).

[19] See Perry Education Association v. Perry Local Educators' Association, 460 U.S. 37, 45 (1983) ("The State may also enforce regulations of the time, place, and manner of expression which are content-neutral, are narrowly tailored to serve a significant government interest, and leave open ample alternative channels of communication.").

[20] In re Kay, 464 P.2d 142, 146–47 (Cal. 1970).

Of course, the anodyne description above obscures the many, many challenges in applying these rules to actual protest situations which are often emotionally fraught, fast-moving, and highly chaotic. For example, the rule of "content neutrality" demands treating like cases alike—if one group has been allowed to (say) occupy the campus quad, another group with more controversial politics can't be prohibited from engaging in the same conduct even if in concept an evenly applied "no occupying the quad" rule would represent a reasonable "time, place, and manner" restriction. But "the same conduct" will often be the sticking point—if the first group only picketed for a few hours and the second pitched tents and stayed overnight, is that "the same conduct" or not? Similarly, a rule against a shout-down cannot encompass hostile questioning or combative audience response—but when does the latter bleed into the former? There is room for discretion, and where there is room for discretion, there is room for controversy. These difficulties typically fall upon the heads of the frontline administrators tasked with enforcing free speech policies in the field, who are left holding the bag when they inevitably fail to resolve on the fly controversies that even in hindsight provoke sharply divergent interpretations and conclusions.

And the more that a university presents its free speech policies as mimicking First Amendment standards, the more these choices sit upon a knife's edge. In California, for instance, the "Leonard Law" prohibits universities from punishing students for any speech that would be protected from governmental sanction under the First Amendment—in other words, not just allowing but requiring California universities to adopt First Amendment strictures.[21] This adds a significant layer of complexity to any decision a college might make in seeking to regulate student protest. It's at least plausible that some forms of "significant" disruption can be penalized without running afoul of constitutional protections. But even with the benefit of hindsight—to say nothing of the in-the-moment judgment demanded on the scene—it may be difficult to determine with absolute confidence when a protected protest converts into a proscribable substantial disruption. Guessing wrong in one direction marks the university as permitting a toxic culture of disruption and shout-downs; guessing wrong in the other opens it to legal liability for violating protesters' free speech rights.

[21] Cal. Educ. Code §94367 ("No private postsecondary educational institution shall make or enforce a rule subjecting a student to disciplinary sanctions solely on the basis of conduct that is speech or other communication that, when engaged in outside the campus or facility of a private postsecondary institution, is protected from governmental restriction by the First Amendment to the United States Constitution or Section 2 of Article I of the California Constitution."). *See also* Cal. Educ. Code §66301 (same for public universities); Cal. Educ. Code §48950 (same for public and private high schools).

Yet as difficult as these determinations are, I want to suggest that the problem confronting campus speech regulators runs considerably deeper than the legalistic (or quasi-legalistic) interpretative questions of how to apply X rule to Y factual scenario. The rules surrounding protests recognize both the important free speech value of protests and the important free speech value of limiting certain kinds of protest. On top of that, however, the previous section identified a similar bifurcation in the practical deliberative value of protests—they can be important and salutary as means of compelling consideration of questions that otherwise struggle to get on the deliberative agenda, but they also can be troubling and worrisome as a means of jumping the queue and diverting deliberative resources to whoever chants the loudest, while simultaneously channeling conversations toward a venue that is inhospitable to many deliberative virtues (open-mindedness, reciprocal exchange of reasons) we think are important to confronting fraught issues in a fair-minded way.

Protests, both in their subject matter and in their comportment, can and usually do touch on ethical questions which a university might feel it is important to register an opinion on. A university might not be permitted to prohibit rude or dismissive questioning (that falls short of heckling) by audience members to a controversial speaker, for instance, but it can try to inculcate a value of respectful engagement through means other than censorial sanction. Campus administrators confronting an emergent protest situation have to apply the rules fairly, but they also have to balance the ethical values surrounding protest, which, like the deliberative virtues discussed in prior chapters, are not reducible to hard-and-fast rules but rather are matters of better and worse climates and dispositions.

In the ethical domain, campus protest regulation is a matter of asking what sort of speech is properly facilitative of a climate where people feel broadly comfortable sharing a wide range of views, including on potentially contentious topics. These concerns are often characterized as a matter of facilitating "free speech culture": an environment where relevant stakeholders are tolerant of diverse and divergent views, even ones they sharply disagree with, and create space where such views can be aired freely and respectfully.

Like the term "tolerance" itself,[22] "free speech culture" has an ambivalent relationship with the First Amendment. Though it bootstraps onto the legal imperative of "freedom of speech," the practices frequently condemned as malignant

[22] See Wendy Brown, *Regulating Aversion: Tolerance in the Age of Identity and Empire* (Princeton University Press, 2006), 11 (noting how "tolerance" is associated with the First Amendment even though the term never appears in the constitutional text, is rarely if ever legally codified, and thus almost exclusively "functions politically and socially, but not legally, to propagate understandings and practices regarding how people . . . can and ought to cohabit").

by "free speech culture" are not illegal and, indeed, are typically legally protected by the First Amendment.[23] Nonetheless, they are thought to be antipathic to a healthy environment for the exchange of ideas and so are indicted on that basis. Overly harsh or vitriolic condemnation of certain speech again cannot be banned, but it can be viewed as an exercise of poor judgment which should be judged harshly.[24] The same might be said for rude or uncivil speech.[25]

The ethical dimension of speech regulation is germane to protests as well. There are many ways of protesting a speaker that do not seem subject to prohibitory rules (i.e., they are not shout-downs or analogous acts) but which in context are seen as harmful to the broader ethos of intellectual exchange that, particularly in a university setting, should be cultivated. For example, holding up vulgar protest signs doesn't obstruct a talk and thus seemingly cannot be deemed a "substantial disruption" under any standard. Nonetheless, the choice to display such signs seems out of line with the speech environment a university should hope to facilitate. A protester who protests in this way can be legitimately thought of as a juvenile or even toxic actor, even if their behavior is absolutely shielded from prohibitory sanction. Another example might be an activist who literally protests every talk he or she even slightly disagrees with, refusing to engage in any sort of intellectual exchange in any circumstance where he or she does not already align with the speaker. The activist has the right to do that, but that sort of intentional epistemic siloing is deeply malformed and properly viewed disdainfully.

Educational institutions have long been thought to play a special role in inculcating certain ethical values related to speech and debate. Justice Felix Frankfurter, for instance, described the "special task of teachers" as fostering "those habits of open-mindedness and critical inquiry which alone make for responsible citizens, who, in turn, make possible an enlightened and effective public opinion."[26] In the context of law schools in particular (but probably

[23] See Mary Anne Franks, "The Lost Cause of Free Speech," *Journal of Free Speech Law* 2, no. 1 (2022): 353 ("[A]mong the most important aspects of the right to free speech protected by the First Amendment is the right to criticize the speech of others, even in harsh ways."); Erica Goldberg, "Competing Free Speech Values in an Age of Protest," *Cardozo Law Review* 39, no. 6 (2018): 2166 (noting that content moderation policies that would be instances of unconstitutional viewpoint discrimination if imposed by government are constitutionally insulated from regulation when imposed by private parties, even though they arguably impose similar costs to "free speech").

[24] See, e.g., Nadine Strossen, *Resisting Cancel Culture: Promoting Dialogue, Debate, and Free Speech in the College Classroom* (ACTA, 2020), 8 (arguing that "pressure by private sector individuals and institutions can silence or punish our speech . . . as effectively as government could do, if not more so," but conceding that "free speech culture . . . embodies speech protections that go beyond what the First Amendment literally requires").

[25] Though it is worth noting that Mill expressly rejects the attempt to limit the protection of free speech to that which is "temperate, and do[es] not pass the bounds of fair discussion." John Stuart Mill, *On Liberty* (1859), ed. Elizabeth Rapaport (Hackett, 1978), 50.

[26] Wieman v. Updegraff, 44 U.S. 183, 196 (1952) (Frankfurter, J., concurring).

applicable in any academic environment), Eugene Volokh has written about the important role the university plays in cultivating a spirit of intellectual engagement and exchange.[27] For example, an effective advocate must allow herself to be exposed to her opponents' strongest arguments. This is not necessarily a natural instinct, for there is an inherent anxiety in taking seriously arguments that *strongly* support positions that one deems to be wrong-headed or even immoral.[28] Nonetheless, as Richard Bernstein observed, "The basic condition for all understanding requires one to test and risk one's convictions and prejudgments in and through an encounter with what is radically 'other' and alien. To do this requires imagination and hermeneutical sensitivity in order to understand the 'other' in its strongest possible light."[29] "Critical engaged dialogue," he continues, "requires opening of oneself to the full power of what the 'other' is saying. Such an opening does not entail agreement, but rather the to-and-fro play of dialogue. Otherwise dialogue degenerates into a self-deceptive monologue where one never risks testing one's prejudgments."[30]

Much of the ethical criticism of campus protest activity takes the form of concern that students are insufficiently attuned to these values. Protesters seeking to drive off dissident or minority views from campus discourse can be seen as attempting to convert an "epistemic bubble" (a circumstance where certain relevant voices are not present) into an "epistemic echo chamber" (a circumstance where these voices are actively targeted for exclusion).[31] If one believes that many elite law schools lack significant opportunities to see conservative ideas articulated (i.e., they are liberal epistemic bubbles), then certain campus protests—even leaving the proscribable shout-downs aside—can be seen as the enforcement arm that ensures these ideas cannot be aired or considered in the normal processes of intellectual academic engagement (thus creating the echo chamber). The problem identified here is not necessarily that the protesters are incorrect to view the target of their acrimony as holding wrong or even immoral beliefs. The ethical challenge, rather, is in the protesters obstructing the consideration of these (potentially wrong, immoral) beliefs via the preferred deliberative mechanism of fair consideration and open-minded engagement.

[27] Eugene Volokh, "Free Speech Rules, Free Speech Culture, and Legal Education," *Hofstra Law Review* 51, no. 3 (2023): 631–40.

[28] *Id.* at 632 ("Considering such arguments—which, by hypothesis, one considers to be deeply wrong, morally or factually—can make one angry. Thinking about them, and taking them seriously, is an unpleasant experience (indeed, can make one feel dirty or disloyal). The temptation is to not consider those arguments, to gloss over them, and at least to subconsciously underestimate them.").

[29] Richard J. Bernstein, *The New Constellation: The Ethical-Political Horizons of Modernity/Postmodernity* (MIT Press, 1992), 4.

[30] *Id.*

[31] See C. Thi Nguyen, "Echo Chambers and Epistemic Bubbles," *Episteme* 17, no. 2 (2020): 141–61 (articulating the difference between these two concepts).

As discussed in Chapter 7, while it is incorrect to say that there is no basis for concern here, it is also easy to exaggerate just how cloistered academic spaces are and how insulated students, particularly minority students, are from allegedly challenging or competing perspectives. But even recognizing these practices as potentially problematic, unlike the prohibitory register we cannot say that these ethically questionable practices are inappropriate per se. This is not just because they lie beyond the power of formal sanction, though that is important to emphasize given how frequently commentators *do* urge that formal sanctions be imposed for protests whose sin, if there is one, falls solely within the ethical domain. But beyond emphasizing that prohibitory sanctions cannot be imposed on speech and protest activity that falls under the ethical register, we also cannot view speech activities that themselves are expressly geared at limiting or chilling the speech of others as inappropriate per se because it is incontestable that in some circumstances speech like this *is* ethically appropriate. Protesting speech is an argument that the speech in question is "beyond the pale," and while that is a fuzzy phrase, all of us have some notion of speech that is not just wrong but goes beyond that which should be accorded respectful engagement. Even if we cannot prohibit Holocaust deniers from giving speeches on campus if they're invited by duly authorized community members,[32] we can and probably should deny them the legitimacy that they crave by *not* treating them as equal contributors to the field of ideas and therefore not respectfully "debating" their points (which, in turn, is why so many persons of this ilk frame their provocations as a demand: "Debate me!"). In the case of Holocaust deniers, it may well be perfectly ethically appropriate to treat them with overt disdain and dismissiveness. The point of the "protest" here is to intentionally withdraw the rules of social cooperation which govern how we debate "normal" issues, emphasizing the abnormal and fringe character of Holocaust deniers.[33] For similar reasons, we cannot say that angry or discourteous responses are always out of line.

What is fair to say is that university environments should cultivate a norm of respectful intellectual engagement, where the sorts of practices that would be justified as against Holocaust deniers are not the community's move of first resort when faced with any controversial speech whatsoever.[34] Universities should, in

[32] See, e.g., Robert M. O'Neil, "Academic Freedom to Deny the Truth: Beyond the Holocaust," *Minnesota Law Review* 101, no. 5 (2017): 2072 (noting how academic freedom protects the right of a Northwestern University electrical engineering professor to promote Holocaust denial).

[33] See Hayward, "Disruption," 451 (explaining how acts of disruption can force items onto the public agenda that might otherwise be suppressed); Frances Fox Piven, "Interdependent Power: Strategizing for the Occupy Movement," *Current Sociology* 62, no. 2 (2014): 226 (noting that persons lacking traditional resources of power nonetheless can sometimes exercise considerable influence via their ability "to withdraw or threaten to withdraw from systems of institutionalized cooperation").

[34] See Volokh, "Free Speech Rules," 631 (explaining why law schools, in particular, should seek to cultivate "a culture of free speech and openness to contrary ideas" as essential both to democratic citizenship and to the practice of training new attorneys).

other words, cultivate a strong *disposition* toward respectful engagement and interaction, with dismissive nonengagement remaining an exceptional outlier. But precisely because we cannot say universally that such responses are never justified, the ethical register resists the imposition of bright-line rules. Judgment in the ethical register will, by necessity, always be case-by-case and always have a considerable element of subjectivity—regarding both what is considered "respectful intellectual engagement" in the first place, as well as when it is appropriate to withhold that respect outright. This doesn't necessarily mean that universities are wrong to even try to cultivate the right balance, only that when they do so, they will inevitably be making contested value judgments and will open themselves to criticism from parties that do not share in those judgments.

What Do We Expect of Academic Speech Enforcers?

Given all of this, what do we desire from administrators tasked with enforcing university rules and standards surrounding free speech? As it stands, we are seeing on this question a dangerous confluence: on the one hand, we don't know what we want, and on the other hand, we're very confident that we do know what we want. Our decisive assertions about what free speech clearly demands mask deep, lingering uncertainties regarding how different registers of speech regulation ought to interact with one another.

One highly publicized incident that crystallized these concerns came in early 2023, when the Stanford Law School chapter of the Federalist Society invited Fifth Circuit Judge Kyle Duncan to give a talk on campus.[35] Judge Duncan was

[35] I draw my account here from a variety of sources which reported on the incident shortly after its occurrence. See, e.g., David Lat, "Yale Law Is No Longer #1 For Free-Speech Debacles," *Original Jurisdiction*, March 10, 2023, https://davidlat.substack.com/p/yale-law-is-no-longer-1for-free-speech (offering an early account of the protest including interviews with several student attendees); David Lat, "The Full Audio Recording of Judge Kyle Duncan at Stanford Law," *Original Jurisdiction*, March 15, 2023, https://davidlat.substack.com/p/the-full-audio-recording-of-judge (providing an audio recording of the event); Foundation for Individual Rights and Expression "Transcript of Stanford Law Shoutdown of Judge Kyle Duncan," March 9, 2023, https://www.thefire.org/research-learn/transcript-stanford-law-shoutdown-judge-kyle-duncan-march-9-2023 (providing a written transcript of the event); Foundation for Individual Rights and Expression, "Stanford Administrator Remarks at Event Featuring Fifth Circuit Judge Duncan," March 9, 2023, https://www.thefire.org/research-learn/stanford-administrator-remarks-event-featuring-fifth-circuit-judge-duncan-march-9 (providing a transcript of Dean Steinbach's remarks); Rod Dreher, "Exclusive: US Judge Kyle Duncan Interview," *Rod Dreher's Diary*, March 12, 2023, https://roddreher.substack.com/p/exclusive-us-judge-kyle-duncan-interview (transcribing an interview of Judge Duncan by Rod Dreher following the event); Mark Joseph Stern, "A Trump Judge's Tantrum at Stanford Law Was Part of a Bigger Plan," *Slate*, March 13, 2023, https://slate.com/news-and-politics/2023/03/trump-judge-kyle-duncan-stanford-law-scotus-audition.html (recounting the protest); Aaron Sibarium, "'Dogs—t': Federal Judge Decries Disruption of His Remarks by Stanford Law Students and Calls for Termination of the Stanford Dean Who Joined the Mob," *Washington Free Beacon*, March 10, 2023, https://freebeacon.com/campus/dogshit-federal-judge-decries-disruption-of-his-

controversial for what many perceived as his strong anti-LGBT bent (including, among other things, repeatedly and intentionally misgendering a transgender litigant in a judicial opinion).[36] That Judge Duncan was going to face a protest was known in advance and likely impacted how he comported himself on arrival. One eyewitness characterized the judge as "looking for a fight. He walked into the law school filming protestors on his phone, looking more like a YouTuber storming the Capitol, than a federal judge coming to speak." And from the outset of his presentation, he was vigorously, loudly, and profanely heckled, so severely that he was unable to functionally present at all.

Eventually, Tirien Steinbach, Stanford's associate dean for diversity, equity, and inclusion, stepped in to try to facilitate Judge Duncan's talk. Her mediation had two notable characteristics. First, she affirmed Judge Duncan's right to speak and informed the protesting students that they had to "give space to hear what Judge Duncan has to say." Stanford has rules prohibiting shout-downs of invited speakers, and the students were in breach of that rule. Second, she appeared to endorse the protesters' "on the merits" assessment that Judge Duncan was a problematic actor potentially worthy of protest, suggesting he opposed the "humanity" of LGBT persons and indicating—via her infamous line "Is the juice worth the squeeze?"—that it might be a better outcome if Judge Duncan did *not* exercise his acknowledged right to speak. Following this intervention, the shout-down part of the protest died down, but Judge Duncan's presentation was irretrievably toxified—students waving hostile signs and asking ad hominem questions, Judge Duncan acting with sneering derision and berating even the reasonable and substantive questions he did receive.

As the dean of Stanford Law, Jenny Martinez, put it, "Other than someone who hoped to create a meltdown for the cameras to capture, no one can be happy about what happened." Both the dean of Stanford Law School and the president of the university apologized to Judge Duncan for his treatment.[37] Judge Duncan, for his part, defiantly refused to apologize for his conduct during the

remarks-by-stanford-law-students-and-calls-for-termination-of-the-stanford-dean-who-joined-the-protesters. *See generally* Paul Caron, "Stanford President and Law Dean Apologize to Fifth Circuit Judge for Disruption of His Speech," *TaxProf Blog*, March 13, 2023, https://taxprof.typepad.com/taxprof_blog/2023/03/stanford-president-and-law-dean-apologize-to-fifth-circuit-judge-for-disruption-of-his-speech.html (collecting commentary). I discuss this incident more fully in Schraub, "They Managed a Protest," 623–29.

[36] See United States v. Varner, 948 F.3d 250 (5th Cir. 2020).

[37] Letter from Marc Tessier-Lavigne and Jenny Martinez, March 11, 2023, https://eppc.org/wp-content/uploads/2023/03/letter-from-Stanford.pdf.

proceedings.[38] Dean Steinbach's role in the proceedings came in for especially harsh criticism, with Judge Duncan demanding her termination.

But what, exactly, did Dean Steinbach do wrong? Was it failing to enforce the prohibitory rule against shout-downs? But she did articulate that rule, insisting that the students had to "give space" for Duncan to speak. Was it endorsing the students' substantive assessment of Judge Duncan as a speaker? That, obviously, represents a potentially ill-advised foray into holding a normative preference, in tension with the idea that the university should remain viewpoint-neutral. But it also can be read as an effort to enforce (albeit by suasion, not by coercion) certain ethical commitments. And many commenters have argued that just as universities are obligated to enforce prohibitory rules against (for example) shout-downs, they also carry a duty to try to inculcate (albeit not by formal sanction) certain ethical rules as well. For example, Henry Chambers argues that when an authorized campus group invites a speaker whose presence is "not consistent with the university's values, ideals, and principles," other campus officials and stakeholders should urge the group to reassess.[39] If the group declines to do so and cannot adequately defend its choice of speaker, it "should be encouraged to understand that it has squandered an opportunity to advance the university's mission—the search for truth and dissemination of knowledge."[40] This approach, he clarifies, is meant to stand in opposition to any formal "punishment . . . or retaliation" against the group; the group retains its formal free speech right to issue the invitation.[41] It is instead an example of a university attempting to promote, without resort to formal sanction, the sort of free speech culture it thinks is beneficial and conducive to a functioning academic environment. Volokh similarly urges that "[l]aw schools should do all they can to communicate"[42] the ethical values of free speech culture—which is to say, they should *not* adopt a posture of institutional neutrality toward them, notwithstanding that these values are predominantly not reducible to First Amendment–style prohibitory rules.

So, do we *expect* administrative staffers to attempt to engage in such encouragement—for example, to make appeals that community members refrain from speech practices that are antipathetic to a functioning free speech

[38] Stuart Kyle Duncan, "My Struggle Session at Stanford Law School," *Wall Street Journal*, March 17, 2023, https://www.wsj.com/articles/struggle-session-at-stanford-law-school-federalist-society-kyle-duncan-circuit-court-judge-steinbach-4f8da19e ("It's true I called [the Stanford students] 'appalling idiots,' 'bullies[,]' and 'hypocrites.' They are, and I won't apologize for saying so.").

[39] Henry L. Chambers, "Curating Campus Speakers," *University of Richmond Law Review Online* 53, no. 5 (2019): 14–15.

[40] *Id.* at 15.

[41] *Id.*

[42] Volokh, "Free Speech Rules," 631.

environment? Or, pushing in the other direction, do we think administrative staffers should be *forbidden* from making such attempts (and are failing in their job if they do anything *other* than clearly state and enforce the prohibitory rules)?

Both positions are unattractive, for different reasons. On the one hand, expecting staffers to encourage the ethical rules inevitably requires them to make subjective appraisals that will be highly contentious. Consider interventions that center around trying to inculcate norms of respectful engagement. Even if we agree that this is an ethical rule worth enforcing, it still raises difficult questions in application. Who is being "respectful," and who isn't? If there is conceded lack of respect, is this one of the situations where lack of respect is warranted, or is it not? Even Judge Duncan expressly agreed that "sometimes anger is the proper response to vicious behavior," albeit unsurprisingly in the course of validating his own disrespect toward the Stanford students and not vice versa. The lack of bright-line rules means these decisions will always be subject to second-guessing and debate, even when made in good faith. And the invocation of substantive ethical commitments necessarily places considerable pressure on the content- and viewpoint-neutrality that undergirds why our First Amendment–inspired limits on prohibitory regulation are appealing in the first place. Indeed, to some extent academia faces this problem more acutely than does the government. While the state cannot coercively enforce a favored viewpoint, there is no constitutional problem with government expressing in its own voice a preferred ideological position.[43] By contrast, one of the most prominent and influential explications of how academic freedom intersects with official university position-taking, the 1967 Kalven Report, sharply warns against the practice: the university "is a community which cannot take collective action on the issues of the day without endangering the conditions for its existence and effectiveness."[44]

On the other hand, forbidding staffers from encouraging the ethical norms will in many cases not suffice to create an intellectual climate that is in practice facilitative of a meaningful exchange of ideas, even as everyone avoids the

[43] See Pleasant Grove City v. Summum, 555 U.S. 460, 468 (2009) (observing "it is not easy to imagine how government could function if it" were unable to express substantive opinions).

[44] Harry Kalven Jr., John Hope Franklin, Gwin J. Kolb, George Stigler, Jacob Getzels, Julian Goldsmith, and Gilbert F. White, "Kalven Committee: Report on the University's Role in Political and Social Action," University of Chicago, November 11, 1967, https://provost.uchicago.edu/sites/default/files/documents/reports/KalvenRprt_0.pdf (suggesting that there must be "a heavy presumption against the university taking collective action or expressing opinions on the political and social issues of the day, or modifying its corporate activities to foster social or political values, however compelling and appealing they may be"). Recently, the American Association of University Professors (AAUP) controversially repudiated this conclusion of the Kalven Report, concluding instead that academic freedom does not compel a university to adopt a posture of institutional neutrality. AAUP Committee A on Academic Freedom and Tenure, "On Institutional Neutrality," AAUP, February 2025, https://www.aaup.org/report/institutional-neutrality ("Committee A therefore rejects the Kalven Report's argument that 'there is no mechanism by which [the university] can reach a collective position without inhibiting the full freedom of dissent on which it thrives.'").

outright prohibitory misconduct. Dueling disdain, intentional provocations, ad hominem pseudo-engagement, and vulgar mockery all are permissible, albeit not characteristic of an ethically healthy deliberative climate. Many prominent defenders of campus free speech recognize this. But if we believe that staffers are *forbidden* from encouraging the ethical rules, then the actual rule is that universities are institutionally *precluded* from seeking to avert that sort of intellectual climate. By the same token, if we wish the staffers to try to inculcate these ethical values, they necessarily are going to make subjective and likely contested judgments about what sort of speech may be protected but nonetheless fall outside the normative behavior the university seeks to promote. This endeavor sits in inherent tension with ideals of intellectual pluralism that are crucial to academic functioning.

So maybe we believe that the university should abjure any effort to enforce those ethical norms and confine itself to flat declaration and enforcement of the prohibitory rules (which are thought to be amenable to articulation in a reasonably objective, bright-line manner). But if we believe the only institutional role for a staffer is to enforce the prohibitory rules, then the equilibrium eventually reached following Dean Steinbach's intervention (no more overt disruption, but a talk characterized by extreme mutual antagonism and disdain) has to be accepted as not just permissible but sacrosanct—Stanford is forbidden from seeking to alter it, because it does formally fall within the confines of the prohibitory rules (notwithstanding Dean Martinez's seemingly inarguable conclusion that nobody could be happy with the event occurring like this). Even once the validly prohibited shout-down portion of the protest ended, Judge Duncan was understandably uninterested in presenting to a crowd that—while no longer in breach of any formal rules—was clearly hostile. But notice now the problem is precisely that Stanford supposedly *needed* to enforce the nonprohibitory (ethical) rules to ensure not just that Judge Duncan wasn't shouted down but also that certain norms of respect and receptivity were observed by the audience. Yet such steps are precisely what Stanford is *forbidden* from taking under the view that Dean Steinbach's only permissible role was to announce and enforce the prohibitory rules. It seems that many critics do want universities to cultivate certain *ethical* norms in their students, norms which are by necessity contestable and value-laden—even if those norms cannot be enforced via prohibitory sanction. But once the school makes that choice—to single out certain types of protected speech and say "You may have the right to say this, but as an institution we think your exercise of that right is ill-advised, unwise, or even an outright failure in your ethical duties as a university student"—then we struggle to articulate what Dean Steinbach did wrong beyond substantive disagreement with the content of her ethical commitments.

And leave aside for the moment institutional efforts to expressly engage in ethical speech regulation. Even if a university limits itself to enforcing prohibitory bans, these decisions still may exert aftershocks that extend well beyond limiting proscribable speech. What happens when (we will stipulate) valid prohibitory bans also deter protest activity that, to the extent it is problematic at all, should be addressed only by ethical or prudential persuasion?

In 2022 there was a flurry of controversy regarding the degree to which Yale Law School was hospitable to conservative speakers, culminating in an announcement by several federal judges (most notably Fifth Circuit Judge James Ho) that they would refuse to hire Yale Law graduates as clerks.[45] Among the triggering events was a panel featuring (among others) Kristen Waggoner of the right-wing Alliance Defending Freedom, whose presence allegedly prompted shout-down efforts by protesting students.[46] A year later, Waggoner returned to Yale Law School on a panel with former ACLU president Nadine Strossen and Yale Law professor Robert Post. In contrast to the protests that greeted Waggoner in 2022, the 2023 event went "without a hitch."[47] Not only were there "no ear-shattering chants, no profanity-laden signs, and no ad hominem questions," Strossen observed, but "[t]here was not even a peaceful protest" associated with the event.[48] The dissident opinions on Waggoner were instead shunted into a "counter-event" hosted by the law school's OutLaws chapter.[49]

This outcome was widely lauded as a victory for free speech culture.[50] But the conflation of "ear-shattering chants" with "profanity-laden signs" and "ad hominem questions" raises some troublesome issues. The former is a valid subject of a prohibitory ban on shout-downs. The latter two likely are not. We can say perhaps without qualification that to the extent Yale Law was successful in eliminating the former, it was an unambiguous victory for free speech. By contrast, to the extent Yale Law suppressed "profanity-laden signs"

[45] See Joe Patrice, "James Ho Cancel Cultures Yale Law FedSoc Because Other Students Are Mean to Yale Law FedSoc Students," *Above the Law*, September 30, 2022, https://abovethelaw.com/2022/09/james-ho-cancel-cultures-yale-law-fedsoc-because-other-students-are-mean-to-yale-law-fedsoc-students.

[46] David Lat, "Is Free Speech in American Law Schools a Lost Cause?," *Original Jurisdiction*, March 17, 2022, https://davidlat.substack.com/p/is-free-speech-in-american-law-schools. Whether there actually was a "shout-down" is disputed. Lat observes, "If you read the [conservative] Free Beacon's coverage, you get the sense of an out-of-control mob; if you read the [Yale Daily News's] coverage, you get the sense of quiet, non-disruptive protesters. . . . Based on what I've heard from folks who were there, the truth lies somewhere in between." *Id.*

[47] Aaron Sibarium, "Yale Law School Bars Press from Free Speech Panel. Yes, Really," *Washington Free Beacon*, January 24, 2023, https://freebeacon.com/campus/yale-law-school-bars-press-from-free-speech-panel-yes-really.

[48] *Id.*

[49] David Lat, "A Controversial Speaker Returned to Yale Law—You Won't Believe What Happened Next," *Original Jurisdiction*, January 26, 2023, https://davidlat.substack.com/p/a-controversial-speaker-returned.

[50] *Id.*

and "ad hominem" questions—indeed, ensured there was "not even a peaceful protest"—then it seems Yale didn't just ban illegitimately disruptive protest; it also functionally squelched perfectly lawful forms of protest.

Is that problematic? Maybe; maybe not. In part, the answer depends on why the Yale students did not launch "even a peaceful protest." It seems unlikely, after all, that no Yale students felt moved to protest this speaker, or that they were all busy with other things. More probable is that the students were deterred by the steps Yale had taken to proscribe the illegitimate, censorial forms of protest (like the shout-downs), such that they no longer felt confident they would not be sanctioned even if they abjured *those* protest forms and "merely" elected to engage in ethically and prudentially questionable—but free speech–protected—activities like profane signs or ad hominem questions. If this is the case, then Yale's conduct looks more worrisome—its prohibitory efforts spilling over to capture speech that should remain protected.

But a spillover deterrent effect is not the only explanation for why Yale students' protest activities changed so dramatically from 2022 to 2023. Another explanation is that, in the intervening year, the law school had successfully inculcated its students with a set of free speech values which caused them to endorse the law school's own ethical judgments regarding the validity of those forms of protest. Under this explanation, the students didn't protest via profane signs and ad hominem chants not because they feared formal penalties but because they'd been successfully educated not to utilize their free speech rights in such a fashion.

Is *that* problematic? Again, the answer is less clear than one might hope. At one level, one could argue that this is exactly what law schools (and advocates of "free speech culture" more generally) believe should be happening. Formal recognition that students are *allowed* to protest in dubious fashion is paired with a vigorous ethical critique of the choice. Where that critique is taken up and internalized by the university stakeholders we have a quintessential free speech success story.

But notice that this outlook depends on—indeed, valorizes—the position that universities are entitled to make substantive value judgments regarding "good" and "bad" speech within the category of legally protected speech, promoting the former and discouraging the latter. This stands in opposition to another potential principle, which is that once one leaves the realm of legally proscribable speech (shout-downs and the like), the university must maintain a studious neutrality among all different forms of protected speech. If this is so, then the university cannot prefer (for example) audience questions to be respectful rather than insulting any more than it can prefer a given speaker be respectful of LGBT citizens rather than insulting toward them. Consequently, those who are pleased to see the university successfully intercede to tamp down these toxic or inappropriate forms of protest cannot claim to be endorsing this sort of neutrality. They must believe that, so long as the university does not utilize formal penalties or sanctions as part of its endeavors, it is appropriate or perhaps even essential that the university single out certain forms of protected speech for condemnation and opprobrium in the hopes that the relevant speakers will voluntarily refrain from acting in the disapproved fashion.

Yet if we adopt that view, then it's no longer clear what Dean Steinbach did wrong (aside from any substantive moral disagreement one might have regarding the ethical assessment of Judge Duncan's speech). Dean Steinbach did explicitly defend Judge Duncan's formal right to deliver his remarks—she made clear that there was no possibility of using formal sanctions to preclude his speech. She also signaled, however, that the content of Judge Duncan's speech fell outside the ethical parameters that the law school sought to encourage. That judgment seems to be what has drawn the most ire as a departure from "free speech culture"—but it is precisely the move that "free speech culture" advocates insist upon in praising academic administrators who successfully suppress legally permissible but arguably inappropriate protest practices.

At most, one could fault Dean Steinbach for not being more explicit that the students who were violating the prohibitory rules would face formal sanction. But the fact is that after her intervention, *that* form of protest (the arguable shout-down/heckling) did stop. If Dean Steinbach's only valid interest was eliminating the legally proscribable speech—and nothing else—then her intervention was a rousing success, precisely because (perhaps unlike what happened at Yale) it *only* brought an end to the proscribable speech and had no discernable impact on the speech practices—most notably, the mutual discourtesy exchanged between speaker and audience that stemmed from their obvious shared loathing of one another—that are immune from formal sanction even as they seem clearly toxic to a healthy speech environment. On the flipside, if we indict Dean Steinbach for trying to do more than articulate the formal regulatory prohibitions on the grounds that outside of that realm Stanford cannot legitimately make evaluative appraisals of "good" versus "bad" speech, then Stanford likewise has no valid cause to even *disapprove* of anything that happened after Dean Steinbach's intervention—all of which, toxic as it was, falls well outside the terrain of speech that can be formally proscribed. Contrary to the Stanford Law administration's suggestion that nobody could be happy with how the events at the law school transpired, taking this view seriously would mean that the law school would be *obligated* to remain stoically impassive at practices like ad hominem questions, profane signs, and disrespectful dismissiveness.

In short, one can say, in accordance with what seems to be the majority view, that the 2023 Yale Law event was a free speech success story insofar as Yale Law students refrained from engaging in both proscribable protests (like shout-downs) and formally permissible protests (like ad hominem questions) that nonetheless are antagonistic to the type of free speech culture Yale hopes to cultivate. Indeed, I'm inclined to agree with that position. But if one adopts that position, one does so only by conceding that the law school is not, should not be, and likely cannot remain wholly neutral within the category of First Amendment–protected speech. Rather, even within the category of protected speech, the law school has an interest in encouraging, facilitating, and promoting certain types of speech and discouraging, disavowing, and suppressing others. And once that concession is made, one cannot categorically object when law school actors take steps—short of formal penalties—to discourage speech they view as antipathetic or toxic to the broader intellectual environment they wish to cultivate.[51] The propriety, or not, of such judgments must instead rest on far murkier and subjective case-by-case judgments pitting the individual interest in having a specific view articulated against the structural damage such articulations might pose to the broader communal deliberative architecture—an architecture that, inconveniently, cannot be held together solely by a posture of pure hands-off liberal neutrality.

Finally, to say that a regulatory body is obligated to affirmatively prohibit a given course of conduct does not answer the question of how severe the sanctions should be for the violation. It is common to argue not just that universities should (must) prohibit shout-downs but also that the sanction for students who violate the prohibition should (must) be suspension or expulsion. Certainly, we might think that if sanctions are too low, the functional result is to permit speech disruption so long as students are willing to pay a minimal cost. (Imagine a rule that purports to prohibit disrupting speech and then lists as its sanction "Any person who disrupts a speech shall be fined $5.") But even for behavior that is generally agreed to be impermissible, it is not the case that universities are obligated to impose the maximum possible punishment—and this is true even if harsher punishment might discourage certain violations that a more lenient regime fails to deter. There is always a marginal increase in deterrent effect as one imposes progressively more draconian sentences, but this does not mean that all wrongs must be given infinite punishment. Policymakers rightly take account of other considerations, including the relative gravity of an offense and the possibility of deterring legitimate conduct—and importantly, they do so *knowing* that adopting a more lenient tone means sacrificing some measure of deterrent effect.

Put differently, minimizing the number of speech disruptions is a worthy goal of rules which seek to prohibit speech disruption—but it is not the *only* goal, and a prohibitory regime does not intrinsically fail in its obligation to ban

[51] See David Schraub, "Academic Freedom versus Academic Legitimacy," *FIU Law Review* 9, no. 1 (2013): 71–72 (arguing that the requirements of academic freedom do not prevent university actors from condemning certain forms of academic speech as illegitimate, but only provide "a constraint on remedies").

disruptive speech solely because it would be conceptually possible for a harsher regime to minimize disruptions still further. Perhaps it is reasonable to think that some speech disruptions are so dangerous to the mission of an academic institution that it is proper to meet them with the academic discipline equivalent of the death penalty (expulsion).[52] But it is possible for a reasonable university to balance the equities differently, perhaps not finding the wrong to be quite that grievous, perhaps thinking the speech value of the protest carries considerable weight as well, perhaps worrying that such heavy sanctions hanging over student heads will deter legitimate, protected (but edge-case) protest activity, perhaps worrying (in the opposite direction) that perceived over-policing may invite backlash and escalation rather than submission, or perhaps simply viewing these incidents as teachable moments that can be better redressed by the tools of education and professionalization than by the blunt instrument of punitive injunctions. Without attempting to resolve the proper balance here, it suffices to note that the significant possibility of disagreement on these issues further blurs certainty around when and in what contexts an academic institution fails in its obligation to promote a healthy speech environment even within the prohibitory register.

The student protests surrounding Israel's war in Gaza provide an emphatic demonstration of the limits of taking a purely and uncompromisingly punitive approach to disruptive student speech. What turned into a nationwide phenomenon of pro-Palestine campus encampments was widely credited as originating at Columbia University, beginning the same day that Columbia president Minouche Shafik testified before Congress regarding campus antisemitism.[53] Seeking to avoid the fate of two of her Ivy League predecessors, whose answers to questions regarding how calls for "genocide" of Jews would be treated under campus conduct policies were widely criticized as overly "lawyerly,"[54] Shafik promised swift and uncompromising action.[55] The next day, police raided

[52] See Laura Ann Rosenbury, "When Student Protest Goes Too Far: I'm the President of Barnard. This Is My Line in the Sand," *Chronicle of Higher Education*, March 3, 2025, https://www.chronicle.com/article/when-student-protest-goes-too-far (defending the expulsion of masked protesters who disrupted a class on the history of modern Israel by "taunting and loudly speaking over the professor, distributing antisemitic flyers, and refusing to join the discussion even when the professor graciously invited them to sit in on the class").

[53] AP, "Timeline of the Nationwide Protest Movement That Began at Columbia University," May 6, 2024, https://apnews.com/article/israel-palestinian-campus-protests-timeline-f7cd3abe635f8afa4532b7bed9212b56.

[54] See "Liz Magill, UPenn President, Resigns after Antisemitism Testimony Draws Backlash," *PBS News Hour*, December 9, 2023, https://www.pbs.org/newshour/education/liz-magill-upenn-president-resigns-after-antisemitism-testimony-draws-backlash (noting the widespread criticism of University of Pennsylvania president Liz Magill's contention that "[i]t is a context-dependent decision" whether calls for genocide are punishable, which ultimately led to her resignation).

[55] See Nicholas Fandos, Stephanie Saul, and Sharon Otterman, "Columbia's President Tells Congress That Action Is Needed against Antisemitism," *New York Times*, April 17, 2024, https://

the encampment and arrested over 100 protesters. Far from quelling the protest campaign, however, this decision caused an explosion of copycat encampments to emerge on campuses across the country. These encampments have been dealt with in different ways. Some universities have sought to negotiate with the protesters, promising various forms of consideration regarding demands to divest from Israeli companies or military contractors.[56] Others have followed Columbia's lead and cleared the encampments with force.[57] Many have canceled graduation or commencement exercises;[58] several have had commencement or graduation speakers cancel on them.[59]

To give a full accounting of the encampment protests and the university response to them, and the related free speech issues, is a book in itself. But some brief remarks can be made. Most important, the protests are a "they" and not an "it"—even within the encampments (to say nothing of across them), there is a wide range of views expressed and behaviors practiced. Many of the protests have been nonviolent,[60] but some have not been, including attacks on Jewish students presumed to be Zionists[61] as well as violence enacted by pro-Israel counterdemonstrators against pro-Palestine protesters.[62] Some campus

www.nytimes.com/2024/04/17/nyregion/columbia-university-president-nemat-shafik-hearing.html (describing statements in President Shafik's testimony, including disclosing student and faculty discipline decisions and suggesting the school might punish community members for speech deemed antisemitic, as "part of an all-out effort on Wednesday to persuade a House committee investigating Columbia that she was taking serious action to combat a wave of antisemitism following the Israel-Hamas war"). Shafik resigned from her position at the end of the summer. Alan Blinder and Sharon Otterman, "Columbia President Resigns after Months of Turmoil on Campus," *New York Times*, August 14, 2024, https://www.nytimes.com/2024/08/14/us/columbia-president-nemat-shafik-resigns.html.

56 See Andrew Lapin, "After Making Deals with Protesters, Universities Are Granting Hearings on Israel Divestment," JTA, May 10, 2024, https://www.jta.org/2024/05/10/united-states/after-making-deals-with-protesters-universities-are-granting-hearings-on-israel-divestment.

57 Bruce Shipkowski and Michael Casey, "Police Arrest Dozens as They Break Up Pro-Palestinian Protests at Several US Universities," KXAN, May 10, 2024, https://www.kxan.com/news/national-news/ap-police-dismantle-pro-palestinian-tent-encampmentIsrael/Palestine conflict:pro-Palestine encampments-at-mit.

58 Alaina Demopoulos, "US Students Blast Cancellation of Commencements: 'A Slap in the Face,'" *The Guardian*, May 9, 2024, https://www.theguardian.com/us-news/article/2024/may/09/gaza-protests-university-commencement-ceremonies-students-react.

59 Riley Rourke, "Colson Whitehead Cancels UMass Amherst Commencement Speech over 'Shameful' Protest Arrests," *CBS News*, May 10, 2024, https://www.cbsnews.com/boston/news/colson-whitehead-umass-amherst-protest.

60 See Lois Beckett, "Nearly All Gaza Campus Protests in the US Have Been Peaceful, Study Finds," *The Guardian*, May 10, 2024, https://www.theguardian.com/us-news/article/2024/may/10/peaceful-pro-palestinian-campus-protests (concluding that the vast majority of the protests have not experienced violence more serious than vandalism or pushing and shoving).

61 See Ronny Reyes, "Jewish Yale Student Journalist Stabbed in the Eye with Palestinian Flag during Protest," *New York Post*, April 21, 2024, https://nypost.com/2024/04/21/us-news/jewish-yale-student-stabbed-in-the-eye-with-palestinian-flag-during-protest.

62 See Josh DuBose, "L.A. Police, Possibly FBI to Help Investigate Violent Attack on UCLA Encampment," KTLA, May 6, 2024, https://ktla.com/news/local-news/fbi-and-l-a-police-to-help-investigate-violent-siege-on-ucla-encampment.

disciplinary measures were enforcements of long-standing time, place, and manner rules, but others appeared to represent ad hoc alterations of policy based on objection to the content or viewpoint of the protests.[63] There is, unsurprisingly, wide dispute regarding the amount of antisemitic expression and activity among the protesters,[64] a dispute which speaks to larger controversies and disagreements over the contours of antisemitism and its relationship to anti-Israel or anti-Zionist activity, but there is little doubt that there is some nontrivial measure of antisemitic sentiment extant within the protests[65] even as it is also the case that it is unfair to tar a broad collective with individual acts of bigotry where many protesters are clearly motivated by nothing more sinister than heartfelt humanitarian concern for the safety and dignity of the Palestinian people.

It is also important not to discount the genuine difficulties university administrators faced in determining how to respond to the protests. Rigorous dissent, including through the medium of public protest, is an essential component of academic freedom and does not cease to hold that value because it makes some students uncomfortable.[66] Nonetheless, a university has very legitimate interests in enforcing content-neutral time, place, and manner restrictions on

[63] See Aubrey White, "IU Changes Policy Day before Encampment Arrests," Indiana Public Media, April 26, 2024, https://indianapublicmedia.org/news/legal-action-may-be-necessary-after-students-faculty-banned-from-iu-campus.php.

[64] The *Columbia Spectator*, in collaboration with *New York Magazine*, published an oral history of the Columbia encampments that offers a range of perspectives, including that of the protesters as well as that of Jewish students who felt victimized by the protests. See Isabella Ramirez, Amira McKee, Rebecca Massel, Emily Forgash, Noah Bernstein, Sabrina Ticer-Wurr, et al., "Our Campus. Our Crisis. Inside the Encampments and Crackdowns That Shook American Politics," *New York Magazine*, May 4, 2024, https://nymag.com/intelligencer/article/columbia-university-protests-israel-gaza-campus.html.

[65] See, e.g., Katherine Rosman, "Columbia Bars Student Protester Who Said 'Zionists Don't Deserve to Live,'" *New York Times*, April 26, 2024, https://www.nytimes.com/2024/04/26/nyregion/columbia-student-protest-zionism.html; Steven Vago and Isabel Keane, "Anti-Israel Protester Screams 'Go Back to Poland' at Demonstrators with Israeli Flag outside Columbia, Harrowing Video Shows," *New York Post*, April 21, 2024, https://nypost.com/2024/04/21/us-news/anti-israel-protester-screams-at-demonstrators-with-israeli-flag-outside-columbia-u-go-back-to-poland. There have also been documented instances of racist activity directed by counterprotesters at pro-Palestinian demonstrators. *See* Kiara Alfonseca, "'Racist' Actions from Counterprotesters at University of Mississippi Prompt Investigation," *ABC News*, May 6, 2024, https://abcnews.go.com/US/racist-actions-counterprotesters-university-mississippi-prompt-investigation/story?id=109958356.

[66] See AAUP, "In Defense of the Right to Free Speech and Peaceful Protest on University Campuses," April 29, 2024, https://www.aaup.org/media-release/defense-right-free-speech-and-peaceful-protest-university-campuses (defending "our students' right to protest and to express their political convictions" as part of the "critical evaluation of different points of view and the questioning of even the most deeply held beliefs"); Geoffrey R. Stone, Marianne Bertrand, Angela Olinto, Mark Siegler, David A. Strauss, Kenneth W. Warren, and Amanda Woodward, *Report of the Committee on Freedom of Expression*, January, 2015, https://provost.uchicago.edu/sites/default/files/documents/reports/FOECommitteeReport.pdf [https://perma.cc/3YJ9-DU65] ("Although the University greatly values civility, and although all members of the University community share in the responsibility for maintaining a climate of mutual respect, concerns about civility and mutual respect can never be used as a justification for closing off discussion of ideas, however offensive or disagreeable those ideas may be to some members of our community.").

the occupation of public spaces, even where the violations of these restrictions are nonviolent.[67] Allowing a particular faction to set up ideological checkpoints of indefinite duration to determine which community members are and are not allowed to move freely across campus is, or should be, intolerable for obvious reasons.[68] And as noted above, while the decision of some university leaders to negotiate an end to the encampments by offering various concessions to pro-Palestine demonstrators has been praised in certain quarters, it has also been met with severe criticism by some Jewish leaders who believe that it functions to reward violations of campus policy while disadvantaging community members who have not aired their concerns via the mechanism of protest.

What cannot be gainsaid, however, is that the specific response exemplified by President Shafik at Columbia—aggressive, no-holds-barred punitive measures spearheaded by police intervention—has proven to be a resounding failure under any plausible metric for what a "successful" resolution to the protests might look like. If the goal was to restore order and normal operations on campus, it failed. If the goal was to cow violators of campus speech policies into obedience, it failed. If the goal was to quell pro-Palestine protests more broadly, it failed. If the goal was to make Jewish students feel more secure, it failed. If the goal was to assuage partisan critics of higher education, it failed. If the goal was to demonstrate evenhanded commitment to content-neutral principles of free speech regulation, it failed. To the extent some believed that any response to disruptive speech that falls short of immediate, maximalist punitive sanction is tantamount to betraying free speech itself,[69] that view has been firmly and decisively falsified. There are, it turns out, excellent reasons why a university administrator attuned to facts on the ground might elect to respond to even policy-violating speech disruptions with something other than implacable, overwhelming force. I do not know if Dean Steinbach has offered, or was asked, her

[67] See Anthony D. Romero and David Cole, "Open Letter to College and University Presidents on Student Protests," ACLU, April 26, 2024, https://www.aclu.org/news/free-speech/open-letter-to-college-and-university-presidents-on-student-protests (acknowledging that "universities can announce and enforce reasonable time, place, or manner restrictions on protest activity" so long as they are "content-neutral" and "leave ample room for students to express themselves").

[68] See Jenny Jarvie, "'Are You a Zionist?' Checkpoints at UCLA Encampment Provoked Fear, Debate among Jews," *Los Angeles Times*, May 9, 2024, https://www.latimes.com/california/story/2024-05-09/are-you-a-zionist-checkpoints-at-ucla-encampment-provoked-debate-among-jewish-students. In August 2024, a federal judge enjoined UCLA from permitting "exclusion of Jewish students based on religious beliefs concerning the Jewish state of Israel" from "ordinarily available programs, activities, and campus areas." Frankel v. Regents of the Univ. of Cal., No. 2:24-CV-04702-MCS-PD, 2024 WL 3811250, at *8 (C.D. Cal. Aug. 13, 2024).

[69] See, e.g., GianCarlo Canaparo, "That Tantrum at Stanford Law School and What to Do about It," *Washington Examiner*, March 14, 2023, https://www.washingtonexaminer.com/opinion/beltway-confidential/2779105/that-tantrum-at-stanford-law-school-and-what-to-do-about-it (arguing, in response to the Kyle Duncan incident, that "the only way to stop this problem is through appropriate punishment. Lessons about why free speech and rational debate are important to the practice of law will not work").

thoughts on how universities have been responding to the campus encampment crisis. But few could begrudge her if she felt some measure of vindication.

The big-picture problem is simple: prohibitory rules, modeled on the First Amendment, can in concept adhere to principles of liberal neutrality that permit institutions (like universities) to avoid resolving contested issues of policy or propriety. Unfortunately, prohibitory rules on their own are too austere to actually prop up the sort of academic environment and intellectual culture of exchange we want in a university context. Recognition of this shortcoming is the entire impetus behind the "free speech culture" concept. But enforcement of the ethical rules inevitably impinges on the liberal neutrality that the prohibitory rules are trying to instantiate—it requires substantive judgments regarding "good" and "bad" speech.

In the face of that paradox, we do not actually know what we want. We have not developed a cohesive view as to when and whether academic staffers on the scene should try to promote a particular "culture" of speech, even if that means attacking certain speech practices that are not validly the subject of formal prohibitions, versus when and whether staffers should limit themselves solely to enforcing express regulatory prohibitions—and nothing else. Our own confusion, unsurprisingly, means that the staffers trying to make on-the-ground enforcement decisions are faced with an impossible task—they are forced to unravel a puzzle that defies easy resolution even when presented in the cool tones of abstract academic inquiry, to say nothing of the hurly-burly of rapidly evolving chaos.

At some level, the project of this book is to explain why these putatively "easy" free speech questions are actually quite hard rather than to provide definitive answers to them. Indeed, if there is one takeaway across the entirety of the book, it is that once we step outside the realm of governmental regulation, the corpus of free speech rules contained in First Amendment doctrine have surprisingly little to tell us about how to handle free speech controversies. The real goal is to develop a healthy deliberative ethos around speech, and that ethos is one that recognizes the importance of open-minded listening but also the important freedom not to listen. That tension is not one that can be reduced to hard-and-fast rules about avoiding censorship. It instead takes the form of trying to cultivate certain deliberative virtues, so that the legitimate and incontestable interest in avoiding some speech, some of the time, is not abused to denigrate and degrade our collective deliberative capacities altogether.

Conclusion

Free speech, it often seems, has a great many fair-weather friends. An advocate insisting one day that college is about encountering tough new ideas and is incompatible with any notion of a safe space may the next day be found bemoaning Marxist professors indoctrinating students with un-American values. The same activist who pens column after column articulating how a hostile environment and microaggressions silence certain student voices may suddenly discover the appeal of a hyper-legalistic definition of "censorship" when called upon to defend a disruptive student protest shouting down a controversial speaker. The same political movement which trumpeted an executive order guaranteeing "free and open debate on college and university campuses" now pushes a wave of legislation seeking to ban critical race theory and a full-throttle campaign to extirpate DEI from public life.[1] Appeals to open discourse are simultaneously everywhere and nowhere, the province of every political faction and none of them. Virtually everyone claims to support the value of genuine consideration, but it does not take long for virtually everyone to find their cases of exception.

Is this simply hypocrisy? Sometimes it is. Everyone comes to the table with certain value commitments; everyone comes to the table seeking to suppress certain thoughts they would rather not think. Too often our natural instinct is to construct our social world to avoid hearing certain types of claims, or at the very least unquestionably inhabit a social world which feels comfortable to us precisely because it effortlessly enables such avoidance. And, more dangerously,

[1] Compare Executive Order 13864, "Executive Order on Improving Free Inquiry, Transparency, and Accountability at Colleges and Universities," American Presidency Project, March 21, 2019, https://www.presidency.ucsb.edu/documents/executive-order-13864-improving-free-inquiry-transparency-and-accountability-colleges-and with Russell Vought, "Memorandum on Training in the Federal Government," White House, September 4, 2020, https://www.whitehouse.gov/wp-content/uploads/2020/09/M-20-34.pdf (directing federal agencies "to begin to identify all contracts or other agency spending related to any training on 'critical race theory' [or] 'white privilege,' and "identify all available avenues within the law to cancel any such contracts and/or to divert Federal dollars away from these un-American propaganda training session[s]"); Cathryn Stout and Gabrielle LaMarr LeMee, "Efforts to Restrict Teaching about Racism and Bias Have Multiplied across the U.S.," *Chalkbeat*, July 22, 2021, https://www.chalkbeat.org/22525983/map-critical-race-theory-legislation-teaching-racism; Collin Binkley, "Trump Administration Gives Schools a Deadline to End DEI Programs or Risk Losing Federal Money," AP, February 18, 2025, https://apnews.com/article/dei-critical-race-theory-colleges-diversity-db8317ad37931558dd5a396cf5ab3d42.

Deliberation, Dismissal, and Democracy. David Schraub, Oxford University Press. © Oxford University Press (2025). DOI: 10.1093/9780197816424.003.0011

we can create conditions where we feel justified in dismissing certain claims—refusing to even consider them substantively on their merits. When abused, this tendency toward dismissal breaches our duty to listen to our fellows and fails to respect members of marginalized communities as epistemic agents.

But we would go too far if we said that dismissal was solely a matter of bad actors—individuals failing to respect the dignity of marginalized others seeking to join in the dialogic conversation as equals. For one, it is the unremarkable truth that we could not give full consideration to every claim even if we wanted to. There is an unavoidable scarcity in deliberative resources that compels us to come up with some mechanisms for distribution. Moreover, it is far from clear that we should want to fully consider every single claim. Are we wrong in dismissing the Holocaust denier, the social media troll, the shock jock provocateur, or the manifestly uncredible conspiracy theorist? As a deliberative problem, dismissal resists easy resolution not because it is always wrong but because it sometimes isn't.

What is fair to say is that we must cultivate a *disposition* toward engagement and against dismissal. Dismissal will often be unavoidable and may sometimes even be appropriate. But it should never be our discursive tool of first result. Ironically, even justified dismissal may require expending a fair amount of energy engaging in consideration. Precisely because dismissal is sometimes a valid option, it requires great strength to abjure resorting to it simply when convenient. Dismissal exists as a temptation, a siren's song which holds out the promise that we can stay cocooned in what is comfortable and comforting without ever being forced to step outside of our deliberative comfort zone. Resisting this temptation is not predominantly a matter of crafting better rules; it is a matter of cultivating the internal virtues and temperament of intellectual courage. "If we would guide by the light of reason," Justice Louis Brandeis wrote, "we must let our minds be bold."[2]

As much as this disposition toward consideration is an important personal virtue, however, it is also essential to acknowledge and protect institutional and systemic contexts where dismissal can be circumvented. Protests are one opportunity for circumventing dismissal—protests often are directed precisely at overcoming a reflexive (and otherwise difficult to challenge) refusal to even consider certain challenging or discomforting claims. The judicial system is another such venue—courts are spaces where, for a limited but nonetheless important set of claims, decision-makers are compelled to listen and compelled to give reasons. In either context, avoiding dismissal does not entitle one to or guarantee a substantive victory. But it does at least enable certain hard thoughts to get on the deliberative table.

[2] New State Ice Co. v. Liebmann, 285 U.S. 262, 311 (1932) (Brandeis, J., dissenting).

Even as I acknowledge this deliberative niche occupied by courts, though, I hesitate to give it too much weight. The questions grappled with in this book have overwhelmingly been discussed in legalistic terms—in the American context, as questions of First Amendment doctrine. I am a law professor who teaches constitutional law, and so I am susceptible to this instinct even though I strongly believe that the actual operative dilemmas are far more likely to be questions of ethics and virtue than ones of law and juridical rights.

Yet I still believe that there is something about law that can serve as a model for deliberative virtue outside the courtroom. Legal scholarship frequently asks what other disciplines—economics, psychology, philosophy—have to teach us about law. This book suggests that law has something to teach us about the ethics of our everyday discursive interactions. It is not, as some argue, that we should mimic First Amendment standards in our personal deliberative lives. That ambition is impossible to realize and fundamentally misunderstands the purpose of the First Amendment itself, which is to *shift* regulatory judgment over speech from public to private actors. It is one thing to say that the government should have no right to block publication of a given book; it is quite another to tell an editor that they are indulging in censorship when they decide a submitted manuscript is not up to their measure of quality.

The usefulness of law, rather, is in how it embodies a particular set of deliberative virtues that are worth aspiring to even outside the courtroom. Deeply embedded in legal culture are a series of important deliberative norms that make fair argument and adjudication possible. These include the right of all sides to present arguments, the importance of fairly weighing evidence, and the obligation to take seriously even uncomfortable claims. In a political climate where many Americans worry that we are becoming epistemically siloed—stuck in like-minded bubbles, unwilling or unable to even contemplate arguments from communities foreign to our own—these virtues often feel in short supply. The focus on dismissal—the legal concept analyzed as a discursive practice—can help point the way to more expansive and more just modes of interacting across political and cultural difference.

In *The Subjection of Women*, John Stuart Mill resorts to legal metaphor in describing the difficulties faced by those who seek to challenge settled opinion: "They must be fortunate as well as unusually capable if they obtain a hearing at all. They have more difficulty in obtaining a trial, than any other litigants have in getting a verdict."[3] That legal thinking is valuable not simply as a means of securing formal rights and remedies at the end of a filed case is perhaps why this metaphor resonates so clearly. The lessons of the law extend beyond the

[3] John Stuart Mill, *The Subjection of Women* (Hackett, 1988), 2.

boundaries of the law. The example of the courtroom can also inform our everyday deliberative practices, pushing us to be less close-minded, less arrogant, less partisan—less dismissive—toward the ordinary hard thoughts that a functioning democratic citizen must force herself to think.

Index